Phil Rostron, who collaborated with Barry Fry on this book, has been a sports journalist for over 30 years. He began his career with the *Oldham Evening Chronicle* in 1967, and after spells with the Oldham Press Agency and the *West Lancashire Evening Gazette* in Blackpool he embarked on an 18-year association with the *Daily Star*, becoming one of Fleet Street's longest-serving sports editors. He is currently chief sports writer of the *Yorkshire Evening Post*, covering the fortunes of Leeds United.

D1350831

BIG FRY

The Autobiography of Barry Fry

CollinsWillow

An Imprint of HarperCollinsPublishers

First published in 2000 by
CollinsWillow
an imprint of HarperCollins*Publishers*
London

First published in paperback 2001

1 3 5 7 9 8 6 4 2

A CIP catalogue record for this book is
available from the British Library

ISBN 0 00 218949 6

Set in PostScript Minion by
Rowland Phototypesetting Ltd, Bury St Edmunds, Suffolk

Printed and bound in Great Britain by
Clays Ltd, St Ives plc

The HarperCollins website address is
www.**fire**and**water**.com

Photographic Acknowledgments
All photographs supplied courtesy of Barry Fry with the exception
of the following: **Allsport** 16t, 16c **Empics** 4c, 10t, 12c, 15c, 15b, 16b
Mirror Syndication 4b **Popperfoto** 4t, 9b **Press Association** 15t

*To my wife Kirstine,
and my children Jane, Mark, Adam,
Amber, Frank and Anna-Marie.*

Contents

Acknowledgements

This book would not have been possible but for the support of my family. To my late mum Dora and dad Frank, thanks for all the sacrifices you made for me and your encouragement and understanding in trying to help me fulfil my dream. My wife Kirstine has been a rock, my best ever signing, while her mum Gisela and dad Andy have always been there for me.

I was fortunate enough to be at the birth of each of my six children Jane, Mark, Adam, Amber, Frank and Anna-Marie, and I can honestly say that the experience is better than scoring at Wembley! Since the days they were born they have all, in different ways, brought so much pleasure and enjoyment into my life. As have my three grand-children Keeley-Anne, Yasmin and Louis and the best son-in-law anybody could wish for in Steve. I count my lucky stars that I have been surrounded by such a wonderful group of family and friends through my rollercoaster career in football.

Finally, thanks to my publishers HarperCollins and the man who helped me put my thoughts down in writing, Phil Rostron. It's been a privilege working with such professionals.

FOREWORD

Sir Alex Ferguson

I am privileged to have been asked to write the foreword to the autobiography of a man whom I cannot bring to mind without the thought prompting a smile. This is not because Barry Fry is a figure of fun, but because of his larger-than-life character, happy-go-lucky nature and reliance upon humour to soften the blows which a life in football can inflict with uncomfortable regularity.

Barry is a man for whom football is a blinding passion, displayed in his every thought, word and deed. He is one of the rare birds in the game in that he is highly respected by almost all of his fellow professionals for his vast knowledge, unquenchable enthusiasm and unflinching adherence to the ideals in which he believes.

He is a very popular manager among managers. Barry may not have been at the helm of a Premiership club but that, in itself, is surprising in many ways because he has achieved success in one way or another at each of the many he has managed both in non-league football and in the lower divisions of the Football League.

A staunch member of the League Managers' Association, he shows as much enthusiasm for its affairs as he does in his day-to-day club involvement. We operate in an industry which all too often does not meet its obligations when there is a parting of the ways between clubs and managers, and there is a real need for voices as powerful as Barry's to be heard if an equilibrium is to be achieved. Some managers are fortunate enough to walk straight into another job once they have been shown the door, but there are many others who do not enjoy the same fortune for one reason or another. They need protection, with due and full severance pay a priority, and Barry, who knows a thing or two about such matters, works tirelessly towards these goals.

Thoughts for the welfare of others are typical of the man and his self-deprecation is very endearing. Having walked into Old Trafford as a young boy to become one of the original Busby Babes, he says that the only reason Barry Fry did not make it as a player was Barry Fry. He is perhaps being a little hard on himself with this observation. The fact is that the crop of youngsters with whom he was competing for places at the time was exceptional, as has regularly been the case at Manchester United, and it is no disgrace that he failed to break through into the big time.

There is no disputing that he was a smashing little player – you don't get schoolboy international caps and headhunted by Manchester United if you are no good – but Barry didn't get the breaks. Simple as that.

An incongruity in football is the number of great players who do not aspire to be, nor become, top managers and a corresponding number of distinctly average players who achieve tremendous managerial success. In my own case I was never anything more than a run-of-the-mill player and the same could be said of the likes of Bill Shankly and Bob Paisley, but playing is one thing and managing entirely another. Barry is in the category of people who have done better as the man in charge than he did as the one taking the orders and his feats in winning championships and cup competitions are not to be underestimated. In any walk of life you have to be special to achieve success and there is no doubt that Barry Fry is a very special man.

He takes us here on a roller-coaster ride which reflects his colourful life. Hold on to your hats and enjoy the journey. Then, when you think about Barry Fry in the future, I defy you to do so without a smile on your face.

CHAPTER ONE

Who'd be a football manager?

Raindrops trickled down the window of the prefabricated building that was my office on the winter's day that a familiar red Lamborghini drew to a halt in the parking bay outside. The magnificent machine was just one of the success symbols flaunted by the highly charismatic Keith Cheeseman, who had recently assumed control of the Southern League club Dunstable Town. This was my first managerial position in football and I felt privileged to be the individual charged with the task of transforming the fortunes of a club which, for eight successive seasons, had finished stone cold bottom of the league. I was in a fairly strong position in that things could hardly have got worse. Or so it seemed.

I was just a few months into the job and the chairman's arrival on this dank Tuesday was the signal that this was to be no ordinary day. Up until now he had never been near the ground in midweek unless we had

1

a game. And even then he did not come to all the games because he got bored with them.

My first thought as he got out of the car was 'What the hell is he doing here?'

As he came into my office I offered him a warm greeting.

'Hello mate, what brings you here?'

He replied that he had come to meet somebody and seemed disappointed when I said that nobody had arrived.

I offered him a cup of tea, which he rejected, and he waved aside my invitation to sit down. He was on edge and started to prowl the room. Even though he was always naturally on the go, there was something different about his demeanour.

After a while a Jaguar pulled up alongside the Lamborghini, giving this dilapidated little outreach in Bedfordshire the incongruous appearance of a classic car showroom. We watched as the driver emerged and walked to my office. His polite knock on the door was answered by Cheeseman.

'Ah, I've been waiting for you.'

'I'm Keith Cheeseman. Please come in.'

And with that greeting the chairman slammed the door shut. In a lightning-fast move he had his visitor pinned back against the door with his forearm tight against his throat. He hastily frisked this hapless man and, as I recoiled in horror, Cheeseman tried to make light of the situation.

'Just checking that you aren't bugged or carrying a gun,' he laughed.

Now I'm just a silly football manager and I feared something approaching a siege might be developing, but Cheeseman just said: 'Barry, I've got to speak privately to this man. Have you got the keys to the boardroom?'

Confirming that they were in my car, I went to get them as they made their way to the boardroom at the other side of the ground. I caught up with them and as they stood on the halfway line they surveyed an advertising hoarding belonging to a particular finance company.

I was never introduced to the visitor, who boomed at the chairman: 'You can take that board down straight away. That goes for starters.'

Cheeseman put his arm round him and smiled.

'My boy, that's just cost you three quarters of a million. I'd leave it there if I were you.'

And with that I let them into the boardroom where, I presumed, they concluded whatever business they were up to. None of what had happened and been said made any sense to me but I was left with the distinct impression that something was amiss.

A few days later I was given a much bigger indication of the type of man I was working for. We had a home game on the Tuesday night and in the afternoon I took a call from Cheeseman in which he said that he would not be going to the match. I said that was fair enough, but there was more. He said that after the game he wanted me to do him a favour and go to meet him.

'I'm only in the country for five minutes,' he said 'but I want to see you before I go. I'll ring you when the match is over and let you know the location.'

I didn't raise an eyebrow because it was not unusual for him to be abroad on business. I often went to his office in Luton before one of these trips for him to hand over some cash or to sign some cheques.

When his telephone call came there was something quite sinister about it.

'Right,' he said, 'I want you to leave and bring with you a case that somebody has dropped at the ground during the game. When you get to the roundabout at Houghton Regis go round it two or three times and make absolutely sure that you are not being followed. Then shoot off all the way down the A5, get on the M1 at the end and come off at Scratchwood Services. I will meet you there.'

'Keith, what the hell ...'

'I'll explain it all when you get here,' he interjected. 'Just make sure you have got the bag.'

I asked the secretary, Harold Stew, whether someone had dropped off a bag from the chairman's office and he confirmed that it was in one of the other offices. So I picked up this big bag, a briefcase, and put it in the boot of my car.

It was with a very nervous look into my rear mirror that I pulled away from the ground and onto my unscheduled journey. I approached the Houghton Regis roundabout with his words ringing in my ears, but I just thought how ridiculous it would be to keep going round and round it and completed the manoeuvre normally. From there, though, I could hardly keep my eyes on the road ahead because I was looking so many times into the mirrors. It was frightening how often I thought one car, then another, then another was tailing me. Paranoia was sweeping over me.

I was overcome with a sense of relief as I arrived unscathed at Scratchwood, yet there was still a feeling of foreboding about the contents of the case and what kind of situation I might soon be walking in to.

Cheeseman answered my knock at the door and welcomed me into a room inhabited by two other members of the finance company and three other people who acted as legal representatives and advisers.

As well as being a member of the Dunstable Football Club board, one was also the manager of the finance house. I hadn't seen him for some time and greeted him warmly. But when I asked if he was well he answered: 'Oh, I'm terrible. I've been out to Keith's place in Spain and all hell has broken loose.'

Cheeseman broke in here and asked me, 'Have you got the case?'

'Oh yes, I forgot. It's in the boot of my car.' He asked for the keys and off he went to get it.

His exit allowed a resumption of my chat with the pale-faced money manager.

'We've got some problems. I've got to get out of the country.'

I pointed out that he had just been abroad.

'I know,' he replied, 'but I've got to go again and for longer this time.'

Cheeseman returned with the case, put it on one of the beds and threw it open. Well, I have never seen such money in all my life. It was crammed full of foreign notes amounting to goodness knows how much.

'What the hell's going on?' I asked the chairman nervously.

'I'll tell you later. We have just got to look after him now.'

Trying to lift the atmosphere I asked if anyone was having tea or coffee or a beer, but Cheeseman said abruptly: 'No. You can go back now.'

'But I thought you wanted to see me?'

'No, I only wanted this,' he said pointing to the money.

I left more than a little concerned. I was 28 years old, terribly naive in the ways of the business world, desperate to make an impression in my first job in football management as a player-manager and here I was, witnessing twice within the space of a week, some very suspicious activities involving the very person I should be able to rely upon for all kinds of things, my chairman.

I drove home stony-faced and with my head swimming. I thought about what had gone before with Cheeseman and things slowly began to add up.

There was, for instance, the Jeff Astle fiasco. This man had been a legend in his time at West Bromwich Albion and it was considered a fantastic coup when I signed him for Dunstable. The ultimate professional, he had been working for Cheeseman's building firm in the Midlands and after two months he came to me and said that he didn't like the situation of living and working such a distance from the club.

Keith urged him to move south, pointing out that he was selling his home in Clophill and moving to a mansion in Houghton Regis. It might be an agreeable solution if Astle were to buy his house.

It was an amicable arrangement for Jeff, too, and he moved in. It was not long, though, before he started to come to see me and say: 'I still haven't got the deeds to that house, Baz. What am I going to do?'

At the end of that season and the beginning of the next campaign – Jeff had scored 34 goals for me – I had had my first blazing row with the chairman. Jeff found out that on the property in Clophill there were no fewer than 35 mortgages that had never been paid. He didn't get the deeds because they were never Cheeseman's to give. There had been this second mortgage and that second mortgage. How the hell Keith managed it, I don't know.

Jeff told me this and I said that if that were the case then he could go. Graham Carr, the Weymouth manager, had wanted to buy him and offered £15,000, but I said that if Cheeseman had done him out of any money, then as far as I was concerned he could go for nothing and get himself looked after in terms of a signing-on fee and any other inducements.

The mortgages totalled £200,000 on a house Jeff thought he had bought for £14,000. I let Jeff and his wife Larraine go to Weymouth for talks with the intention of trying to sort out the mortgage situation. But when I mentioned it to Cheeseman he just huffed and puffed and bluffed and blamed it on anybody and everybody else. He told Jeff everything would be all right but the player himself was far from convinced and I sold Jeff to Weymouth so that he could get back at least some of the money that he had forked out. Nowhere near the full amount, but some of it at least.

He went reluctantly because he was happy playing for Dunstable and was a great hero with the fans. No doubt prompted by Jeff's displeasure at the house situation Cheeseman came to see me one day.

'This Astle ... he ain't doing this, he ain't doing that, he ain't doing f**k all,' he blasted.

But I stopped him in his tracks.

'Keith, I've sold him.'

'You've what?' he screamed.

We were on the pitch and he's a bloody big geezer and we were face-to-face snarling. I've never seen a man so consumed with anger. Knowing what I know now, I was bloody lucky to get away with what I said to him next.

'You don't f***ing treat my players like that. You'd better treat my players right because if you f**k them up like that, mate, I'm no longer with you. My loyalty is to my players. I've sold him, he's gone and there's f**k all you can do about it.'

I was sure he would sack me after this tirade, but he didn't. Yet Jeff had gone, which was heartbreaking. This episode had brought on further inclinations that things were not quite right at the club. Yet Keith was never around. He was always in Australia, America, Tenerife, London, the West Midlands. So rarely in his office in Luton and even more infrequently at the club.

From another perspective, it was great. He would ring every now and then but, by and large, he didn't bother me. As long as the club was ticking over he remained in the background. He just paid the bills and if I saw him and needed money he would leave me readies, otherwise he would leave a sheaf of cheques, sign the lot and leave it to me to pay what had to be paid. This, at least, was on the playing side. All the other bills went to Betty and Harold in the general office and I never saw them.

It was a deeply worrying time and what I was considering more and more to be the inevitable happened one day when the police arrived on the scene.

I was full time on my own at Dunstable, even running the lotteries. Jeff used to help me sell the tickets and he became a great PR man for the club, but I faced the police alone as one officer began to ask questions like 'Have you got a second mortgage on your property?' and 'Have you ever dealt with this finance company?'

As their line of questioning unfolded I began to put two and two together.

I remembered the last Christmas party. Cheeseman had the generosity to invite not only the players, but their wives, girlfriends, parents, family, Uncle Tom Cobley and all. I could not fathom this, nor his wanting all their names and addresses. It was almost on the scale of the party he threw at Caesar's Palace, Luton – for the entire Southern League!

All the players had loans. All their parents had loans. The names and addresses were not to be invited to a party, they were to be the subjects of loans. It was a genius idea. Brilliant. A great scam, and it would have worked. Keith had all the money coming in, but he was greedy, always wanting to go off at tangents and bring in this, that and the other. He wanted to go out and buy a nightclub with George Best, for instance. All hell broke loose and he was arrested. I couldn't find him. Nobody could find him. We didn't know what was going on, but then everything came out of the woodwork. Every five minutes it seemed there was a knock at the club door.

'You owe me ten grand.'

'You owe me fifteen grand ...'

'I did that building work and I haven't been paid.'

'I did the floodlight work. You haven't paid me.'

'You owe Caesar's Palace for that big party.'

All of a sudden, a club going along nicely, top of the Southern League, are in deep trouble. Our man, whom we can't find, owns the club lock, stock and barrel. The only thing I can do is to sell players. I had to sell Lou Adams, George Cleary, Terry Mortimer; Astle had already gone. I had to sell anybody I could. The lads didn't have any wages and we didn't have a penny in the bank. Cheeseman always paid us in readies. So in my second year as a manager I had gone from top of the tree to an absolute nightmare. I started with a crowd of 34 people – we used to announce the crowd changes to the team – but with Cheeseman's arrival in the summer and putting up the money to buy players and us getting promotion, the average gate went up to 1,000. Now we were facing disaster. The taxman was after us, the VAT man was after us, everybody was after us ...

All the players and I had to give statements to the police. Cheeseman said to me once: 'Barry, this was a good thing gone wrong. We were just unlucky. I'll get out of it, no problem. The finance manager did nothing wrong, he couldn't get out of it. I blackmailed him. I had him by the bollocks.'

When he got arrested he changed his story. He said that he knew nothing about it. It was the finance manager's idea and it was down to him. The police came to see me and told me that and I said I had to go with the finance manager because I was once in a room with Cheeseman and he admitted he had done it all. I told them that he wasn't turning it round like that and I would go to court and say that.

I was in court and Keith came in. It was the first time I had seen him for six months and he threw his arms around me.

'Hello Basil,' he greeted me affectionately. 'How are you doing?'

I told him I was there to give evidence against him.

'You've got to do what you've got to do in this world, ain't you boy!'

He was unbelievable. Never ever down, the geezer.

The police, when interviewing me, had said: 'Well, you took these loans out and unless you confess you're in big trouble.' I said: 'I can't confess. I don't know what you're talking about.'

And I really didn't, but because everybody thought Keith and I were so close, it appeared to them that I was in on the whole scam. Socially we saw each other now and then at big functions and that's all. There was never a one-to-one. We were not close – I hardly ever saw him. He was always running down the stairs to jump in his car to go to the airport.

'You, you bastard,' he'd say. 'I didn't want to see you.'

'Keith, I've got no money,' I would plead.

With that he'd open his briefcase and pull out a wad of notes.

'That will do you for now. Stop pestering me.'

He was a dream chairman at first. Then he went inside and you can imagine what happened then. Because I was having to sell all my players before the transfer deadline, we tumbled from top of the league to eventually finish fifth. We would have won it if we had all been able to keep together, but a different issue altogether had emerged. It was no longer about winning. It was about surviving.

I couldn't pay the players any wages. Because we owed the players so much money, I had to turn to my old mate George Best. I told him that we had floodlights, hadn't paid for them, were in the shit, the chairman was going to prison and Harry Haslam, manager down the road at Luton, had said he would provide us with opposition in a friendly.

Bestie, good as gold that he is, came and guested for us and pulled such a big crowd that we were able to pay the players the six weeks wages they were owed. George never got a pound note for his friendship, loyalty and generosity and it's rewarding for me to reveal the other side to his character when all he took for so long was so much criticism.

At the end of the season we were kicked out of the league. We broke our necks to get out of trouble but because our guv'nor, who had all the shares, was inside, and we had debts that we could not possibly honour, we were sent down a division. From there Dunstable Town went into liquidation. They formed a new company but after Cheeseman went I had five or six different chairmen who came in to try to save the club but none of them succeeded.

In the end Bill Kitt, a local man who had made a few bob and who was the latest in the line of possible saviours, said he was going to give all the players a tenner – only the ones who played, not the substitutes – and after this, his first match, away at Bletchley, I was asked by the press what I thought about his generous gesture.

I went up to the boardroom where Bill was having a drink.

'Do you want a whisky, Barry?'

'Whisky?' I huffed and threw it all over him – what a waste of a drink – but I was Jack The Lad and raving, mocked his offer of a tenner and then, I'm afraid, I got hold of him. I should not have. Next morning the club called an emergency board meeting and sacked me. But what was I to do? After all I had been through I could not stand idly by and be told that my players were going to be paid a measley £10 for their efforts. It was a sick joke. Bill and I are the best of friends now but, at the time, I could have knocked his lights out ...

There had been a long period of uncertainty before Cheeseman and his crew were all arrested. What Cheeseman had done was this. When he was at the football club he used all the names and addresses of players, officials and supporters – as many names as he could gather – to fund his other businesses to get loans out.

He was paid by the council every month a substantial amount of money. He was a director of a construction company with many contracts, and the beauty of these contracts was that he was being paid by the council so that it was rock solid, gilt-edged money paid on the button. The trouble with Cheeseman was that he was never happy with just a good, going concern like his construction company. He always wanted something else.

He got the finance manager to do a few straight loans and then they became fictitious. The guy just got him the money the next day. It wasn't a problem. The monthly debits were coming in regularly on a standing order for the straight ones but as the invented ones got bigger and bigger in number, alarm bells must have started to ring everywhere.

At one point the man in the respectable position tried to get out of the mess but Cheeseman told him that if he turned his back on the scam he would stitch him up by saying that it was he, and he alone, who was responsible. Poor bloke. One minute he was getting record sales and pats on the back for doing great business; the next he's in the deepest shit.

He was a nice guy who simply got in over his head. He couldn't get out of it. His assistant manager obviously knew about it and it was clear to him and everybody else who knew the fall guy that he was heading for a nervous breakdown.

Cheeseman got him out of the country and into his place in Spain where, after a week, he called to say that he was enjoying it. So Cheeseman would tell him to stay another week, and another week, and of course the manager's absence from the office meant that paperwork was piling up.

The managing director, the man Cheeseman had had by the throat in my office, arrived at the office one day to find a lot of accounts which had not been paid. So he began telephoning a few people to tell them that they had missed out on the current month's repayment instalment on their £2,000 loans. A typical conversation would follow.

'What £2,000 loan?'

'Well, that £2,000 loan you have had for the past seven months.'

'But I haven't got one.'

'But you must have. You've been paying it.'

'I haven't been paying it. Not me.'

There were more than a few too many of these. I lived in Tiverton Road, Bedford then and was to discover that there were eight loans in variations of my name, Fry, Friar, Frier and so on.

The beans were spilled when the assistant manager broke down in tears and told his managing director precisely what had been going on.

In 1977 Cheeseman stood trial at Bedford Crown Court for having made bogus loan applications totalling nearly £300,000, using the names of the club's players and others he got from the phone book. He was jailed for six years.

Soon after his release he was jailed for three years for blackmailing a bank manager into advancing him £38,000 against fraudulent US bonds, an Old Bailey case in which the Duke Of Manchester, Lord Angus Montagu, stood in the dock with him on criminal charges. The Duke was acquitted and left court with the judge's admonishment that he had been 'absurdly stupid' ringing in his ears.

In 1992 Spanish police raided Cheeseman's villa in Tenerife and arrested him. He was wanted for extradition on charges of laundering £292 million worth of bonds stolen from a City of London messenger in the biggest robbery in history. At the time it was thought the bonds were unusable, but Cheeseman was arrested at the request of the FBI, who were investigating attempts to launder them.

He jumped bail a few days after an associate of his was shot dead in Texas and, two months later, when a headless body was found near a layby in Sussex, it was suspected that Cheeseman might have met a similar fate.

It was at this point – I was by then manager of Maidstone – that I received a bizarre telephone call from the police. The conversation went like this:

'Barry Fry?'

'Yes.'

'Did you used to be manager at Dunstable?'

'Yes.'

'Was Keith Cheeseman your chairman?'

'Yes.'

'Could you recognise Mr Cheeseman?'

'Of course I f***ing could.'

'Could you recognise Mr Cheeseman with no arms?'

'Yes.'

'Could you recognise Mr Cheeseman with no legs?'

'Yes.'

'But could you recognise Mr Cheeseman without his head on?'

I checked that the calendar was not showing 1 April before replying: 'Sorry, mate. I didn't know him that bloody well.'

About a month later I got a call from the same officer.

'Mr Fry, I am pleased to report that the body we found is not that of Mr Cheeseman. It is of somebody else.'

I obviously had not seen him for ages and I could not resist asking what Mr Cheeseman had been up to. The officer told me: 'He deals with the wrong kind of people.'

I hadn't heard from him for years until, three months into my tenure at Peterborough in 1996, I picked up the telephone.

'Hello my old son,' came a familiar voice on the other end. 'How are you doing? You're in a bit of trouble aren't you?'

It was Cheeseman again. I said that we hadn't got any money, if that was what he was referring to.

'I've got plenty for the both of us, Barry.'

I asked what he was doing at that point in time.

'A bit of this and a bit of that but I won't talk over the phone, I'll come and see you.'

We arranged that he should come to our home match the following Saturday and that he would bring his lady for lunch. He looked good, but always had done. He was invariably immaculately dressed in a designer suit, crisp shirt and eye-catching tie and always wore shades.

He said he had been in America and last weekend had been with Gloria.

'Gloria who?

'Estefan, of course.'

Then they had gone on to a party and Frank said this and Frank said that.

'Frank who?'

'Sinatra.'

Of course. Now he had become a great namedropper. He gave me his business card, which prompted me to ask what he was currently doing. He said that he was making fortunes through setting up venues for pop concerts and that was why he had been anxious to meet up with me at Peterborough.

'You want some money, don't you?' he asked, rather needlessly.

I told him that we were desperate for cash.

'We'll hire out the ground. I'll bring some top people over,' he said.

'Keith, I'm not being funny but it might be a flop.'

He assured me that everything would be all right because he would pay the money up front and he proceeded to stay in Peterborough for two months. He made it clear that he wanted to buy the club and I arranged meetings with all the directors. He came to league games and youth games and talked to this person and that within the club. He liked the fact that we owned the freehold on the ground and that we had several promising young players who would ensure progression on the playing side.

He got really into it, bringing his accountant into things and acting as though it was a foregone conclusion that he would own the place. One or two people were getting a bit hot under the collar and then one night he invited us all out for a meal. He talked freely and openly

19

about the City of London heist, asserting that he got on with all the coppers because he knew them so well, claiming kinship with the mafia bosses and asking if we had seen the television documentary about him.

Nobody had seen it, but I later viewed a video copy that he had given to me. I, in turn, showed it to all the directors of the club and to anybody who is squeamish or a bit nervous it is very frightening. It centres on the world's biggest robbery and, after they had seen it, there was no way the board wanted him in their club.

The round-up to the piece is an interview with him in which he is asked: 'Well, that's the world's biggest robbery. Is that you finished with crime now?' He smirks and says: 'No. I want to top that.'

Well how do you top it?

The atmosphere in the boardroom when they came to discuss the proposal was icy. It was dead in the water and Keith knew that. He had had his card marked and when he called me to ask what had happened I told him.

'Keith, you frightened them to death.'

He said that he had to go to Luton and would pay a social visit to me at home on the way back to his hotel before I set off for my day's work at the club.

As he was nearing my place he called on his mobile phone to check my exact location and I asked my great pal Gordon Ogbourne, who has been with me for 20 years as kit manager at various clubs and whom I trust implicitly, to go to the end of the drive and just wave him in.

We had tea and sandwiches and he said that he was not prepared just to accept what had happened. He was not giving it up that easily. He wanted the club and was going to get it.

After half an hour of reinforcing his ambition we both decided that it was time to go our separate ways for the day ahead and I said that I would follow him out. We reach the main road from my drive and he turns left, I turn left. We get to the lights and he goes straight on, I go straight on. At the next lights he turns left, I turn left. Then as he goes straight on to pick up the A6 to Luton, I turn left to get on the A421 to Northampton. I had no sooner reached this main highway through a little village than my mobile phone rang. It was my wife, Kirstine.

'Stop at the nearest phone box and ring me back at the neighbour's house over the road,' she said with some urgency.

I protested and said that whatever she had to say she should just say it.

But she insisted. 'Barry, I ain't being funny. Stop at the nearest phone box and ring me back. Immediately.'

Realising that something strange was happening, I did as she said.

What's going on?' I asked from the phone booth.

'You ain't going to believe this, Barry. I've got our neighbour over here. I think you'd better come home. She has had people with guns with telescopic sights in her garden. They are following you.'

'Following me? I'm in a phone box. There's nobody here.'

'I don't mean you,' she said. 'I mean Keith.'

So I put the phone down on Kirstine and called Keith on his mobile. I relayed the message that when he pulled into my driveway a white van turned up in the drive of the house opposite and that there were men with guns.

Understandably, the neighbour was petrified because she could see what they were tackled up with. They even knocked on the door and she didn't know whether to answer it or not. She decided not to, but they said they were police and that she should ring the station to verify their presence.

She did this and the officer who answered the phone said that he knew nothing about it. Well, she was in a panic now and didn't know what to do. Thankfully, with two men with rifles on the other side of the door and her quivering, her phone rang and it was a return call from the police to say that, contrary to the information previously given to her, they did know about the situation. It was nothing to do with them, said the caller, it was Interpol.

Armed with this information, she opened the door to them and they presented their badges with the reassurance that they were just observing somebody.

In my conversation with Cheeseman I continued.

'They're following you.'

'Not me, mate,' he replied with typical bravado. 'You must have been up to no good Barry.'

That's the way he plays it. So bloody cool.

I met him the next night at the home of Rinaldo, an Italian gentleman who lived in Peterborough and owned a night club of the same name. Cheeseman wanted to buy his property which was on the market for £750,000. That was the last I saw of him for some time.

A couple of months after that I had a phone call, again from the police in London, to ask if I had a phone number at which they could get hold of him, but I could not help them. The officer said there had been a few complaints about Keith and they were searching for his whereabouts. Did I have a previous address for him? All I could tell them was that he had stayed at The Butterfly Hotel, and that I had a mobile phone number for him which was no longer applicable.

Then I had the manager of The Butterfly phone up.

'You know Keith Cheeseman, don't you?'

I said I did (only too well, by now).

'He's left an unpaid bill of £3,500 here.'

I could not help but laugh. Uncontrollably. Then a finance company (ho-ho) called with an all-too-familiar opening line. 'Do you know Keith Cheeseman?' Apparently he hadn't paid the last five instalments on a car loan.

Keith Cheeseman is the greatest conman I have ever known; possibly the world has ever known. When you were out with him he always had loads of readies and he was the most generous man with tips you could wish to meet. One day at The Dorchester Hotel in London

23

he gave the porter £20 just for taking the bags to his room. A waiter brought an ice bucket and he gave him £20. Then he gave a taxi driver a £20 tip when he took us less than a mile round the corner.

He was such good company that you would have thought butter would not melt in his mouth. Yet in a roll-call of 20th Century villains he would have to be near the top of the league.

If my first job in management was a roller-coaster ride, it could hardly have prepared me better for the long and winding road ahead.

CHAPTER TWO

'Practice son, practice'

Pilgrims Way, Bedford, was part of a council estate of prefab housing originally designed to last for 10 years, though they must have been made of strong stuff because my father actually lived there for 49 years and 11 months before they finally brought in the bulldozers. For me, it was wonderful to be resident there as the most popular kid in the block, entirely due to our being the only household to possess a proper football. My dad worked as a Post Office engineer for 40 years while mum was employed at a television rental company called Robinsons and also for, as I called it, the 'knicker' factory. This was, in fact, a lingerie outlet called Hallwins.

I went to Pearcey Road School from the age of five and it was here that my lifelong obsession with the wonderful game of football began. I got into the school team when I was eight and in those days I used to wait for dad after coming home from school, looking anxiously over our little fence in readiness for him to appear on his way home from work. Football quickly consumed my entire young life. I would say to dad, 'Will you play football with me?' almost before he could get to the front door.

There were plenty of fields down at the bottom of the street and it was greatly pleasing that dad encouraged me and all the kids round our estate to kick around with a football. We were the first to have a posh ball with laces and it was amusing at Christmas time and when the kids had birthdays. They would all come round to our house and ask, 'Can Mr Fry pump our ball up?' They didn't know how to lace it up, either, and dad was an expert on that.

I was an only child and it must have been comical for the neighbours to see dad and I emerge from our front door. He was like the Pied Piper. As we walked down the street, bouncing the ball, the other kids would emerge, one by one, and by the time we had reached the fields there were enough bodies for a 12-a-side game. We would use milk bottles or jackets for goalposts and the games were never-ending. Dennis Brisley, who was a bit older, was one of the boys I was friendly with. He just used to love football and played until he was 45. He was a super-fit man. Ken Stocker, another one of the knockabout boys, was in my school team and it's a coincidence that two of my best pals, he and Dennis, were right wingers. Tommy McGaul was another one of the crowd. He had two brothers and they all used to come down to the green to play.

Dad was trainer for the Post Office side as well as playing for them and whenever the GPO had a game I would take the day off school and go and support him. He was obliged to wear glasses because a bomb in the war had sent him flying, but it was frightening and almost farcical to see him playing in those spectacles. Born in Dover, he had been a navy man. Mum was from Jarrow and there was as much a contrast in their personalities as there was in their geographical roots. Dad was always the serious one, a stalwart of the school of rigorous discipline, whereas mum liked a joke a minute. Both had big families.

There had been no football on television in the days of my early youth and, anyway, we did not possess a television set. But in 1954 Wolves were to be shown on television playing Spartak Moscow in a friendly and I went to the house of a neighbour, Terry Mayhew, whose mother was Irish, to watch it. I was spellbound, mesmerised. Tilly Mayhew later told my mother: 'I asked Barry if he wanted a drink and he was just oblivious to the question. He just kept staring at the screen.' I became a mad Wolves fan, so much so that mum knitted me a scarf with all the players' names on. I've still got it all these years later! I was besotted just through watching them on television. Billy Wright was my idol. Not only was he captain, but he was a gentleman and conducted himself correctly. Everything about him was pure magic. I kept a scrapbook on Wolves and a separate one dedicated entirely to Billy Wright. Among the team there was

Swinbourne, Clamp, Deeley, Flowers, Delaney, Hancocks, Mullen, Murray and Broadbent. Peter Broadbent was another one of my favourite players. He had such grace about him. Their names were all on my scarf, but when it came to the captain he was given his full name. The stitching says 'Billy Wright'. I don't know why I loved him so much because he played in that unexciting position of centre-half. He was, however, the England captain and that may have had something to do with my boyhood admiration. I was also incredulous at how high he could jump for a little man. Dad was later to take me to London to see Wolves play whenever they came south.

You can imagine the scene then, years later, when I'm in a garage at Barnet, filling up my car. Another man pulls in, jumps out and he comes over to me and I instantly recognise him.

'Hello Barry,' he says. 'You're doing a wonderful job down at Barnet.'

It was none other than Billy Wright. Imagine, my hero says that to me! I was so awestruck that I nearly squirted him with all this petrol.

'You wouldn't believe this mate, but you're my idol.'

He smiled. 'I've been watching your progress down at Barnet at close quarters and you have done fantastic.'

I asked how he knew about what, to him, must have been such a rudimentary matter.

'I only live down the road,' he said.

So Billy and his wife Joy were living so close without

my ever knowing, even though at the time I knew he was working for Central Television. I was further able to indulge my hero worship because, on occasions, I used to get to sit in the Royal Box at Wembley alongside Billy, who was a director at Wolves. He always looked after me in those circumstances.

My favourite carpet game as a kid was tiddlywinks, though I played it in a manner which can hardly be said to have been traditional. I turned the tiddlywinks into massive football matches – red tiddlywinks versus blue tiddlywinks; black tiddlywinks versus yellow tiddlywinks. I would put two Subbuteo goals at either end and this massive tournament would start and go on all day.

One of my earliest memories of football is of the so-called 'Matthews Final' in 1953, the FA Cup Final at Wembley between Blackpool and Bolton Wanderers. Dad's football connections with Elstow Abbey and the GPO allowed him access to one ticket to stand behind the goal and he gave me a tremendous thrill when he announced that he was taking me. After our journey by train and tube he put me on his shoulders as we mixed with the thronging crowd and walked down Wembley Way. I was to remain in this elevated position – even though I must have felt like a sack of potatoes by half-time – right through the match. Dad wanted Blackpool to win it; everybody wanted Blackpool to win it because of Stanley Matthews. They may have called it the Matthews Final but I have never understood why because Stan Mortensen scored three goals.

I was the envy of all my schoolmates and, indeed, I have been at every Cup Final since. I was always very keen to collect autographs and after the matches I used to stand outside Wembley and try to figure out a way to get to the team coaches. I couldn't get in because of those big doors. Then I discovered that if you went down one of the long tunnels from inside the stadium and avoided being stopped you would eventually get to the buses. So it became my practice to do this. Dad would be looking everywhere for me and it would not be until both buses pulled out, and I had got all the autographs, that we were reunited.

Another of my indulgences was to jump the perimeter fence and get a bit of turf which would then be in a bowl in the garden for ages.

Throughout my school years I was never interested in any of the lessons, only in sport. I used to get the slipper a lot. When I was aged 11, and in my first year at Silver Jubilee, one particular teacher who hated my disregard for education would say, 'Come out here Fry!' and I would say, 'No.' In those days the desks had ink wells in them and in one of this gentleman's lessons I threw one at him. But this prank rebounded horribly when he sent me to see the headmaster.

'Right Fry,' he said. 'You're not playing for the school team on Friday.'

He could not have taken a worse course of action. Six of the best with the slipper would have been preferable. I begged him and cried my eyes out, but all to no avail.

That slaughtered me. I was captain of the school team and became a prefect, to be identified by the red and white braid on the black jacket of the uniform, later on in life. I was urged by the headmaster, Jack Voice, to put as much effort into education as I did into football and I determined to at least try during lessons. I began to get a prize a year for English, not because I was ever going to raise a challenge to William Shakespeare, but because I tried. It was made clear to me that if I didn't concentrate and I became a pain in the arse I wouldn't be allowed to play football. There could have been no greater incentive. Really, I had no interest in school whatsoever but if they had told me to jump over the moon in order for me to play football I would have jumped over the moon.

I missed the one solitary game and that was it. It taught me a lesson. It was 'three bags full, sir' after that.

Jack Voice was the one who put me on the straight and narrow. He certainly knew my Achilles heel and he had no trouble with me after that. He said he was aware that I didn't like school but emphasised that while there were lads who succeeded at football there were a lot more who did not and therefore I should try because you would never know when you needed to fall back on education. As I am only too well aware now, for all the stars such as the Beckhams and Owens of today, there are a million who get released and hit the scrapheap.

All the teachers encouraged me in the sporting arena because, after all, it was good for the school to have one of their pupils representing them outside. Whether it was cricket or football, whoever was in charge just gave me my head.

As a boy I once had a conversation with Stan Matthews. I managed to get onto his team bus and asked him to sign his autograph.

'What are you doing here?' he asked.

'I'm watching you. It's fantastic.'

He asked how old I was and I told him I was 10.

'You shouldn't be here, you should be playing. Practice son, practice.' Stan has since passed away and I joined the rest of the football world in mourning over his death.

It soon became apparent to me that you can't be a softie and be a good footballer but I remember being frightened to death at Pearcey Road one day. I was going home for dinner and suddenly became aware that a bloke was following me. I was convinced he was chasing me and wanted to murder me so I ran into the house of a couple who fortunately were in at the time. I didn't want to go back to school. They had to get a kid called Brian 'Trotter' Foulkes to look after me, get me across the road and make sure I was all right. I must have been the youngest kid in the country with a minder. But eventually you had to look after yourself. As I got older and a bit more successful football wise, people who were not so interested in football thought I was cocky and big headed and all that. You always get bullies trying to pick a fight or sort you out and I fought like everybody else though with me it was an instinct, a reaction. I was always a scrapper, really, because you had to be to survive. The alternative was that people would walk all over you. I was as placid a kid as I am a man but when too much gets too much you hit out at people. I never went looking for a fight but I certainly wouldn't run away from one.

Football being my only interest in life, I always got hot-off-the-press copies of *Roy of the Rovers* and *Charlie Buchan's Football Monthly*. I would get up in the morning and hope that I was early enough to play Wolves v Manchester United at tiddlywinks and when I got home I couldn't wait for dad to come round the corner. Now my kids do the same to me but I say, 'No, I can't. I'm mentally and physically drained.' Dad must have had such patience. There are days for most people when you have been to work and you simply can't be bothered playing head tennis. My little 10-year-old, Frank, will say, 'Well just give me a few headers, dad.' I tell him to kick it against a wall instead.

I used to say to my dad that I wanted a wall to kick a ball against and we didn't have one. He got me this magic thing with a ball on the end of some elastic and you'd kick it this way and that and it would always come back to you. Mind you I broke a lot of things in the house. Mum went mad and dad would tell her to leave me alone. They had World War III and I would sneak off.

I never knew the meaning of being bored. I either played football and when I came back it was time for bed, or I played a full league table of tiddlywinks. There would be a goal scored and me making an almighty racket, while mum and dad sat there listening to the radio in the other room. The decoration in our front room was rosettes and other football memorabilia. Normally parents wouldn't allow those things in the room where guests were entertained, but my mum and dad were very understanding. The front-room carpet would be covered with all my 'players' and my parents were so considerate that if they wanted to go to the toilet they would walk all the way round the house to avoid the living room so that they would not disturb my game. The sacrifices they made – you don't appreciate it at the time. My bedroom was also full of Wolves momentos.

When I was 12 there was a brilliant article in the local paper. Because I'd been to Wembley so many times since turning eight, the only thing I ever dreamed about was actually playing there. In this feature my dad was quoted as saying, 'It's Wembley or bust, isn't it son?' Dad had taken me to internationals, FA Cup Finals and amateur cup finals between the likes of Crook Town and Bishop Auckland, so by that time I had gained a real feel for the place. There were the old songsheets and such like and I just loved going to that magical place.

Mum and dad were bringing up their only child in a sublime area for sporting activity. The local hamlet of Elstow was proud of its pristine village green and I would play cricket as well as football there. Dad was also trainer of Elstow Abbey, a men's team in the Bedfordshire and District League. I played for them at the age of 14 against all the village sides and I would have to look after myself although some of the lads, particularly our centre-half Maurice Lane, and Charlie Bailey, would not allow the opposition to take liberties with me. They didn't mind me being kicked, because that was all part of the game, but if there was any sign of a rough house they would look after me. If you were in the trenches you certainly wanted Maurice with you. I appeared for them in a cup final at Bedford Town's ground. At school at Pearcey Road I had played in a cup and league-winning team, scoring 60 goals in one season, and was in the Bedford and District team when I was eight. When I moved up to Silver Jubilee School I was soon into the Beds and District Under-13 and then Under-15 teams. It was a period in my life when I walked to school and ran home!

Dad, as always, encouraged me in my football passion. He would come and park outside school in his lorry and watch me play and he was even known to have climbed up a GPO pole to get a good vantage point. These were Friday afternoon matches, after the last lesson in school, and in my playing days in the Bedford and District side we played on Saturdays and went all over the country together.

At 14 I was picked for London Schoolboys. I know the saying that Big Brother is watching, but how the hell a boy 56 miles away in Bedford is selected to play for London is beyond me. Then, in what was a wonderful year for me, I had trials for England Schoolboys. They were organised as Southern Possibles v Probables and

Northern Possibles v Probables and then South v North and for the first of these I was down as a reserve. As luck would have it, somebody didn't turn up and I got a game. I must have impressed the right people because I was called up for the next trial and then the other. As a kid you never know how these things come about, but it was announced in school assembly one day that I had been picked to trial for England. I went on to play for England schoolboys six times and the most memorable of these was in front of a 93,000 crowd at Wembley against Scotland on Saturday 30 April 1960. Among my England team-mates were Len Badger, the Sheffield United full back, Ron Harris and David Pleat, while George Graham played for the opposition. My international selection was terrific for Silver Jubilee school because I was the only Bedford boy ever to have been picked for England. A convoy of buses left the school for Wembley and later the headmaster insisted on a photograph being taken of the entire school with me wearing my England cap.

I used to wonder what it was all about when the other kids would say they were going to Blackpool for the week or Great Yarmouth for a fortnight, for we never had a holiday. Never once. Aunts, uncles and mates all had cars and forever seemed to be darting here, there and everywhere, but for me it appeared that the Bedfordshire boundary lines indicated some kind of electrified fencing to keep us in there, with the rest of the world a no-go zone. I never knew why this was the case but it has since become clear. After all the years dad worked he was allowed four weeks' holiday, then five, then six but never used to take them. What he did instead was to build them up, because he felt that at one time he might have to pack up work, or take a long period of time off, to look after mum. He had to look after his family and do the best he could for them. When retirement came upon him it became apparent that he could have finished a year earlier because of all the time due to him that he had in the bank.

Mum, Dora, died a month after my son Mark was born and it was very sudden. It was as though she had been clinging on to life just so that she might see him. I was at Bedford Town as a player and I worked for the chairman, George Senior, in the mornings. He had a cafe down the London Road and had all these breakfast rolls to get out for a lot of local companies. I couldn't cook, so I was just serving or cutting rolls and putting cheese and ham in them. About 7.30am dad came in with Maurice Lane. He and Maurice often popped in but this day he came in the back way. He never did that. He said he'd been up all night with mum and she was in pain and at the hospital in Kempston, where I lived at the time. Dad said mum had said that I was to get on with work, but I wanted to go to the hospital to see her. He said there was nothing to worry about, but it did concern me. After half an hour I said I wanted to go. At Bedford I used to go round in a van collecting from the sale of lottery tickets. This night I went to hospital with dad, a week before Christmas on a Friday, and mum was obviously in a lot of pain. She had her face screwed up and complained of feeling cold.

I was in the room alone with her for a while and she kept saying that I had to go to work. I felt very uncomfortable. When dad came back I asked if he'd seen the nurse to sort out her coldness and he just said: 'No'. The bell ending visiting hour was going in no time, so I kissed her and she said: 'Go to work.' Dad had to pick up her mate from Hallwins. She was a Scottish lady called Jenny Denton who was getting the bus to Biggleswade from where she would catch the train to Scotland for New Year, so mum was on about dad not forgetting the passenger and me not forgetting to go to work. I went first. Dad had a car then, which I bought for him. I just wanted to go home and not go to people's houses. My house was only five minutes away. I walked in the front door and Anne, my first wife, said the hospital had just rung to say my mum had died. My reaction was to turn round and put my fist through a pain of glass in the window.

'You've got it wrong,' I said.

My dad wasn't on the phone. He worked for the company for 40 years and never had a phone. Can you believe that?

I was 26. I didn't even know mum was ill. My first thought was about dad taking this lady to Biggleswade, so I jumped in the car, got there taking one route to find the bus for Scotland had gone and coming back another route without seeing my dad. I stopped at a club, run by my mum's sister, Alice, which my dad sometimes popped into for a drink. I saw Auntie Alice and asked if she had seen my dad and she said: 'No, why?' I said: 'My mum's dead.' She screamed. I was in a daze. 'Our Dora' was all she could say. I was trying to find my dad and couldn't. I called at a couple of pubs in which he would usually be having a drink with his mates but nobody had seen him. They all knew he was going to take this woman to Biggleswade. I just went home. I was telling Anne the story when there was a knock on the door and it was my dad.

'I've been looking for you everywhere. Mum's dead.'

'Yeah, I've been expecting that,' he said.

Just like that.

We went back to the hospital. Upstairs the curtains were drawn and by this time it was 10 o'clock at night. I could hear people near mum breathing and you didn't know she was dead. I went a bit crazy. Dad calmed me down and took me to the pub opposite the hospital. He said there was nothing I could have done. That was the way she wanted it. She knew she was bad but just tried to forget about it. She had being going to London for years for chemotherapy treatment and there was no way you could have known this unless you had been told. She was always as white as a freshly-starched tablecloth so there was no reason to suspect that anything was wrong.

I was due to play for Bedford the following day and

I said to dad that I would have to pull out of it. He fixed me with a stare and said: 'You won't. The last thing your mother said to you was to go to work. That's your work. Now go to work.' I did, but I may as well have been on Mars for all I could remember about the game. I didn't know whether I had had a touch, scored or not scored; whether we won, drew or lost. I was in a daze. It had been important to dad that I carried out her last wish and, in retrospect, I can understand his attitude to the whole situation. Whatever you give to your parents should come naturally and not because they are dying and you want to tell them again that you love them.

For 25 years I just blanked mum's death from my mind. I broke down terribly at her funeral. She is buried in Elstow and, even though I think about her a lot, I don't go to her grave. I can't explain the reason. People deal with the loss of somebody close in different ways and I have my own way. Dad, Frank, still lives in Bedford. He comes to all the games, with my son-in-law, Steve, taking him along. Though I live in Bedford I don't see him as much as I'd like to. He's a great father like that because where a lot of old people moan that you should go and see them, he never makes reference to it. He knows that I'm very busy both at work and with my family.

I'm afraid that I do not possess any of his qualities and I wish I did. He is a lot better a man than I will ever be. He has got principles, I have none. He has respect, I have none. He is disciplined, I am not. And, talking of discipline, he is responsible for having made me such a good runner. Whenever I crossed him as a youngster he would take off his belt and threaten me with it. He never used it. The threat was always enough and I would be off like greased lightning.

I heard him swear only once, and that was when I had the audacity to laugh when those dreadful glasses of his fell off when he went up for a header one time. I got a clip round the ear for that for good measure.

It will be a source of some amusement to those who know me that I grew up never once hearing a swear word in the house. I have no other vocabulary and I cannot offer an explanation for this. When I was at school everybody thought I was a cockney. The teachers used to tell me that I was uncouth, whatever that means. I didn't even know what a cockney was. Now that I do, I am happy to issue an invitation to those of that breed who wish to learn from the Fry Academy of Blasphemy.

CHAPTER THREE

New boy at Old Trafford

During that 12-month spell when I was playing for England Schoolboys I could have signed for any club in the country except, perversely, Wolverhampton Wanderers. The Molineux management was just about the only one not to make an approach of any kind, and had they done so I would have found myself in something of a dilemma.

I trained with Bedford Town and their manager Ronnie Rook, the old Arsenal centre-forward, wanted me to sign for them, though I soon had reason to fix my sights much higher. During the holidays, as a 14-year-old about to leave school in the summer, Manchester United's chief scout Joe Armstrong invited mum, dad and me up to Old Trafford for four days. They wanted to sign me as an apprentice professional and took me up there to show me the kind of digs in which I would be resident. At this stage in life I had, of course, never been away from home and it was important that my parents were happy with the projected arrangements.

On the particular day of our arrival United had a youth game. Joe introduced us to the assistant manager, Jimmy Murphy, and the boss, Matt Busby. They looked after my parents while Joe took me along to Davyhulme Park Golf Club, where the lads were having a pre-match meal before the game. Such meals in those days consisted of a steak with an egg on top and I duly sat down to enjoy the fare. You dare not have a steak these days – it's pasta now, but back then the menu was different. I sat next to Nobby Stiles, who was captain of the youth team, and in less time than it took to eat the meal he had sold Manchester United to me. He had so much enthusiasm for the club, with dedication and loyalty gift-wrapping his every word in praise of Joe, Jimmy and Matt. I joined the lads on the coach back to Old Trafford, was introduced to everybody and just wished that I was playing that night. I could not have been looked after any better. I was in the dressing room and then behind the dugout and was made to feel part of the set-up from the word go. I was to discover that this was the way they always did things at Old Trafford. The following night we were taken to the top show in town in Manchester and in the middle of the third day my parents took one look at their starry-eyed son and asked what I wanted to do. I was due at Chelsea and West Ham the following week just to have a look around, but I said: 'I don't want to do anything else. I want to come here.'

Mum broke down in tears. My parents were brilliant. They never offered unwanted advice like taking some time to think about it, nor cajoled me into joining a London club much closer to home. They made me feel that the decision was mine and mine alone but, in fact, Manchester United had made my mind up for me. Their public-relations exercise was first class. I had watched that youth team match among a crowd of 35,000 and a three-quarters full Old Trafford was more than enough to impress any aspiring youngster. I had Jimmy Murphy telling me that I would be out there playing the following year and the package was sold lock, stock and barrel without me even having kicked a ball during our stay. When Joe Armstrong came to our house with the invitation to Manchester, he might as well have issued the same invitation to Mars. I didn't know where Manchester was – I was never very good at geography at school. It may have been a foreign land as far as I was concerned. Joe had watched me playing for England Schoolboys and, after the games, would always come over and shake hands and tell me that I had played well. But he was just one of many influential people who used to hang around and I was offered many things. My family had never been used to having money and it was something I didn't care much for at that stage. That was a good thing because it meant that a purely footballing decision was to be made.

Afterwards the lads would ask how much you had got for going there, saying they had received this, that and the other, but I literally did it for nothing other than the privilege. Dad later told me that after I had agreed to sign they sent down railway tickets so that he could watch me in whichever match I played.

My last few months at school felt interminable as I savoured the prospect of going to Old Trafford. What I have never understood is the 'local boy done good' factor didn't register with the Bedford newspapers. I'd lived there all my life and yet there was never a mention of a move which had to reflect well on the town. I have since been involved a lot with the press and so I know the way it works. For instance when I was at non-league Hillingdon, I was God. I could walk on water. I saved them from relegation and we beat Torquay in the FA Cup and hardly a day went by without there being some mention of me in the paper there. But for some reason, the locals in Bedford missed out on the good news.

Anyway, northbound I went. My first digs were with Mrs Scott at Sale Moor, a lovely district of Manchester. She lived there with her sister and both were absolutely nuts about Manchester United. A lad who had played for Scotland Schoolboys called Mike Lorimer also resided there. We would get the bus in to training every day and the whole thing was the complete opposite of what I had expected. We would arrive at the ground at nine o'clock having had a breakfast of a raw egg in milk. This would come up more often than it stayed down, but the club insisted on starting the day with this concoction and to make sure the rule was adhered to the landlady would stand over you while you drank it. I thought we would be playing football morning, afternoon and night. But the first task of the day was to help the groundsman sweep the terracing. Then you would clean all the baths and toilets before moving on to clean the boots. You did everything, it seemed, except play football. We moved on to training in the afternoons but I hated those morning chores. Of course it was all part of the education process, but in those days I never cleaned my own shoes, never mind someone else's boots. It was something of a disappointment. You leave school and think 'Great, I'm going to be a professional footballer with Manchester United' but the reality is that you're like some old cleaning lady with mops, buckets and brushes. Any small consolation I was able to take from this unexpected facet of the occupation was that I was at least cleaning the boots of two immortals in Nobby Stiles and Johnny Giles. For the first couple of years they looked after me wonderfully. The routine was that the new kid on the block would have two more senior players assigned to him and I was fortunate to have this pair.

United had a reserve team, A team, B team and youth team and I went straight into the youths, whose only games were in the Youth Cup, and the A team, having virtually bypassed the B team. At the end of those first two seasons we went to Switzerland for a tournament in Zurich which featured all the big European teams. I was 15 and 16 and, suddenly, a whole new world had opened up to this former Bedford 'inmate'.

Travelling to that first tournament entailed me getting onto an aeroplane for the first time in my life and it was not until some time after that I was able to get my feet back onto the ground, because we won the tournament and I scored the winning goal against Juventus. I was through on goal and smashed the ball into the net and when, in celebration, I went to retrieve the ball out of the back of the net to take it back to the centre circle, it caused an affray. Half of the Italian team jumped on me and I emerged with half of my shirt missing and my number eight floating away on the breeze. This was my first bitter experience of Italians and there were to be more in later life. We won the tournament the following year, too.

Another dream was fulfilled when, at the age of 16, I was picked for Manchester United reserves. The fixture list could not have been kinder if I had compiled it myself, because I made my debut at no other venue than Molineux, home of Wolverhampton Wanderers. I don't know whether my failure to score was down to nerves, inability or a lack of desire to hurt my favourite club, but we won anyway. Before I was 17 I had played a dozen reserve games which, at that time at Manchester United, was almost an achievement of the impossible. One of the games in which I played was a night match at Anfield, where I was given the friendly greeting as I stepped off the team coach of spit in my face accompanied by someone shouting, 'Piss off, Fry!' It was a daunting experience for one so young. I wondered how the agitant even knew my name. At the time it slaughtered me, yet it taught me what to expect. First the

Italians, then the Scousers ... there is another side to football. So often there are examples of abnormal behaviour brought on by the passion which the game engenders. In no other sphere of life can there be such a collective will to win.

One March day in 1962, a month before my 17th birthday, Matt Busby called me into his office.

'You have done brilliant, son. The whole staff are very pleased with your progress at Old Trafford and I have decided to offer you a two-year professional contract.'

He added that he did not want me to worry over whether or not I would be taken on and that he wished to give me advance notice of his intentions. This was a lovely stroke and, to an extent, a relief because so many kids, myself included, were wondering what might become of them. The signing of this contract did not mean much in monetary terms. There was a few quid more, but the maximum wage of £20 a week was in place then and I was to receive £12 8s 0d (£12.40) and £8 in the summer. At the time Matt was writing a column for the *Manchester Evening News Pink* and when we returned from Zurich after winning that second tournament trophy he wrote that, in Barry Fry, United had on their playing staff the northern Jimmy Greaves. I had been scoring a lot of goals, right enough, and I had made the most progress of all the apprentices who had joined at the same time. My big moment had arrived.

United were still in the process of rebuilding after the devastation and heartbreak of the 1958 Munich air disaster. On that dreadful day I had gone home from school to hear the breaking of the news of the tragedy on the radio. The newscaster had barely got the words out of his mouth before I burst into tears. Like many others, I cried all day and night and for days afterwards. Before United had travelled to Germany they played in London on the Saturday and won by a big margin with a sensational performance. Having been to Wembley so many times I had been privileged to see Duncan Edwards, Tommy Taylor and Roger Byrne and I had all their autographs. It was almost as if I knew this trio who lost their lives personally. I was not a Manchester United supporter then, but I have always passionately supported England and those who played for England. The crash had a profound effect upon me.

Everybody in the country, and a lot of countries throughout the world, felt very sorry for Manchester United. When they played Bolton Wanderers in the FA Cup Final that year, there was almost universal support for them. I was in the crowd at Wembley and watched as they lost 2–0 to a couple of Nat Lofthouse strikes. Jimmy Murphy had done a brilliant job in getting them there. Matt Busby was practically at death's door in hospital and Jimmy had everything to sort out, not least the immediate rebuilding of the team. It was an achievement in itself just to have got them to Wembley.

When, two years later, I walked into Old Trafford the pall of Munich was still hanging over the place. Jimmy, Joe Armstrong and John Aston were always speaking with warmth about the players who were lost out there; how genuine and wonderful they were as people as well as footballers. They always emphasised that. The older players like Bobby Charlton, Harry Gregg and Bill Foulkes simply would not talk about Munich. It was too painful. A funny atmosphere was created whenever Munich was mentioned and it became almost a taboo subject within the club. The hurt was just too deep. In Jimmy Murphy's dealings with the older apprentices and the first-year kids, however, he would use Munich as an illustration of how triumph could overcome adversity. He was great for Manchester United. With his aloofness and the tremendous respect he was shown by everybody, the manager, Matt Busby, was always the boss while Jimmy was the one filled with fire and passion. They were a terrific team. Busby didn't hand out many roastings but when he did you knew full well that you had been told off. Jimmy, on the other hand, was always sounding off. He would pack the skip for an away trip and there would always be a bottle of scotch stashed in between the freshly-laundered shirts, shorts and socks. I once witnessed him take a swig during his half-time team talk and shower all the players as he tried to emphasize a point he was making. Jimmy was the Welsh team manager at this time and he spoke in glowing terms about the country and his admiration for the players, particularly Cliff Jones and John Charles. Cliff was the greatest winger out there, known and universally admired for his spectacular diving headers. I played with him later at Bedford

Town and I could relate to him because I had heard so many stories about him. Two of us would converge upon him in training as he flew in from the wing and he would simply and effectively knock us both out of the way as he went through in barnstorming fashion. He was only little, but very strong. He would have made a great jockey.

When I had played 15 or so games for Manchester United reserves I thought I had truly arrived. I was a professional now, and instead of going in at nine o'clock, I sauntered in at ten o'clock or half past. There would be training for an hour and a half and, after 12.30, you would have nothing to do for the rest of the afternoon. The routine for the older lads was to go to the races at Haydock, the now-defunct Manchester, York or Chester and, unfortunately, it became a regular occurrence for me to jump into their cars and go along with them.

My first-year digs, in which Mike Lorimer had a room to himself and I shared with Eamon Dunphy, were with Mrs Scott, but when I returned from my home in Bedford to renew the arrangement, having failed to write to her or telephone in the summer, I knocked on the door expecting to be greeted with open arms. This was far from the case. Unfortunately I had forgotten my manners. She rasped: 'What are you doing here?' I told her that I was back and ready for the new season only to be informed that someone had taken my place. I rang Joe Armstrong, who ticked me off big time. I was a bit naive about the ways of the world and, apparently, I should have sent her a cheque. As far as I was concerned, though, the club paid for the accommodation; I had never dealt with money. It was all a bit strange.

My room-mate Eamon, who had played for the Republic of Ireland schoolboys when I played for England schoolboys in a 2–2 draw in Dublin, was everything I wasn't. For a start, he was intelligent. He had a healthy understanding of religion and politics and showed me a facet of life which I never knew existed when he came home with me to Bedford one weekend. On the Sunday morning he was up at the crack of dawn to attend mass at 7am. Eamon was able to talk authoritatively on a whole spectrum of subjects about which I knew nothing, yet his cerebral dexterity got him into a lot of trouble at Old Trafford. He would get on people's nerves and, small though he was, he ended up in many a fight. All hell broke loose one day when he made a snide comment to the goalkeeper Harry Gregg, who was from Northern Ireland. Harry, a huge man, lifted him eight feet into the air and was clearly going to punch his lights out. Now, I see this and go running over from the five-a-side game in which I am involved to rescue the situation. King Kong could not be humoured. This time he lifted us both to the same height, one in each hand, and crashed our heads together with such force that we both saw stars.

Eamon's trouble was that he had an opinion on everything and almost always expressed it. There are at least some things I think which I like to keep to myself, but not him. What he believed he could not hold back and this led to further confrontation with Wilf McGuinness. Worse, it led me into confrontation with Wilf McGuinness. He and I must have had four fights, and each time they had nothing to do with the combatants and everything to do with Eamon Dunphy. It was always a case of him sending McGuinness, who was a tough guy, smashing into the advertising boards around the five-a-side pitch or uttering some obscenity in his direction. I would go in to sort out the ensuing altercation and it would go up between the two innocent parties. It got to a stage where McGuinness said: 'I want to see you, Fry. Upstairs.' Off we went, just the two of us, and we proceeded to batter hell out of each other. When it was over we wondered where it had all started in the first place. We both said that neither of us had a problem with the other, determined that Dunphy was the root cause and shook hands at the very moment that we espied the culprit walking over the bridge with his arm around a tasty-looking bird.

Myself and Wilf, a great character who had the misfortune to suffer one of the worst broken legs the game has ever seen, became mates. He was another with a real passion for the club.

Saddled with the problem of being housed for my second season, I became aware that Dunphy had been as ignorant as I and was in the same situation. Joe Armstrong said that Bobby Charlton, who lived in Stretford, was getting married and was leaving his digs with Mr and Mrs Jim Davenport. I would take his place there in a fortnight's time but, meanwhile, was to share temporary accommodation with Dunphy next door to another Irish lad, Hugh Curran. At the Davenports I was joined by Ken Morton, who had played for England schoolboys, and Denis Walker, an older pro who knew everything. They were good days. I had my first car from Jim, who worked on the railways and who I always called 'The Governor'. Now we were within five minutes' walking distance of Old Trafford, just down the back alley and over the bridge. You didn't have to get up so early. I had had lots of driving lessons and the day dawned when Jim came to change his car for a better one. He said that he wasn't getting much from the garage for his, a cream Hillman Hunter, and that I could buy it if I fancied it. We did a deal on the never-never and he was so kind that I don't think I ever paid for the car and he never mentioned it. I passed my driving test – at just the ninth attempt. Every time I failed it was for a different reason and I could never understand it. I hadn't killed anybody; nobody had even suffered a life-threatening injury. I drove the car to Bedford and back many times without incident and, in those pre-motorway days, it would take ages all the way down the A6. Mrs Davenport took a keen interest in my progress and every time the car pulled up outside her house after a test she would look out of the window and question whether I had passed by means of a thumb's up and an expectant look on her beaming face. I would return the thumb's up sign and slowly turn it into a thumb's down and she would say: 'Oh no, not again. Why this time?' She would be more disappointed than I was.

As the time was approaching when I would take my test for the sixth time I was very anxious and I asked the lads for some general tips and hints. Bobby Charlton came up with what sounded like a bright idea. 'You know what you should do Baz,' he said, 'you should wear your Manchester United blazer.' To impress the examiner further, I even put on my club tie. There was no way I could fail. I drove well and after 20 minutes we pulled into a layby and I was oozing confidence when he began asking questions about the Highway Code. I felt that I had got them all right and was crestfallen when he uttered those immortal words: 'Mr Fry, I am afraid that you have failed to reach the required standard.' With that, he got out of the car and as he was closing the door he bent down and added: 'By the way, I'm a Manchester City supporter.' It caused a riot of laughter when I related this at The Cliff training ground the following day with Bobby saying to me, 'Barry, you must be the unluckiest guy walking.'

In the early hours of one morning I was awakened by a severe bout of coughing followed by a heavy thud. Mrs Davenport was on the floor, covered in blood, and she could not be attended by Jim, who was working a night shift. I called the doctor and her daughter, Sylvia, and she was diagnosed as having cancer. Her death soon afterwards was the first I had to cope with and it was very difficult. You become very close to those with whom you live and while Sylvia was kind enough to offer alternative accommodation to Ken Morton and myself, I did not like leaving The Governor on his own. Some time later I read that he had been killed, hit by a train on the railway for which he had worked for over 40 years.

It has been a lifetime regret that, as a footballer, I never fulfilled my promise – the has-been that never was. Although I had this great ability and started at the top with England schoolboys and Manchester United, I did not have a career. As soon as I signed professional forms, I went the wrong way. Those trips to the racecourse would be followed by a meal, then an outing to one of the local dog tracks at Salford, White City and Belle Vue. I was bitten deeply by the gambling bug and a further distraction was the Manchester night life. The next port of call after the greyhounds would be one of the night clubs and life became a merry-go-round of these glamorous playgrounds.

Noel Cantwell, who had joined Manchester United from West Ham in time for the 1963 FA Cup Final, arrived as the kind of philosopher and deep thinker about the game which was the trademark of players brought up in the Upton Park academy. He could not believe how off-the-cuff things were at Old Trafford. The essence, and often the sum total, of Matt Busby's team talks would be: 'We are better than them, go and express yourselves,' whereas Noel had been accustomed to long tactical debates. United went into this Wembley final against

Leicester City, with Cantwell the captain, as underdogs, yet emerged emphatic 3–1 winners. I was with the party, enjoying the sumptuous five-star hotel treatment before the game, and the atmosphere on the return train journey to Manchester was electric. A big card school was soon convened by Maurice Setters and others and my penchant for gambling, which by now was almost compulsive, was very much to the fore. We were playing brag, a game in which money is won and lost in the blink of an eye, and my stake was a fiver blind. Anybody who knows the game will tell you that it takes either nerves of steel or a suicidal tendency to strike so big a wager in that fashion. It was neither to me. I was 18 and had plenty of money with nothing to spend it on. I had saved everything for a couple of years, my digs were paid for, I never went out. For two years I dedicated myself to becoming a professional footballer; for the next two years I came dangerously close to careering off the rails. The warning signs were there. Instead of reading the national newspaper back pages and all the football coverage as I had so far done, I began taking the *Sporting Life* every day instead. It was not long before I was interested not only in what was running that day but what was running the following day as well. You don't realise it at the time, but it soon becomes an obsession. At The Cliff you only had to look over the wall and you could see the horses at Manchester racecourse. One of the problems as a professional footballer is that you have too much time on your hands and you have to do something. I did gambling. At the time it was something I enjoyed greatly. I had no responsibilities and it didn't matter if I did my bollocks. There would be two carloads of players going to the races and from there the rest would go home whereas I would head for the dogs, perhaps seeing Alan Ball, who was a regular at the Salford track.

One day I was waiting at the bus stop outside Old Trafford and Matt Busby drew up in his car. He asked me where I was going and when I told him that my destination was Manchester races he said: 'Jump in.' I had been having treatment for an injury and the other lads had gone on ahead of me.

'Do you like racing?' he asked me.

I told him I loved it.

'Listen, son,' he said, 'it's like women and it's like drink. It is fine in moderation, but don't ever let it get to grips with you.'

It was the best bit of advice anyone had ever given to me ... and I took no notice whatsoever.

Since then I have seen so many players who have been paid millions of pounds end up without a pot to piss in. I never had a million pounds to start with, but all through my life gambling has cost me to some extent. Gus Demmy was the top bookmaker in Manchester and I would see him at all the various meetings. I got to know him quite well and in the end he gave me a job chalking up the prices in his main betting office in the afternoons. I never made any wages because I used to do them all behind the counter, but I was in my element. In those days I had a Post Office account from which I was making withdrawals on a regular basis to fund my gambling. It soon whittled down from a few thousand to nothing and it was a frightening experience to look at the opening and closing balances. Even if I won, it was a case of loaning the money from the bookmakers for just a couple of days before I gave it back to them. But I got a great buzz out of it.

When we were abroad with United we used to get a daily allowance of £10, so you only needed to be away for 10 days to have a tidy sum to look forward to. They were in a different league with that kind of perk. The trouble is that once you leave, everything is an anti-climax. Looking back, it is true to say that I stopped working at my game. I ceased to focus. I still played in the reserves, but other, younger players were leapfrogging me. One such player was Willie Anderson. Another was George Best, who went straight from the A team into the first team.

George and I got along great and still do to this day. There have been various occasions on which he has come to my rescue in times of strife and who would have thought that would be the case when as a slight, shy boy he walked into Old Trafford a year behind me? The omens were not very good for George when he became homesick after a day, went back to Belfast and Joe Armstrong pursued him and dragged him back, yet he was the most naturally gifted footballer I had ever laid eyes upon. Despite his lack of size and weight he would beat people for fun in training, which infuriated some players. They would shout: 'Cross it, get the ball across ...' and they would moan and groan when he didn't. The boss and Jimmy Murphy would tell them to leave him alone, adding that he would learn with time when to cross. More fuel would be poured onto the fires of his detractors when he would beat four men in a spellbinding mazy dribble, go back for more and then lose the ball. What was clear from the outset was that George had the heart of a lion. For a wiry little kid he had this great strength and determination. He tackled like a full-back. There were some real full-blooded full-backs around in those days, like Roy Hartle and Tommy Banks, but even they would have been proud of the challenges delivered by George. It was like being hit by a double-decker bus. He was a genius. I loved him. His terrible shyness meant that he needed a bit more looking after than most and I was more than happy to help in that direction.

I had been going out with a girl called Judith Fish, which was something of a laugh in itself. Fish meets Fry! If we had got married I don't think that either of us could have resisted the temptation for her to carry a double-barrelled surname, which is the current vogue for women. Judith's father Tom, a local big businessman, was a rabid Manchester United fan and I got Denis Law to go along and cut the tape when he opened a garage. All the apprentices were given two complimentary tickets for matches and those not required for friends and family were sold to Tom. It was a few extra quid for the lads and no harm was done. I would buy George's complimentaries and pass them on to Tom. As everyone knows, George became a star overnight and rightly so. The beauty about George is that he has had so many bad things written and said about him – he can do 99 good things for people and one bad thing will have him on the front, back and middle pages of every newspaper – that while the temptation must have been to lay low he has kept smiling through. He has been brilliant to me, always keeping in touch despite his having reached the dizzy heights and me having never got off the ground in terms of playing careers. The only sad thing about him is his having packed up at the age of 27.

George's career did not really start to blossom until after I had left Old Trafford in the 1964/65 season. It was to be three more years until their famous victory in the European Cup and he entered the realms of superstardom as 'El Beatle'. By this time I had gone into management and he was in that surreal world of agents, advisers and hangers-on which was brought about as much by his inability to say no to anyone as people wanting to be associated with him.

To demonstrate just how different class he was, my cousins Karen and Pauline Miller were obsessed, like thousands of other girls, with George and wanted to meet him. Manchester United were playing a night match at Luton at the height of his popularity and, even though I hadn't seen him for a few years, he greeted me warmly when I went into their dressing room and agreed to see the girls after the game. The lads, meanwhile, were saying: 'Hey Barry, you still backing those f***ing losers?' and having a laugh. That's football for you. George emerged later and greeted Karen and Pauline, who haven't washed their hands since.

The parting of the ways for me at Old Trafford was, indeed, a sad moment. Just as he had done in much happier circumstances a couple of years previously, Matt Busby called me into his office at the end of April 1965, with my contract due to expire at the end of June. I was 19 and I honestly thought he was going to offer me another contract. All players do. One of the strange things about football is that even if you are a crap player, or even a decent player whose game has turned to crap, you cannot see it yourself. You always think you are better than you are in reality.

'Barry,' he said. 'You haven't progressed as much as we would have liked you to have done. Other players who were not as advanced as you have now overtaken you.'

He added that Bolton Wanderers had made an approach for me.

'We won't charge any money,' Matt said. 'We will give you a free transfer so that you can get yourself looked after.'

He urged me to go home and think about it for a day or two, putting me under no pressure, and the following day I went to see Noel Cantwell, the club captain. I told him what had happened and he said: 'Don't go to Bolton, go to Southend. I know the manager there, Ted Fenton, who used to be my boss at West Ham. I'll get in touch with him and give you a glowing report.' This confused me even more and for a few days I was in a daze. For the first time in my life I felt a failure. Although Matt had not said as much, I felt that Manchester United no longer wanted me and the fact that he was allowing me to talk to other clubs only reinforced this viewpoint.

George Martin, the chief scout at Bolton, came round to my digs and told me that they had permission to talk to me with a view to joining them. United, he said, were going to release me anyway. They were words which felt like daggers through my heart.

On many occasions I have been offered big money by the media to criticise Matt Busby, but there is no way I would ever do that. Matt Busby is not the reason I failed. Barry Fry is the reason I failed. All Matt did was to give me good advice and the opportunity to join the biggest club in the world. Lots of players have got chips on their shoulders when they leave clubs, because they feel they have more ability than those they have left behind. Many are right to hold that view. But those who remain are invariably more dedicated, more focused. Such players are often bitter and twisted. Not me. I look in the mirror and see a man who let himself down, not one who was let down by others.

As George Martin spoke I reflected upon the two appearances I had made for United as a first team reserve – there were no substitutes then and you only got to play as a reserve if someone went down ill just before the match. The first of these was at Ipswich, where all sorts of things were running through my mind in the dressing room. One thought was that, as 12th man, if I had accidentally trodden on someone's toes, breaking a couple in the process, I would get to make my debut through his misfortune. I thought better of it. Ipswich won the game 4–2, with Ray Crawford and Ted Phillips sharing their goals and Bobby Charlton scoring both for United.

The second match was at Sheffield United and this was most memorable for the police bursting into the Manchester United dressing room after the game. 'You can't come in here, mate,' I shouted to one of them, but they brushed me aside and made straight for Dave Gaskell, who was our goalkeeper at the time. He had been taking some stick from the home fans during the game and responded by pulling his shorts down and showing them his arse.

You know, I would have kissed Gaskell's arse for a first-team debut for Manchester United. But it was never to be.

CHAPTER FOUR

Bankruptcy and on the scrapheap

The massive shock to my system caused by my departure from Old Trafford was compounded when it became clear that I had upset Noel Cantwell and, for the first and only time in my life, I had a falling-out with my father. I telephoned my dad to give him the news that I had signed for Bolton Wanderers and to say that he was stunned is something of an understatement.

'Who did you talk to about this?' he asked, clearly upset.

I told him that it was my own decision and that I had consulted no one.

'I thought you might have had the decency to discuss it with me.'

My protestations that I had received a £5000 signing-on fee seemed to irk him even more.

'What good is money?' he demanded. 'Money has never meant anything to you. What are you doing? You should have come home to mull this over.'

67

And with that, he bashed the telephone down on me.

Noel, meanwhile, had been true to his word and gone to the trouble of contacting Ted Fenton, who had apparently been happy to discuss the situation. But my mind was swimming and I just didn't bother to follow up Noel's lead. He let it be known that he thought I should have acted more responsibly.

So it was against that very negative background that I embarked upon the next step in my career. I bought myself a brand new Datsun and everything went very well in a pre-season build-up in which I was a member of the Bolton senior squad, though I failed to make the team for the first couple of league games. They got off to an inauspicious start, with results going against them, and then they dropped Francis Lee for me. My debut was in a home match against Coventry City, who were managed by Jimmy Hill, and unfortunately I was unable to stop the bad run of results as we were beaten. My third consecutive game was at Cardiff, who had that marvellous team which included Ivor Allchurch, John Charles and Mel Charles. In our team were Freddie Hill, Wyn Davies, Gordon Taylor, Roy Hartle and Eddie Hopkinson in goal – a strong side and one in which I was to score my one and only league goal in a 3–1 victory. It was a headed goal in which I beat the mountainous John Charles to the ball. I ask you, men like him and Davies, as big as houses, and I score with a header!

We flew back to Manchester after the game and as I walked down the aeroplane steps I began to feel the after-effects of a crunching tackle I had received from Mel Charles. Suddenly, I could hardly walk. The pain was terrible. Forty-eight hours later we were due to play away at Middlesbrough. I still lived at Mrs Davenport's and on the Sunday morning I walked round the corner to get some treatment from Jack Crompton, the United physio. He said there was no chance of my being fit enough to play. We were leaving Bolton at 11 o'clock the following day and by nine I was on the treatment table at Burnden Park. Then I tried to run round the track and it was hopeless. I couldn't walk, never mind run. The physio told me to go and take a bath and as I soaked, feeling sorry for myself, the door opened and in walked the manager, Bill Ridding.

'What's the matter with you?' he inquired sternly.

I told him that I had done my groin.

'I used to use that excuse to get out of things when I was in the Army,' he replied, and walked out.

Fuming, I jumped out of the bath and set off in the nude in pursuit of Ridding. Of course, the floor was slippery and I doubled or trebled the damage that had already been done to my groin, but there was no stopping me.

'Oi, what did you say? What the f**k are you talking about? Excuse? I don't need any excuse. I've only just got into the f***ing team. I don't want to be left out of it. I've just scored on Saturday. What are you on about?'

It was the worst thing I could have done. He never picked me again. It had been, I suppose, an unseemly event. As I reached screaming pitch, people were emerging from every door in the building to see what was going on and the manager being bawled out by a new player without a stitch on was not what they might have expected.

Franny Lee was back in the team at Middlesbrough and Bolton lost 4–0. It remained, however, a great dressing room. Nat Lofthouse was in charge of the reserves, to whom I had now been consigned. He kept telling me that I was doing well and then they would have Franny being picked for England and Wyn being called up by Wales and I thought I must get my first-team place back. It never happened. Instead they would draft in big Eric Redrobe, then Brian Bromley, then somebody else and somebody else, but not me. In the end I got fed up with the situation, so I decided to knock on Bill Ridding's door.

'What's going on?' Nat keeps saying I'm playing well, there are people away on international duty, you are short of players and I'm not getting a look in.'

'I've been told you're crap,' he responded.

With this, silly Basil goes to see Nat Lofthouse.

'You're a f***ing two-faced bastard, you are,' I screamed at him.

In life you realise sooner or later that there are some people you say that to and some you don't. Nat was in the latter category. At least he asked for an explanation.

'You keep saying that I'm doing well in the reserves,' I said, 'and now Bill's just told me that your reports on me say that I'm crap.'

Before I could flinch he had me in a vice-like grip around my throat, dragged me into the manager's office, and threw me to the floor.

'What's this about my reports saying...' He was stopped short by Ridding entering the room.

'Barry,' Ridding intervened, 'leave us, will you. Leave us, please.'

I got up, dusted myself down and listened behind the closed door as a huge row sparked up. Nat had a right go.

'Don't use me as an excuse!' he thundered. 'You tell him you don't like him. You tell him he isn't good enough. You tell him anything, but don't tell him that I have been giving him bad reports when I have not.'

Those fights at Manchester United which were not my fault and those two incidents at Bolton were to have a positive effect on me in my subsequent managerial career. It has always been the case with me that if I have the occasion to say to a player that he is playing crap or has been an empty shirt, and he turns round and has a real go back, I never take offence. They can throw cups of water in my face, they can call me a f***ing c**t, they can even punch me. I would still pick them for the next match. So much is done and said in the heat of the moment in normal life. In football, every moment is heated. For instance at Barnet, where in all probability I first came to the attention of the modern-day football fan, I had in our non-league days a very good player called Robert Codner, whom I got for nothing from Dagenham and later sold to Brighton for £115,000. I had been telling England's non-league representative Adrian Titcombe for some time that he was worthy of an international place and Adrian came along to watch him in a match against Weymouth. In muddy conditions we were 2–0 down and came back to win 3–2, getting out of jail courtesy of two great goals by Steve Parsons with the winner a 30-yard screamer in the last minute. As the players came off the pitch I was shouting from the dugout.

'Well done, Frank. Brilliant. Phil, Brilliant. Well done. Robert, f***ing empty shirt. You're a f***ing waste of time.'

'What did you say?' Codner demanded as he stopped in his tracks.

'You, you c**t. F***ing waste of time.'

He nutted me, there and then, flush on the nose and I was sent sprawling flat on my back in a foot of mud. I got up and as I entered the dressing room I went straight over to Codner and gave him a full-blooded smack across the face. All the lads jumped in, but it soon calmed down and within minutes I got into the bath and sat next to Codner.

'F***ing hell, boss,' he said. 'That hurt.'

'Your head-butt didn't do me a lot of favours either.'

I got dressed and walked down the corridor into the boardroom, where the chairman, Stan Flashman, greeted me.

'Are you all right?' he said. 'I'm banning that c**t.'

'Who?'

'Rob Codner, of course.'

'No you ain't, Stan.'

At this point we were joined by Adrian Titcombe.

'Well, that's buggered that boy's chance for England. He will never play for his country.'

'What are you talking about, Adrian?' I said.

'Codner. He head-butted you.'

'Bollocks,' I replied. 'What makes you think that?'

He said he had seen the incident from the stand, but I countered.

'Look. I had plimsolls on. I shouted something to him which he didn't hear, so he came back to see what I had said. At that moment I slipped. It's knee-deep in mud out there. You can see for yourself. There's nothing wrong with me. Head-butted me – that's a laugh!'

'Oh, all right then,' Adrian said. 'He can play for England.'

And play for England he did.

I never see the point in allowing situations to fester and what happened at Bolton taught me that lesson. Two spats with the manager completely finished me. I have often wondered what would have happened if I had just sat in the bath that day and said nothing to Bill Ridding, but the fact remains that after just a year I was on my way again, this time to my most local league club, Second Division Luton Town.

They had wanted me as a boy, when George Martin

was the manager. He was still in charge and he telephoned me to say that it had come to his attention that Bolton were letting me go on a free transfer and he would like me to go along for a chat. The fact was that I was going home anyway. There was nowhere else to go. When we came face to face all George could say was: 'When you left school you should have come here.' I signed a one-year contract and that season Luton finished within 0.046 goal average of being promoted. Again, though, I didn't play much. I was in and out of the team and I left the club having played a career total of fewer than 20 league games while at three clubs, which was disgraceful for what I had to offer.

At the age of 21, six short years after walking into Old Trafford with the world at my feet, I was on the scrapheap. Finished. Caput. Not a single league club wanted me.

The only club of any description to show even the remotest interest was Southern League Gravesend & Northfleet, who were managed by Walter Ricketts. They had a lot of experienced players like Jim Towers, formerly of Brentford and Tosh Chamberlain, who had been at Fulham, while John Dick, the ex-West Ham stalwart, was the coach. So here I was, living in Bedford and set to join Gravesend, which was almost the other side of the world. And part-time football into the bargain. I joined them purely because I wanted to play football, but it was clear from the outset that I would have to get a job in the Bedford area to make ends meet. A firm called

Advance Linen in the nearby village of Kempston required a driver to make deliveries of those pull-down towels which you see in the ladies and gents toilets at pubs and restaurants and I was successful with my application. I had to do my rounds in quick time because on Tuesday and Thursday nights I had to be at Gravesend for training sessions.

I was inhabiting a totally different world. While in Manchester I had met at a dance the girl, Anne, who was to become my first wife and she was no small part of the equation at this time and in these new circumstances. She had no interest in football, even though she lived in Salford right next to The Cliff, and I told her on the dance floor that I was a bricklayer. It was the kind of lie that only a woman could spot and she asked how I could be a bricklayer with such soft hands. Three years on we married in Salford but set up home in a flat in Bedford. It was a very difficult time. My life had been turned upside down. Instead of getting up and looking forward to work because I loved the running around and the training, followed by the afternoon off and going to the races, I was reporting for duty in a mundane job at 7.45am and rushing to allow time for the two-and-a-half-hour journey to Gravesend. Also, I was newly-married.

Even though they had players who were far more experienced than I, Gravesend made me captain. I had been there for just six months when Walter Ricketts was appointed as assistant manager to Dick Graham at Leyton Orient. He told me straight away that he would be taking me with him and, presto, I was back with a league club. I was buzzing. Dick looked after me, giving us a club house at Gants Hill. By this time we had Jane, our first daughter, but the move wasn't really of any concern to Anne because of her apathy towards football. It would not have mattered to her where we lived. She never came to any of the games and, consequently, didn't mix with football people.

I was never a regular in the Orient team, and in one of my periods on the sidelines something was to happen which would change the course of my life. The players arrived for one game to find that the trainer, the man with the magic sponge, had done a moonlight flit. No explanation. He just didn't turn up. Dick was naturally concerned, but I volunteered to do the job. I allayed his misgivings about my qualification to take on the role by telling him that any silly bugger could apply cold water where it was needed and, anyway, we had a doctor on hand to deal with any serious injuries.

My enthusiasm must have been infectious, because I was given the job. To be honest, I was just so glad to be back in football. I would have put the corner flags out. Anything.

Dick, who had managed Crystal Palace and Colchester very successfully, was a superstitious man and because we won I was the official trainer for the next five games. We remained unbeaten in what was a good run and I was really enjoying myself. I was involved and I was in the dressing room with all the banter which I had missed so badly. Then it came to a point where Dick would call to say that he had a business meeting on a particular morning and would be late in. 'Could you take the training, Barry?' This was a little more daunting. There were players like Cliff Holton, Brian Whitehouse and all the incumbents brought from Palace by Dick; really respected professionals in the game. Here I was, telling them to jump over this and leap over that and do this, that and the other. I was just beginning to enjoy that side of the game when Dick called me in and said: 'Listen, I'm having problems with the board.' He said that Harry Clarke, the former Tottenham Hotspur centre-half and now manager of Romford, had made a bid for me. I was far from horrified about the prospect of a move there, because although they were a non-league side they were in the upper echelons of their division. Dick went on to explain that his problems were such that he was facing imminent dismissal and added: 'I'll arrange for you to buy the house in Gants Hill. If I go, they won't keep you and it is important to me that you are looked after.' He did his best for me, but I was to receive a letter from the club in which they said they were in financial difficulties and that I must vacate the premises.

Clarke offered me as much part-time as I was earning full-time at Orient. Anne and I moved back to Bedford with little Jane and into another flat. We were back at square one, with me facing the prospect of long-distance travel to training and playing part-time football. Now we both went job-hunting. I found employment with the

London-based Initial Towels in a similar capacity to that which I fulfilled with Advance Linen and Anne joined a local financial company. It was not long before I joined her there as a rep. They gave me a car and I began to enjoy this alien role, particularly as I now had the transport to get me to Romford and back. I had a good time at the club, but after 18 months I was tiring of the endless journeys. The best solution seemed to be to join my home-town club, Bedford, and this was duly achieved.

Now I lived and worked in familiar surroundings and the situation was idyllic. At the finance company I dealt in re-mortgaging. Brokers were on 10 per cent commission and some weeks, if things had gone well, they could earn up to £1,000. More often it was £100 or £200, but the thought occurred that, in football, I must be in the wrong game.

At this time a company brought to the area the concept of pyramid selling, a practice whereby individuals would invest at certain levels of the pyramid, say £1,000 or £2,000, and work their way to the top by virtue of the amount of their products they could sell. While still with the finance house I started to attend educational and recruitment evenings hosted by the new company in hotel rooms which they had hired. In no time I was earning obscene amounts of money; so much that I did not know what to do with it. Suddenly I had three Datsuns, because I had recruited my two cousins to work for me and they needed transport, and two racehorses. Football was secondary by now. I was a whizz-kid entrepreneur.

One of the questions on the loan application forms demanded a reason for the advancement and I would advise my clients to cite investment in a new company. Any reason could be put forward, such as home improvements or a new car, but it suited me, as an employee of both firms, to favour the local company investment route. Everything was going along nicely until one of my cousins announced that she was to be married in America. Anne and I took our two small children across the Atlantic for six weeks, having decided to make a holiday of the wedding invitation. We used a house in Detroit as our base and travelled extensively as far as Canada.

On the day that we flew out to the United States a court case was being held locally in which an individual who had taken out one of these second mortgages was to have his house repossessed. For some time he had not only failed to make a repayment on the property but had also amassed a garage full of goods he did not have a clue how to sell. The local paper ran a story taking a sympathetic view towards him, saying that this poor family was being kicked out onto the street, citing this man's naivety as a poor reason to be made homeless.

It could not have been worse publicity for the finance company, who despatched to all their branches from head office a memorandum which said that, with immediate effect, no further loans involving investment in the new firm were to be sanctioned. We, meanwhile, had taken to the skies from Heathrow in the belief that, with a stack of loan application forms being processed, we would be coming home to fortunes. The fates were conspiring against me in another way.

I felt so prosperous now that I took a quarter share in the racehorse Pauldenham, trained by Alf Dalton at Newmarket, and Alf had assured me that he would not run the horse while I was away. He knew how much I liked to be present when the horse ran, such as his most recent outing at Pontefract, where he was strongly fancied. Coming out of the stalls, another horse ran across Pauldenham, who had to be snatched up, and his chance had gone there and then. Yet he finished like a train to be second and would certainly have won but for the interference at the start. Before that Lester Piggott rode the horse at Sandown, where again we thought he could not be beaten, in a four-runner field. He finished stone cold last. So I had done my bollocks on the horse a few times but I felt it was only a matter of time before I recouped my losses and more.

My high spirits on our return from America were soon to be heavily deflated. I could barely open the front door for the mountain of mail awaiting us. Not only was there a sheaf of application forms, the ones set to make me thousands of pounds, with 'Rejected' stamped across them, there was a large bill from Dalton relating to buying back Pauldenham after he had won a selling race. I discovered that, in my absence, he had run the horse back at Pontefract, it won doing handsprings and it had been backed from 33–1 to 12–1. More than that

Glimmer Again, the horse I owned outright, had been sent to run at Yarmouth where, instead of negotiating a bend, he ran straight on, crashed through the running rail and had injured himself so badly that he would never run again. What a mess. What a total, unexpurgated nightmare. I suddenly realised why my father never went away on holiday. Ever since I have always approached them with trepidation.

I lost my house, my cars … everything.

The bank manager was my only potential source of salvation. I made an appointment and told him the whole sorry episode. He said that he had noticed that my account had gone overdrawn but wasn't particularly worried because he knew that I was away and was expecting money on my return. There was no money and no prospect of any. I had been working for myself for 10 months as a mortgage broker. He thought long and hard before recommending that I see a solicitor. I took his advice.

'Have you got a tenner?' asked the legal representative.

I had. Just about.

'You should go down to the court and file your own petition for bankruptcy.'

'You've got to be f***ing joking,' I replied, but he was adamant that this course of action was the only one to take if I were to extricate myself from this dire situation.

I didn't understand the procedure, or its consequences. What I do know is that it was the worst thing I have ever done. Straight away there was someone round to my house to take the rotary arm off my car, so that it is his property and not yours any more. The house is his; the furniture is his; everything you own is his. And because everything was in joint names, my wife lost everything too. The future for Anne and myself as a couple was not bright.

It is in times of adversity that you discover who your real friends are and George Senior, the Bedford Town chairman, helped me out. On the playing side things could hardly have been better. We won the Southern League, scoring 103 goals with me contributing to that total from my midfield role. I was captain and player of the year. He gave me a job in his greasy spoon, George's Cafe, in the mornings, and I added to what was now a meagre income by working for the club's pools operations in the afternoons, delivering to pubs, clubs and individuals. A problem had developed with a property which I owned in Luton. Some itinerants had taken it over and acquired squatters' rights. I wanted to sell it to bring in a few quid but I couldn't get them out, so I passed the burden on to another broker I knew in the town by selling the house to him for a knockdown price. In another property I owned in Bedford my friends Sheila and George Dellar lived on the ground floor with their young family. I suddenly had to be very careful now. I passed everything over to them because otherwise they would have been turfed out. Fortunately for my cousins, their cars were not on my driveway when the man from the Official Receiver's office called.

I went bankrupt for £6,000 and there is no way I should have done that. I just panicked, I suppose, but if I had known then what I know now I certainly would not have done it. Later on in life, when I had got a few quid, I applied for my discharge and it cost me in the region of £18,000. That, to me, is unbelievable. Looked at logically, if I can't pay £6,000 then I certainly cannot pay £18,000. All right, I had had a bit of luck with one or two other things, such as my signing-on fee at Maidstone and a property in someone else's name so that I could wheel and deal with the equity. You can't even buy a house again when you are bankrupt. There are so many complications. They repossessed my home and just sold it without a consideration for me and my family. All they wanted was what they could get out of it. So it was back into rented accommodation for me, Anne and the kids. Not only did that bring a feeling of failure, but the stigma of bankruptcy is awful. Bankruptcy is only a word, like liquidation when applied to companies, but nobody wants to know the ins and outs of these things. They just see you as down and out. It was a terrible time for the family. They rallied round and helped, never wanting to see you without, but it puts a tremendous strain on your relationship. You have moved from a decent home to a not-so-decent home and the kids want to know why. They don't like it. One minute they are being driven around in cars and the next they're on a pushbike. How do you explain it to them? There should be a governing body to which people who get in these predicaments turn for expert advice and help without charging exorbitant fees. The bottom line is that you are in money trouble and the last thing you want is another bill. Every year that you are a bankrupt, a percentage is put onto your debt. It is ludicrous. No common sense is involved at all. But if you want to put the record straight you either pay up or stay undischarged. These days, when I hear the predicaments of some people, I could cry for them because it is a case with me of 'there but for the grace of God go I'. I was lucky to get out of it.

I played for Bedford for three years. During one Tuesday night match I suffered a bad injury and the scar remains to this day. I got a knee in the thigh which, ordinarily, I would have recovered from in a couple of days, but it developed into a haematoma. The following day I was driving on my pools rounds and I literally could not get out of the car at the first stop. My leg was swelling up like a balloon, as though someone were pumping it up, and getting bigger and bigger by the half hour. In severe pain, I managed to drive to the hospital, where the best I could manage was to pip the horn in the grounds until I attracted attention. I was helped inside and when they took a look at my leg I was told it was a blood clot and they would have to operate.

This had to be delayed because I had eaten breakfast. One of the ways in which George looked after me was that after I had finished in the cafe he would cook for me the most gigantic fry-up, which I loved. I had to wait in agony until sufficient time had elapsed and afterwards they told me that there was something wrong with my blood. Instead of bruising and dispersing I was bruising and clotting, which wasn't very welcome news for a 26-year-old footballer. I was on crutches for six months, with my whole leg in plaster.

The season after my recovery I was playing in a five-a-side tournament and suffered exactly the same injury to the other leg. The doctors' concern for my blood abnormality was such that they advised me to stop playing football. Now I may not have been playing at a high level, but it was the last thing I wanted to hear. It frightened me. I did not want to pack in the game but I was apprehensive and naturally took things a bit easier. Back on crutches, I was eating like a pig, not training and getting fat.

CHAPTER FIVE

Cheeseman and the frilly knickers

My journey from Bedford to Dunstable Town as player-manager came via a six-month spell at Stevenage, who had Peter Shreeves as a player and Dave Mackay's business partner Jimmy Burton as chairman. Tony Fear was removed as Dunstable manager in the March, soon after I arrived, and I was asked if I would like to become player-manager. It was with some reluctance that I accepted because they had finished bottom of the league eight years on the trot, although I could not have done any worse and the scope for improvement was immense.

I had two months in which to rescue a situation in which they would be wooden spoonists for a ninth consecutive season and I determined that, whatever happened, we would have some fun and play with a smile on our faces. My first game in charge drew a massive crowd of 34 paying spectators. The second attracted 42 (my family came) and was the birth of what has become a standard joke in football that the crowd changes should be announced to the team.

We finished bottom yet again. When the season had finished a meeting was convened of the committee, which was comprised of nine men and three women. I had told the local press of my plans to liven up things around the club with some high-profile friendlies in the run-up to the following season and the signings of some well-known players. This was the subject for discussion when the door opened and a mini-army walked in. Their leader took centre stage.

'Hello, ladies and gentlemen, I'm Keith Cheeseman and I am the new owner of Dunstable Football Club.'

He introduced his team of advisers and said that he had been with the chairmen of some clubs, such as Harry Haslam at Luton, and been promised the signatures of this player and that player. I got up to walk out, but before doing so I addressed this man who had taken over the room.

'What did you say your name was, mate?'

'Keith Cheeseman.'

I inquired what he did for a living.

'I build houses.'

'I'll tell you what. I don't tell you how to build houses; don't tell me how to build f***ing football clubs.' And with that, I left the room.

He came running after me.

'Oi, you!' he shouted.

I put my face up close to his and said, 'Yeah?'

'You'll do me,' he said and shook hands with me.

'I've read about you wanting to bring Nobby Stiles and George Best down here and I like that. Come into my office tomorrow and we'll have a good chat.'

This conversation was better than any young manager could have dreamed. He told me of his business interests in South Africa and Australia as well as his building companies in Bedfordshire and the West Midlands and it was this last reference which really was music to my ears.

I told him that I was desperate to sign former West Brom and England striker Jeff Astle and it would help if Cheeseman made him a consultant to his company in the area where Jeff was a legend at West Bromwich. He thought this a great idea and asked what else I wanted. I said that we were a crap team and that Ron Atkinson had taken over as manager of down-the-road Kettering, who had just won the league. I wanted three of his players, George Cleary, Trevor Peck and John Hawksworth.

'Any others?' he asked. I said that I fancied Jack Bannister of Luton and Jackie Scurr of Cambridge and, naturally, he wondered what all this might cost.

I related that we would have to give them between £100 and £150 a week, maybe a £500 signing-on fee and an incentive of £500 to win the league. Far from being fazed, he said: 'Yes, we'll sign all those. What about a Christmas bonus for them? If we're in the top six at Christmas, we'll give them a bonus payment.'

This was great. He said he was away so much on business that he would leave me a cheque book with all the cheques signed and I should use them as and when required. I was gleeful, thinking: 'Are you sure?' This was like being a manager in heaven. We managed to persuade Jeff Astle to join us and this was an unbelievable signing for a club like Dunstable. He had once scored the winning goal in an FA Cup Final, led the line for England against Brazil in the 1970 World Cup and could still play a bit, despite two cartilage operations. I was itching to put Dunstable on the map and I said to Keith that what we should really do to put the club into the limelight was to get George Best to play for us. When I was appointed player-manager, George was one of the first people I contacted. I went up to his club, Slack Alice's, in Manchester and told him my glad tidings. He had no idea where Dunstable was and seemed no wiser when I told him it was near Luton.

One of the more irksome aspects of Dunstable Town Football Club was that the nets on the goals were in tatters and there was many a debate as to whether a legitimate goal had been scored or not because the ball would go right through them and bounce along the dirt track. Taking pity on me, George gave me £25 and told me to buy the club a new set of nets. This was great stuff for the local paper and the story made headline news.

As Cheeseman and I discussed plans for the future, he said that he had seen this article and asked if I really knew George Best so well. By now George had fallen out with Tommy Docherty, the manager at Manchester United, and was no longer playing for them. He wasn't playing for anybody. I felt sure that George would turn out for us just as a favour, but my chairman wanted to put it on a business footing and told me to get him at whatever cost and that he might want to go into business with him. Now I felt that he was using me to get to George – some people are like that – and I didn't want to go down that road.

My first impression of Keith was that he was different class. At the Southern League Annual Dinner, where it was the practice for all the clubs to take a table of ten, he took two tables – and we were bottom of the league! He allowed me to drive his Lamborghini as we made our way to stay in the penthouse suite, which was the size of a house, at The Dorchester Hotel in London. Only A-list celebrities frequented this palatial suite; apparently the actor Charlton Heston had stayed there a week previously. When the porter delivered our luggage to the room, Keith gave him a £20 tip. Then he summoned a bucket of ice and gave the room service waiter £20. Next we took a taxi literally round the corner to the dinner – there wasn't even £2 on the meter – and Keith fished for another £20 tip. As he made to hand over the note I intercepted it, put it in my pocket and replaced it with a fiver. The driver still thought his boat had come in. At the function he bought drinks left, right and centre and announced afterwards that we were moving on to a night club. Here again the money was being flashed around and he gave me £60, explaining that I could have the pick of any of the beautiful girls who were lined up like a Miss World parade. I preferred instead to have a few beers with the boys and retired for the night to the luxury of my Dorchester suite. He did not return until daylight and the first thing he wanted to know was which girl I had lavished the money on. I told him that I had abstained and he said I was not getting away with that. We made our way to a lingerie shop close to Harrods and he said that I was to follow his example and buy my wife something from there. So I had to spend the £60 I thought I had got away with and there's no doubt that Anne would rather have had the money than the frilly items I imposed on her.

After all this frivolity it was down in the summer to the business of building a side which I thought capable of taking Dunstable forward. Jeff Astle duly signed for the pittance of £25 a week, I paid £1,500 to Ron Atkinson for his trio – Cleary, who was a prolific goalscorer, Hawksworth, who was the George Best of non-league football with his brilliant dribbling and Peck, a brick shithouse of a Welsh centre-half – and Bannister and Scurr, two very strong full-backs. I promised Keith that we would win the league, reasoning that Cleary and Astle up front would be lethal, Hawksworth would provide them with the service, nothing would get past Peck and the full-backs would be unbeatable. We didn't need anybody else; the rest of the line-up didn't matter. Yet Keith had become consumed with the Best idea and asked me to pursue it.

Back to Manchester I went and when I put the idea to George he readily agreed to guesting for us in a couple of pre-season games but added: 'It will cost you.' I told him Cheeseman would pay him whatever he had to but George came back: 'Not me. Tommy Docherty. I'll play for you all season if you can do the deal.'

United still held George's registration. I didn't know Tommy then, so I went to The Cliff, where the first person I saw was Paddy Crerand, a great guy. I told Paddy the reason for my visit and he took me upstairs to meet the boss. I said that I was seeking his permission to talk to George about playing a couple of games for us and he said: 'No problem at all. He won't f***ing do it, but you see him and come back to let me know how you have got on.' I had no need to seek out George and I went instead to have tea and toast with Anne's relatives Beat and Tom McKinney a quarter of a mile away in territory which was so familiar, returning 75 minutes later when I knew they would have finished training. Docherty was in the bath and I told him that Best had agreed to play for us. 'Who are you playing?' asked the Scot. When I told him nothing had been arranged so far he said: 'We'll play you … you can play Manchester United.' He asked how much Best was being paid and I said that I didn't know. It was a matter for my new chairman whom, I assured Docherty, was a great bloke. So great that he had left me a cheque book with all the cheques signed. That brought a smile to Docherty's face and he remarked that I had a rare breed of chairman.

'I want a grand,' Tommy said. I assured him that would be no problem and promised to contact Keith Cheeseman, whose instructions were for me to go to the Bank Of Ireland in Manchester and the transaction would be faxed to me there, enabling me to pay cash. I took the money to Docherty and passed on Keith's invitation for him and Crerand to join Cheeseman, Astle and myself for dinner in a Manchester hotel that night. The central figure in this deal was the only one missing, because George would not be in the same room as Tommy Docherty. They had fallen out big time. Yet we had a laugh a minute. Docherty is a very funny man. When we left The Doc we went on to Slack Alice's to meet George and everyone got along fine.

We announced the next day that George Best was to play for Dunstable Town and, predictably, nobody believed it. There was further scepticism when, on the day of the match against Manchester United, everybody was there except Besty. He had been on the telephone to me and said: 'I'm calling from the motorway. You aren't going to believe me, but my car has broken down.' My heart sank. An announcement had to be made to the huge crowd of over 10,000 that the kick off would be delayed for 15 minutes to allow time for Best to arrive and this, of course, was met by a resounding groan. It was a remarkable night. Besty turned up and played, the streets of the town were crowded like millennium parties, the club were an item on *News At Ten* and we beat Manchester United, who had George Graham playing for them, 3–2. It was like a fairytale.

Besty came home with me and stayed the night and turned out again for us in our next fixture against Bobby Tambling's Cork Celtic. How things were changing at little Dunstable. Before the Best involvement, when we had signed those three players from Ron Atkinson we went to lunch at midday and emerged from the restaurant at ten past eight that night. Everybody was on such a high.

Not for long. A few days later I got a call from Ron, who said: 'Your cheque has bounced.' I could not get hold of Keith because I didn't know where he was, but fortunately he rang me soon afterwards. When I told him about the dud cheque for £1,500 he asked which cheque book I had used. I related that it was the Bank Of Ireland and he said that he had changed his account before he had left for his latest foreign excursion, promising a new cheque book on his return. 'Just ring Ron and tell him not to worry.' I appeased Ron by saying that I felt he was not the type of man to get egg over his face for that kind of money; that he was a local businessman who seemed to be above board. It was just a mistake. When Keith returned he offered to pay Ron's chairman, John Nash, cash for the players but the new cheque sufficed.

We had a fantastic season, gaining promotion with 105 goals. Jeff Astle scored 34 of them. Basically it was all down to Keith Cheeseman. He was true to his promise of a Christmas bonus for the players, giving them £250 each – a lot of money in those days – for being in the top six.

There was, however, a small blip on the landscape that season. I got into trouble with the league because in the Bedfordshire Senior Cup you were meant to field your first-team players. We were away at Merthyr on the Saturday and I wasn't for cancelling this match to play Sandy in the league and then go up to Merthyr in midweek, so I sent my reserves to Sandy, where we won 5–0 and my first team to Merthyr, where we won 4–0. The Bedfordshire FA hauled me up, warned me, fined my club £100 and kicked us out of the Senior Cup for fielding a reserve side. I had been advised by our secretary, bless him, not to do this, but I was new in management, Jack The Lad, and determined to do things my way.

Then I was in trouble again when I had a bust-up with a linesman. The world and his wife could see that the opposing centre-forward was a mile offside as he was put through and ran on to score. The linesman at first correctly raised his flag but then put it down again and the goal stood. I went up to him and said: 'Oi, either put your flag up and keep it up or stick it up your f***ing arse!' The referee came over to see what was going on and the linesman said: 'He's just told me to stick my flag up my arse.' I protested that the guy was ten yards offside, the linesman had flagged and he, the referee, had not looked over when he was flagging. He banned me from the dugout and reported me. Now I'm up again before the FA, who have already given me a stern warning. They banned me for a month. What that meant was that I was prevented from going to the ground to do my job and I felt this was diabolical. I was incensed by the decision and appealed. This was successful to the extent that my sentence was halved but still, for 14 days, I had been unable to do my full-time job. During this period we had one home game and Keith arranged for me to be there. Well, almost. The club owned a house which overlooked the ground, so I watched the game from the bedroom window. I have never understood how people can sit on football committees and make a decision to deprive you of your livelihood, but I suppose it taught me that rules are rules in whatever walk of life and if you want to get on you must abide by them, however foolish they may be in your view. What was even more alarming on the day I watched a match from a bedroom window was an incident involving Keith. We always greeted each other with a hug, but this time he had with him two very large gorilla-like companions and when I went to make the gesture they stepped in to prevent it. That had been the first indication to me of a lifestyle which demanded minders.

The sack at Dunstable came after two and a half years and my next managerial position was with Hillingdon Borough, another Southern League side. They had played around 15 games and contrived to be bottom of the league despite no fewer than eleven of these matches being at home. So much for home advantage. The Brown brothers, who owned a furniture shop, were chairman and vice-chairman and they were lovely people to work for. Jim Langley, the old Fulham left-back, had been there before me and when I arrived they were resigned to the hopelessness of their situation and said that getting out of trouble was an impossibility. But we had a good season. We went to Torquay in the FA Cup and beat them 2–1, with little Dave Metchick scoring the winning goal with a header, having never previously headed a goal in his life. In the next round we were at home to Elton John's Watford. The papers had a stunted picture of me throwing a poster of Elton into a dustbin – well, it was the silly season around Christmas. We were dead unlucky in that match, leading twice before going down 2–3 on an ice rink of a pitch, but the cup run at least generated a lot of local interest in the club and we went on to finish above halfway in the league, which was regarded as a miracle. When Jeff Brown, the chairman, sent me my wages he put a little note in the packet which said: 'Well done, God!'

In the close season I brought in some new players like Kevin Millett and Robbie Wainwright and I really felt that we were capable of big things. A week before the new season was due to start I received a telephone call at my home, which was still in Bedford. Jim Walker had done marvellous things for my old club, Bedford Town, while managing them but I was to learn in the course of this call that they had parted company. I was asked if I would like to become their manager and that permission had been granted by Hillingdon for them to speak to me. I called Jeff Brown, who said that there was no way they wanted me to go, but they realised that I lived in Bedford and their offer might appeal to me. Hillingdon had, however, put a £1,500 price tag on my head.

It was an awkward time. Pre-season training was in full swing, with battle plans all drawn up, and departures and arrivals at this late stage could be very unsettling. Living in Bedford, I was able to keep up with all the local news and the latest hot potato was that the brewers Charles Wells, who owned Bedford's ground The Eyrie, had given five years' notice that when the lease had expired they could no longer use it. I went to meet the Bedford board, which was 12-strong and made up of accountants, solicitors, Justices of the Peace and businessmen. Individually they were all fine and upstanding and I still go out with some of them for meals. Collectively as a board, though, they were very frustrating. Despite this, the pull of returning to the club was overwhelming and Hillingdon reluctantly let me go. I was in the hopeless position of being unable to sign any players of note, because they were all fixed up at this stage. So I concentrated on building up the youth side, bringing in a 16-year-old goalkeeper, Tony Luff, and a good young player called Rob Johnson on apprentice forms. I later sold Johnson to Luton, for whom he played

350 games including a Coca-Cola Cup Final defeat of Arsenal. He has since been the physio at Sheffield Wednesday.

The Bedford board were adamant that the threat from Charles Wells would not be carried out, despite showing me an exchange of correspondence which made it clear to me that this wasn't a threat; it was fact. Bedford were making all kinds of points about the fans being up in arms about the loss of their stadium and they would boycott the brewery's beer, but the brewery replied that it did not matter what threats were made and that their decision was irrevocable. I made no bones about my views that they should be acting upon a search for a new ground straight away. The board and I were on a constant collision course. We had to play kids and, overall, my task was hopeless. Unsurprisingly, we were relegated. I was terribly outspoken then and a short way into my second season Albert Winter, the chairman, came to see me with his solicitor and I told him the time of day. He asked why I had been giving the board so much stick and I said that while they were lovely people they were f***ing hopeless, with no clue as to what was going on. We were inhabiting different planets. With that, we decided on an amicable parting.

My centre-half at the time was Trevor Gould, Bobby's brother, who was my coach and in a different class to the rest at the club. I recommended that he be given the job of succeeding me and this duly came about. Trevor worked the oracle and got them promotion but, two years later, Bedford Town ceased to exist. Everybody wants to be a success in their home town but, sadly, I was not. The whole episode was one to forget apart from one aspect. There was no way I wanted to go home and be the man responsible for taking them out of the league. That situation, at least, I avoided. I wanted to do precisely the opposite of what the board wanted. I proposed that a local builder be contacted to find a plot of land and erect a new stadium for The Eagles, taking all the time it needed to dovetail with our exit from The Eyrie. There was a magnificent stand there which could have been transferred to the new site but, of course, they knew better ... so much better that the club went bust and never re-emerged for years and years. When they did they had to start at rock bottom.

Throughout the history of football there have been people whose knowledge is limited but who have nevertheless been entrusted with making big decisions. It should never have been allowed and, indeed, they are not in the game nowadays. They have all been found out. But the damage they have caused to many clubs up and down the land is a disgrace. It is a subject which has me seething with frustration. I may not have any money but I have got a lot of common sense and I know about football. They fulfil only one of those criteria and it stinks.

Luton is only up the road from me and was my next port of call. David Pleat was their manager and I worked for him as a scout for a while. He recommended me to the Everton manager Gordon Lee who took me on as a scout for much more money. My best stroke there was to find right-back John Barton, for whom they paid £35,000 to Worcester.

I have never stopped finding and losing players since.

CHAPTER SIX

Backs to the wall at Barnet

When Keith Cheeseman became a guest of Her Majesty, I was approached by another Southern League club, Barnet, to be their manager. I met Ted Hennessey, the vice-chairman and accountant, and Dave Underwood, the chairman, in a little pub in Brickett Wood, Hertfordshire, and though I was very tempted by their offer I felt that my loyalty should be to Dunstable. I don't know why, because I wasn't being paid at the time, but we were doing well and they were exciting times.

Now, while I was scouting for Everton, these two gentlemen came back in for me. I had watched Barnet a few times anyway and during this period Jimmy Greaves was their star player, despite his well-documented drink problem. He was kicking the ball off his own goal line one minute and was popping it in at the other end the next. Jimmy was brilliant for Barnet, just as he had been for Chelsea, Tottenham and England in his younger days. Billy Meadows, the Barnet manager, packed up for some reason and I was wanted as his replacement. When I agreed, it was the start of a long association with the club in two spells spanning 14 years. The first of these was to last for five years and constituted the longest tenure in one place in my working life.

The first season was already halfway over when I joined and Barnet were not doing very well. Jimmy was attempting to overcome his alcoholism and my heart went out to him many times. He would sit alone at the front of the team bus while the rest of the lads were in the bar having a beer and it must have been very difficult for him. A football club was hardly the place to be for a recovering alcoholic and I knew that we would not have Jimmy around for long.

I set about bringing in a host of players from up and down the country, but they didn't know each other and it was important that they gelled sooner rather than later. The Southern League took part in an Anglo-Italian tournament in the March of every year and this presented the perfect opportunity. I told Dave Underwood that we had to go to Italy for the week. It was critical that we finished in the top half of the league, because the following season was to see the formation of what was then the Alliance League and is now the Nationwide Conference, just one rung below Football League status, and we would have missed out if we had finished in the bottom half. The only way we could achieve that, I reasoned, was to go away together and bond – it didn't matter what we did in Italy as long as we did it as a team. Salt of the earth that he was, Dave, who had been goalkeeper for Watford, Liverpool and Fulham, agreed to this, despite the club being short of funds.

As we embarked on the journey to Italy, with a great feeling of comradeship building up, I wasn't to know that the trip would effectively end my marriage. Anne's mother had been ill with cancer for some time. Having at first been given two weeks to live, she hung on determinedly before she died after 11 months and this coincided with our foreign travel. Her funeral took place in my absence and this was not well received. The trip may have done wonders for the club – when we returned we put a run together and stormed up the league – but it did nothing for my family life. On the first night back home we put the children to bed and Anne, stony-faced, wanted to discuss our marriage. In short, she wanted out.

'Listen, Barry, we've been together for 13 years now and through all that time you have always put football first.

'I've got no more feelings for you ...'

I felt that she was in a state of shock caused by the death of her mother, but the situation had been compounded by my not being present at the funeral and there was no doubt about her intentions. She said that she would live her life and I should live mine and though we made some kind of effort at reconciliation over the next few days, with me living at home, the marriage was over. The worst day of my life was when we had to tell the kids. Jane was ten and Mark seven and they took it very badly. I could hardly have taken a more inappropriate course of action when I went to live with my dad. His old school attitudes were such that he demanded to know why I had left my kids. You couldn't tell him that your wife didn't want you any more because, in his view, what she thought and felt did not matter. 'The kids come first and you should go back,' he kept saying. We rowed every night and the situation became intolerable. Anne and I had mutual friends, Pat and Wyn Eaton, and they were aware of what had happened. For a few nights I slept in the front room at their house, mainly to escape the wrath of my father.

At the club Dave Underwood, a wise old owl, was very understanding. I told him everything. One of his friends had bought a house in Dunstable as an investment and the owner said that, as I was a friend of Dave's, I could rent the place, which was fully furnished, for a tenner a week. It was close enough to Barnet and not far from the children, who would come over for weekends despite my inability to cook for them. I was hopeless near an oven but on occasions Wyn would rescue the situation for me. He was a good cook. Domesticity was not my forte, though, and a pattern developed of us abandoning the house in favour of pub lunches.

It was a bad time in my life, but football kept me going and some months later I very fortunately met the lady who was to become my second wife, Kirstine. We went out a couple of times, enjoyed each other's company and the relationship drifted on from there. I had decided to take the kids to Jersey at the end of the following season and Kirstine came with us. She and the kids got along fine. She eventually moved in with me at Dunstable – I had to pay £20 a week then – and she quickly settled into a new lifestyle. Kirstine adopted a paintbrush as a constant companion, transforming the property and slapping on paint wherever it was needed at the club. When Barnet were playing away she prepared all the food and was prepared to muck in all along the way. Things have worked out very well in that when there is something to celebrate, such as the kids' birthdays, Kirstine and I will go out with Anne and her partner, Jay, and have a pleasant evening together. You speak to your pals about their exes and they talk of nothing but war, so it is nice for there to be no acrimony. Anne has said since that, in her view, I am a nice man but that is as far as it goes. She was never interested in football and consequently would never come to the games or involve herself in whichever club I might be a part of. She was more of a career girl, and I am not knocking her for that. She's a bright, intelligent woman and she wanted to further her ambitions.

I'm not bright, nor intelligent, but my football ambitions know no boundaries and it was with some pride that we did well enough at Barnet in my first season there to become a founder member of The Alliance. It was a struggle, though. Two teams were to be relegated in that pioneer season and we finished third from bottom. The following term three were to go down and we finished fourth from bottom. Then four were scheduled for the drop and we finished fifth from bottom. It was survival at its raw edge. In those first five years I derived more satisfaction from escaping the drop by the skin of our teeth than almost anything else in my career, because you knew from day one that it would be a long backs-to-the-wall scrap in which every setback, however minor, was a threat to your very existence. Selling a player always brought a lifeline and I had to do that regularly. One example was Russell Townsend to Northampton for £23,000. These transactions always upset the supporters because all they wanted was a successful team, but things were so bad financially that the chairman and I used to have a competition to see who could ponce the most money off our mates to pay the latest bills.

On a typical morning Dave would shoot off in one direction, I would go the other and we would meet three hours later to compare how many bills each of us had paid off.

'I've paid four,' he would say.

'Crap,' I would counter. 'I've settled five.'

It was scary, but fun, until one morning Dave and Ted were present at a meeting and Ted announced: 'Gentlemen, I have got to resign. The club is trading while insolvent, I'm the accountant and it is my duty to resign.' Dave, head in hands, urged his best friend to hold fire for a couple of weeks until the next board meeting and Ted agreed. The following morning I received a telephone call from Ted.

'Have you heard from Dave?'

I told him that I hadn't.

'I've just received a letter from him,' Ted continued. 'He's resigned as chairman of the football club.'

'What?' I gasped. 'Big Dave? You've got to be joking.'

He wasn't. 'It puts me in the shit as vice-chairman, doesn't it?' Ted went on. 'I've told him that I can't stay on because the club is insolvent and I've got to take the chair tonight.'

I jumped in my car and shot down to Dave's lovely bungalow at Brickett Wood because I was concerned for him. He was in his best suit – his pyjamas. He always said that the first thing he ever did when he got home was to put on his best suit and crash out in the armchair.

I had grown to know him very well. He was into the recycling of newspapers and when he came to see me at Dunstable I would drive him around and he would tell me lots of things about himself. One of these concerned the loss of his son, David junior, in the most horrific circumstances. He played for Barnet and had broken his nose during the course of one match. This broken nose was an embarrassment to him, but one day he won £500 on the club lottery and decided to spend it on having it straightened. He was put under the anaesthetic and never came round. He was just 20, and an only son. This absolutely crucified Dave. The funeral was packed out with famous names like Bobby Moore, Johnny Haynes and Jimmy Hill.

Dave used to organise events for the charity The Gold

Diggers, in which Elton John was involved. Elton once gave a concert in support of the charity in London and it was a great event with people paying £1,000 for this piece of memorabilia and £2,000 for that. When he had finished playing he announced that he would not be signing any autographs for anybody, because he just wanted to have a good night socialising. Dave must have missed that bit because he told me that one of the girls at his office wanted Elton's autograph and asked if I would go and get it. I protested that Elton had just made it plain he would not be scribbling his name but he said: 'Baz, you can get anything. You can sell ice cream to Eskimos. Do me a favour.' Elton had just given it the big finish from the stage and I noticed he was making his way to the toilet. So I followed him.

'Elton, could you sign this please?'

'No I can't.'

'It isn't for me,' I persisted. 'It's for Dave Underwood.'

The star's face broke into a smile. 'Dave Underwood?' he said. 'I'll do anything for Dave Underwood. Give us it here, my boy. Who does he want it to? Where is he?' I told him Dave was at my table and he accompanied me back to where we were sitting. They had a chat and you could see the respect that Elton had for him.

A compromise was made at the club whereby Dave, adamant that he no longer wanted the aggravation associated with being chairman, agreed to remain a board member and Ted agreed to become chairman for three months. It was the most beneficial period in the club's history so far. We reached the third round of the FA Cup, in which we were drawn against First Division Brighton. John Motson came down for BBC's *Match Of The Day,* from which we got some much-needed revenue; we had decent income from an advertiser who was excited by the prospect of his product being on television's biggest football programme; we had a big crowd and we drew 0–0, which meant more money from a mid-week replay watched by 16,000 and which was televised by *Sportsnight,* who also paid well. Brighton, who were managed by Mike Bailey, beat us 3–1 in the replay, with the best goal of the night coming from Barnet's Gary Sergeant. After the game Mike said: 'You've got a few good players,' to which I readily agreed. He confided that he had had us watched twice before the first meeting and we had impressed on both occasions, that we had played well in the goalless draw and that we had excelled ourselves that night. He expressed an interest in three players, Gary Phillips, Colin Barnes and Graham Pearce. He could not afford them all when I told him what I wanted for them, but the following week he signed Pearce, our left-back, for £35,000. It was a magical move for Graham because the following season Brighton reached the FA Cup Final against Manchester United. The match ended in a 2–2 draw and had to be replayed, again at Wembley. This time United won 4–0, but what a transformation for a lad who not long before had been playing non-league football.

This little run of luck also brought about a change in

fortunes for Barnet. All that income from one fixture made an insolvent club solvent and Ted was able to vacate the chair after three months having turned the club round. Tommy Hill, his vice-chairman, took over.

At the end of the season Barnet took a table at a Gold Diggers function. Jimmy Hill, then chairman of Fulham, was also the charity chairman and in his welcoming address he said: 'There's a new breed of manager on the horizon and I don't like him. Where chairmen once got rid of managers, this manager is now getting rid of chairmen. And at an alarming rate, too. He is on his third chairman in four months. Stand up Barry Fry!' I took a bow and it brought the house down.

The fans were not so happy. For five years I had to endure banging on my office window accompanied by chants of 'Fry Out! ... Fry Out!' and I could understand their frustrations. A preoccupation with the balance sheet led some of them to believe that the club was lacking in ambition, yet nothing could have been further from the truth.

Here we were, in this smashing new league, and of course we craved success. Everybody does. We were playing at new venues like Barrow and Gateshead and one Monday evening we had an away game at Altrincham, the crème de la crème of non-league sides and managed by Tony Saunders. Dave knew the Manchester United manager Dave Sexton and was able to arrange a training session at The Cliff on the morning of the match, followed by a steak and egg pre-match meal at Old Trafford.

Imagine that kind of five-star treatment for non-league players. Sexton and Lou Macari came along to watch as Altrincham hammered us 7–0 and the United boss could not have been more supportive after the game. He came into the dressing room and said: 'Never mind, lads. It happens to everybody. You'll bounce back from this. Don't let it worry you. I hope that, at least, you've had a nice day.'

Five days later United travelled to Ipswich – and lost 6–0! On the Monday Dave Underwood came into my office and said: 'I've got to phone Dave Sexton.' Next minute he's on the line to the United boss.

'Hello, Dave. Never mind, mate. It happens to everybody. You'll bounce back from this. Don't let it worry you!'

Really, it's only football people who could do that. In other walks of life you would be so down that you would be inclined to punch somebody on the nose.

Eventually Dave decided to quit not only the club, but his country. He emigrated to South Africa, where his big friend Johnny Haynes was resident, but not before he discovered he had cancer. He died overseas and was followed soon afterwards by his wife Sheila, who was crippled with arthritis. Very sad.

In my fifth year at the club that little gem involving Brighton was all there was to look back on as a positive sign. It was costing chairman Tommy Hill a fortune to keep the club going, the debts were mounting up again and it was really hard work. I had a big meeting with a man called Mike Riley, who owned a local newspaper, in which I pleaded with him to buy the club. He showed more than a passing interest, coming down to the club to look over the place and inspect the accounts, and he felt that he could do things with the clubhouse to make it more profitable. I was convinced that he was going to take it over, but just as that critical stage was approaching he got an offer to go abroad which, he said, was too good to turn down. But he had a suggestion. His best client at the newspaper was a man who spent £1,000 a week with him on advertising. He lived locally in Totteridge, was very wealthy and might be tempted. His name was Stan Flashman.

CHAPTER SEVEN

Stan the Main Man

Everybody had heard of Stan Flashman; I had not. I was taken to his house to be introduced to him by Mike Riley, who dealt with him in all his business with the paper. My host appeared very strait-laced. I told him who I was.

'I know,' he said. 'I read about you all the time in the papers. What do you want?'

I told him Barnet were struggling and asked if he would help.

'I dunno. I'll have a look at it.'

I was hardly filled with optimism, but then he said something else.

'In the meantime, what's pressing?'

I told him that we were due in court the following week to face a couple of actions for late payment.

'Well, here's a grand. I'll pay for those.'

Barely able to contain my excitement, I told him that I would contact the papers with the story that local businessman Stan Flashman had saved the club, but he admonished me immediately.

'Definitely not. I don't want any of that. If you must talk to the papers, tell them that the club has been saved by an anonymous donor.'

I reported to the board that I had met with Stan and there was great jubilation, prematurely as it transpired. First he was coming in and then he wasn't, and I thought that he must be going into the club's affairs with a fine toothcomb before committing himself.

What he would find in the course of his survey would be enough to frighten anybody away from football for life. It was horrendous. Nobody had been paid for six weeks. When I was due a testimonial against Tottenham, Keith Burkinshaw was manager and Peter Shreeves his assistant and they had just got into the FA Cup Final, so it was magnanimous of them to agree to play. I promised the lads that whatever gate receipts were realised would be used to pay their wages. Things were so bad that Kirstine and I worked behind the bar at the club – we could not afford to pay a bar steward. We had discos every Friday, Saturday and Sunday and at 2 am we were wrestling behind the bar, with Kirstine trying to pull the shutters down and me shoving them open again. Anything for a bit more money. Neither could we afford a groundsman. I cut the grass and the pitch would be levelled by means of my car pulling a heavy roller. Then the secretary, Ron Andrews, died in my arms from a heart attack one Thursday night. This was one of our two training evenings, the other being Tuesday, and he turned up as usual in his office, laughing and joking. I had a brief conversation with him and then jumped the barrier onto the field to join the lads for training. Somebody shouted me in and I took one look at Ron, who was foaming at the mouth, before calling an ambulance. I took the journey to hospital with him in the ambulance. He was pronounced dead on arrival. Now I had the job of telling his wife. I went round and knocked on the front door and Eileen smiled.

'What do you want, Barry?'

'Ron's dead, Eileen.'

She laughed. 'You are a one with your jokes.'

I just burst out crying, and she realised then that I wasn't fooling around. Not that you would make light of such a subject anyway. Ron was a sergeant-major type who, on the face of things, was pretty fit. His death came as a great shock, even though he was no longer a young man. He worked for nothing, for the love of the club, and there was no way we could afford another secretary. So this was another discipline which became part of my portfolio. We had another chap, Vic, who would come to empty the one-arm bandits and I would often ask him to bring me £25 worth of 10p coins so that somebody's wages could be paid.

The day of my testimonial dawned and it was slightly embarrassing for me. The opposition was star-studded and we had a very poor side, so I felt that I should do something to try to make us look respectable. I called on my old mate George Best again. He agreed to play but, just as he had done at Dunstable, he was missing when the teams were ready to take the field. He arrived with his son, Callum, having been stuck in traffic, but he made it and that was all I wanted. We lost 6–3, with the final goal coming when I converted a Best cross with a diving header. I was a mile offside, but the ref allowed it, signalling 84 roly-polies from the jubilant goalscorer. Such was the support for the event that I was able to uphold my promise to pay the lads all their outstanding wages and there was even a bit to spare.

Things didn't improve any, though. The clubhouse was forced to close because McMullen's Brewery, which held a covenant, would not allow us to sell any beer other than theirs and we owed them money. They had stopped supplying us until their bills had been met. Lots of other brewers were willing to give us loans, but we could not enter into an agreement because we were beholden to the covenant. No beer was being served, so I begged McMullen's to lift the covenant and they said they would do so for a payment of £12,500. I reported this to the directors, hoping that some of them would come up with the money, but their cupboards were bare. In the meantime Kirstine and I had bought for a very considerate price the house in Dunstable which we had been renting and now owned it. I presented her with a document to sign and when I told her it was for a second mortgage she said: 'Lovely. What are we getting?' Her face dropped when I told her it was to rescue the clubhouse at Barnet, and she asked if I was sure I knew what I was doing. I told her I thought so. The clubhouse was back up and running the minute I handed over £12,500 to McMullen's, just in time for Christmas.

Kirstine is a strange sort of breed, with a German mother and a Scottish father. I had to fight the German and Scottish armies together to get her, but she was worth it. The German tradition is to have what we would call Christmas Day on Christmas Eve and we travelled to Bedford from Dunstable to have dinner with them. When we got home at midnight there was more than a touch of frost in the air. Our Boxing Day fixture was a home match against Wealdstone, with an 11am kick-off. Once again the lads had had no money for four weeks, but it was more serious this time because of the season of the year. I said to Kirstine: 'We've got to make sure the match is on. I'm going to go to the club and roll the pitch.' She looked at me aghast but said: 'I'll come with you.' So we headed for Barnet.

She goes into the office and puts the kettle on while I go into the corner of the ground, get the tractor out and afix the roller to the back of it and drive it onto the playing area. It's now one o'clock on Christmas morning and pitch black. I'm going up and down like a good 'un, whistling and singing away, and I give her a wave as I near the clubhouse. I turn the tractor, with its two lights at the front, to roll the next patch of ground and as I do so I see all these coppers jumping over the fence, shining their torches and making their way towards me. I slowed down as I approached them.

'Yeah?'

'Get off that tractor!' yelled one of them. 'We are arresting you for being drunk and disorderly.'

'F**k off, I'm the manager of Barnet Football Club.'

'Yeah, sure, and I'm George Best. Get off that tractor! All the neighbours around here have been complaining about this drunkard singing Christmas carols in the early hours of the morning. You are under arrest.'

I shut down the tractor and jumped off. The local policeman arrived at the scene of the crime in the nick of time, shone a torch in my face and fortunately identified me to his colleagues.

'Baz,' he said, 'we've got to stop you. We've had so many complaints. There are kids sleeping. It's Christmas morning, for Christ's sake.'

Before I was rudely interrupted I had managed to roll only half the pitch. This looked terrific, all neatly packed so that the ball would just bounce off it, but when I arrived at the ground on Boxing Day the other half was in such a mess that the referee called off the game. It broke my heart.

Things simply could not go on in the way that they had been at Barnet and, from my own perspective, an offer to manage Maidstone could not have been better timed. Maidstone were the Manchester United of non-league football. They had won the Conference on two occasions, the first time being denied admission to the

Football League by one vote. They fell 13 votes short the second time, but they appeared to have a bright future. There appeared to be no obvious reason why they should not be granted League status though their chairman, Jim Thompson, is a Geordie, very passionate and outspoken when it comes to football. He did a highly professional job with his club but unfortunately, with his strongly-held views and beliefs, he seemed to make enemies of some of the powerful people who could have given him what he craved. He was also chairman of The Alliance and did so much for the game, but he incurred much local wrath when he sold the ground and moved the club to Dartford, 20 miles away. This never worked and never had a chance of working.

Unfortunately by the time I arrived there they had lost seven of the players who had been flying the flag for them and were struggling at the bottom of the league. Their manager Bill Williams, who had been so successful, was going abroad and I felt it was a great opportunity for me. I did everything at Barnet, operating on a shoe-string while bringing in various sponsorships, and that had not gone unnoticed by Jim, who wanted me to do similar things for Maidstone. I had to sell the club to people outside the area, which wasn't easy, but there were further opportunities in this direction because we had a dog track at the ground as well. Tommy Unwin, the chairman of Enfield, owned the dog track and paid rent. I could never understand Jim wanting to sell it. I thought it was a backward step. Notwithstanding the exodus of players we got to the final for the first time of the Bob Lord Trophy, in which we lost to Yeovil. Getting to that final was a satisfactory start but again the following season we were struggling, largely because the directors were reluctant to fund the buying of new players. We had a couple of good players, but what used to happen in those days was that you would get the better players to sign a contract and just put it in a drawer. By doing this you felt that you had him, but you didn't really have him.

One day Harry Redknapp, who was then manager of Bournemouth, rang me up.

'Baz, about your player Mark Newson.'

'Yes, he's a brilliant player, H. He can play at the back and in midfield and score goals. He's tops. If I were selling, I would want £300,000 for him.'

'Well, I haven't got £300,000,' he said. 'Do you think if I got him for nothing he would be a good signing?'

I told Harry there was no way he was going to get the player for nothing but he had an answer to that one.

'I've just checked with the Football Association. Mark is in front of me now and he is not registered with you.'

I said I didn't believe he could have done that but Harry said: 'I have. I promise you. I just thought that out of courtesy I would let you know.'

'H, If you've done that I will get the boys to come down and blow your f***ing legs off,' and I slammed the phone down.

I had Jim Thompson in my office within five minutes.

I told him the story of how Mark Newson was now registered with Bournemouth and demanded to know how that could have happened. Jim said that his contract was in the drawer, but as he looked there was no sign of it. My only assumption is that Mark must have retrieved it but, however it went missing we were certainly over a barrel. Jim got on the phone to Harry and started ranting and raving, calling him all the names under the sun, but the fact was that we had lost the player. The next day Jim and I drove down to Bournemouth to see Harry, who said the player had approached them, they fancied him, did some checks and signed him. While I shrugged my shoulders in resignation and with a lot of regard for Harry, who did a brilliant job at Bournemouth, Jim went the other way and pleaded: 'Just give us something, Harry. Anything.' He wouldn't even give us a friendly! Jim threatened that he had got friends in high places and would ensure that Harry never got another managerial position. The fact that he has been in the Premiership with West Ham for so many seasons only goes to show that Harry's mates outnumbered Jim's. Having seethed when this happened, I laughed about it the next day because the fact is that I would have done the same. There are no ethics in football; no ethics between managers. We all feel for one another, but if we can nick a good player we will. And have no conscience about it at all. I may have threatened, in my anger and frustration, to have his legs blown off, but we have been mates ever since. Kirstine and I will go out with him and Sandra for a meal and I see him the odd time at places like Ascot, where he once repaid me for the Newson episode by tipping me a 40–1 winner.

The writing was on the wall for me at Maidstone. I was deeply opposed to the proposed move to Dartford, but Jim wanted me to go to the area and sell all this new advertising while also doing what I was very good at – buying and selling players. Strangely, though, he wanted my assistant John Ryan to coach the team and pick the team. I told him this would never work. The players I bought might not be wanted by John and he might not have wanted to hang on to players I believed should be sold. If that was the way he wanted to run things, I told him, I was not staying. I had joined as manager of Maidstone and if I was no longer manager of Maidstone I was going. He said I had a contract which tied me to a month's notice and I told him he had just got it.

Backtracking, he phoned Kirstine and asked her to try to change my mind, but she knows me better than that and told him it would be pointless. She was right. As well as he had looked after me in terms of salary and a nice car, he failed to understand that I am a football man through and through. Money isn't important. If I could earn another £50,000 because I had sold so many adverts it would not be done for my sake, it would be for the club. I want everyday involvement in football. I want to watch the lads train. I want to be there every Saturday. We didn't fall out, it was just that I couldn't understand him and he couldn't understand me. It was a shame because he was such a passionate man. Years later I cried for the man because, like I say, he had built the Manchester United of non-league football at Maidstone. A couple of years later it had all gone out of the window. They had moved to Dartford, which was no good, and got into money troubles. He was chairman of the Conference and an FA councillor and because the club went pear-shaped he got kicked off the council and banned from football. It was so tragic, because he had a lot to offer.

Stan Flashman, meanwhile, had seen potential in Barnet and taken over the club. Something of a personal vendetta developed in that, for reasons unknown to me, he banned me from their ground. He apparently blamed me for not waiting for his arrival at the club and when I reminded him that I had asked whether or not he would be taking over he had replied in the negative. 'Yes, but you asked me on the wrong day.' Having assumed control, he brought in his friend from Arsenal, Roger Thompson, who was a great coach, and a player of the quality of the former Ipswich star Kevin Beattie. When I left Maidstone Stan called me and asked: 'Do you fancy coming home to Barnet?' There were a few things to get straight. My ban from the ground had been imposed in a letter to me at Maidstone Football Club and I was still angry about that. It was stupid and petty. Stan was the most celebrated, or notorious, ticket tout in the country, depending on which way you viewed it. He had an office in King's Cross, London, from which tickets for all major sporting and social events could be obtained. If it was happening, he had tickets for it. He was a prolific worker, always in his office by seven o'clock. He would be at home by 1.30 pm lunchtime, stripped to his vest and underpants and have a telephone in each ear for many hours of the rest of the day.

Stan made his intentions clear from the outset. He said that he had not got a bottomless pit and there would be no money available to buy players in the first year, yet if it had not been for my own *faux pas* in selling our goalkeeper Kevin Blackwell to Scarborough for £5,000 we would have romped The Conference and gone straight into the Football League. Scarborough, managed then by Neil Warnock, were below halfway in the league table and did not appear to be a threat. I had two very good goalkeepers, Blackwell and Gary Phillips, and when Blackwell went from Barnet to Scarborough he also went from very good to brilliant. Every time I went to watch Scarborough, Warnock would stand up and clap as I approached. I was their lucky mascot, never seeing them lose. They went on to pip us for a place in hallowed territory. Neil has become a good friend since those days. When he left to manage Notts County he took them to Wembley and the play-offs for two consecutive seasons, and both times I walked out with him and his team onto the pitch, having sold him a couple of my players. Neil is a very good manager. After the second of those play-off finals he received a spellbinding offer to go to manage Chelsea with his assistant, Mick Jones. They decided against it, showing loyalty to Notts County, and their reward eight months later was to get the sack It was one of those decisions that most people would regret for the rest of their lives, but Neil has always gone through life with a smile on his face. The tragedy, in my view, is that he would have made a brilliant Premiership manager. He is very clever and passionate and knowledgeable about the game, yet has since been associated with a host of struggling clubs.

Barnet would go on to finish second in The Conference on two further occasions. Having played second fiddle to Scarborough, courtesy of my goalkeeper, our part-timers could not match full-time Darlington, managed by Brian Little, nor Colin Murphy's Lincoln, who were also full-time professionals. There were, however, many successes. We won the Hertfordshire Senior Cup, beating Watford, a couple of times and the Clubcall Cup, which was only in existence for one season. This was for all non-league sides from organisations such as the Northern Premier, the Southern and the Gola and in the final we beat Hyde in a penalty shoot-out at Telford on a Sunday, the day after playing a league game.

There was now a great positive feeling among the fans. When I arrived for my second spell there were barely 200, but with the promise of League football on the horizon 2,000 grew to 3,000 and sometimes 4,000. I started to buy and sell players at an alarming rate. I brought in Robert Codner and Nicky Bissett from Dagenham for nothing and sold them both to Brighton, each for £115,000. Lee Payne came to us on a free transfer from Hitchin and I sold him to Willie McFaul at Newcastle for £125,000. These were all record transactions involving a non-league club.

The 1990/91 season saw the fulfilment of all the club's hopes, dreams, prayers and ambitions when, finally, we won The Conference. This achievement was remarkable when it is considered that in the November, with the season three months old and with six months to go, we sold David Regis and Paul Harding for £150,000 each, Phil Gridelet to Barnsley for £175,000 and Andy Clarke to Wimbledon for £350,000 ... the best part of £1 million worth of talent unloaded and we still won promotion with the highest number of goals in the history of The Conference.

Barnet's first-ever League game was on our home patch at Underhill Stadium against Crewe Alexandra on Saturday 17 August 1991. The fixture attracted a crowd of 5,090 and it was the most explosive start imaginable. Trailing 2–3 at half time, we eventually lost 4–7 in a game in which the defences were clearly on top! Three days later we went to Third Division Brentford in the first round first leg of the Rumbelows Cup and it was a bit quieter this time. There were only ten goals in a 5–5 draw in which we were leading 5–3 with a minute to go. Brentford put us out in the second leg, but we exacted our revenge in the preliminary round of the Autoglass Trophy a week before Christmas when we went to Griffin Park and beat them 6–3. Goals, goals, goals!

They wouldn't stop going in. We beat Scarborough 5–1 and lost to Rotherham 5–2. We beat Carlisle 4–2 and drew with Gillingham 3–3. Our goals for and against columns at the end of the season looked like the Dow Jones Index but, incredibly, we made the play-offs in seventh position, even though most of the players had remained part-time. We had a great squad. There was Kenny Lowe, who lived in Gateshead and travelled down; Spike Carter, who lived in Runcorn and made the journeys; Paul Showler, who lived in Bradford. We could not afford to give these players contracts, so they kept their day jobs. In the first leg of the play-offs at home to Blackpool a crowd of 5,629 watched us win 1–0 when we should have won by four or five. As if that were not enough of a disappointment, Stan Flashman came into the dressing room after the game and burst into a tirade.

'What a load of f***ing rubbish! You're taking the piss out of me, you lot.'

I told him he knew nothing about the game and he made to get hold of me. So I pushed him against the wall and before you knew it we were fighting, with the team jumping in to pull us apart. When there was some space between us Stan shouted out.

'You're sacked. You're f***ing sacked!'

Gary Poole, who was wanted by Peter Shilton at Plymouth for £250,000, tried to calm things down in this mélée and the chairman snarled at him.

'You're sacked, too. I'm going to rip up your contract. You can f**k off!'

And he did. For nothing. All this and we had just won the first leg of the play-offs. Sometimes Stan could be very foolish. He was Dr Jekyll and Mr Hyde. I stormed out and made for the clubhouse, but I was intercepted by the press who were anxious to know what had happened.

'You'd better ask Fatso. He's just sacked me.'

The reporters told me later that he had marched out of the changing room and when asked about the game he was raving about our performance, saying how great it was to win and how we were going into the second leg with a strong chance. This was precisely the opposite of what he had said not 15 minutes earlier. One radio reporter asked why I had been sacked and Stan's reaction was to smash him over the head with his microphone. Three days later we went to Bloomfield Road for the second leg. He would not let us stay overnight, the lads were gutted and the preparation was poor. We lost 2–0, eliminating us on the aggregate score.

The *Barclays Football Club Directory* said in its appraisal of our first season: 'If you want to be entertained with fresh, flowing football, probably laced with some smart finishing and a smile or two, then Barnet is your club. The players mirror the character of their manager and a look at the club's league record shows that his attitude pays off. Eighty-one league goals, plus another 29 in the cups, testifies to that and gave Spike Carter, England's record semi-professional international goalscorer, an amazing 32 goals in his first Football League season and, of course, the much-publicised Garry Bull also

Above: My first eleven. I m just a babe in arms as mum, surrounded by family members, holds me aloft.

Right: Aged seven, with the short back and sides haircut which is now back in fashion.

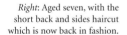

Left: As a schoolboy with some of my football memorabilia. I just loved Wolverhampton Wanderers.

Above: A proud moment for me when representing England Schoolboys against Germany in 1960. I m third left on the front row.

Right: Showing off my ball skills on being selected for Bedford County.

Left: My treasured headed goal for England Schoolboys against Scotland at Wembley. We won 5-3 and 93,000 people were watching.

No. 4.   SATURDAY, 8th SEPTEMBER, 1962.

BARRY FRY (Inside Forward)

When Barry Fry came to Old Trafford from Bedford he had already gained National Honours as a schoolboy. He joined us on leaving school, and we were successful in signing him as an Amateur on the 3rd June, 1960, in competition with several League clubs.

He became an Apprentice Professional on the 29th August, 1960, and full Professional in April, 1962. He is in his third season, and last year made 12 Central League appearances, appeared in every Youth Cup Round, completing the hat-trick twice, against Wigan and Bradford City.

Played a great part in the tour of our undefeated Youth Team in Switzerland during the summer months. Usual position inside forward.

Above: With Eamon Dunphy when we were together at Manchester United.

Left: My profile on the front page of the programme for the match between Manchester United Reserves and Huddersfield in 1962.

Right: All smiles in the Manchester United Youth team. I m second right on the front row.

Left: Chalking up the board prices while working for the bookmaker Gus Demmy in the afternoons in Manchester.

Left: Matt Busby gave me sound advice and the opportunity to join the biggest football club in the world. I ll always be grateful to him for that.

Right: The fantastic Nobby Stiles, one of the senior players who took me under his wing when I arrived at Manchester United.

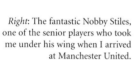

Left: What being at Old Trafford should have been all about for me – winning the FA Cup against Leicester in 1963.

Above: On being let go by United, Bolton Wanderers was my next port of call and here I am, front row right, in their line-up.

Below: I was never a regular in the Leyton Orient team, but being given the job of trainer was something that would change the course of my life.

Left: With Bedford Town when we won the Southern League title. I was captain and Player Of The Year.

Right: What a sight! The ball in the back of the net as I score the winner for Bedford Town.

Below: Manager at Dunstable and I push the wheelbarrow as we build a fence and turnstiles for George Best s appearance.

Right: Jeff Astle signs on the dotted line for Dunstable. I look on with chairman Keith Cheeseman and Jeff s wife Lorraine.

Left: Best of friends – me and Big Ron Atkinson.

Below: George Best between Keith Cheeseman and me when Dunstable played Cork Celtic in a pre-season friendly.

With George Best after his first game for Dunstable against Manchester United. Our non-league heroes won 3-2.

totalled an excellent 27 goals. Most of the side were experienced semi-professionals and many continued with their other careers alongside their "fun in the fourth". Barnet averaged 3,720 for their home games and usually gave great value for money. Apart from their all-round attacking ability the side benefitted from Dave Howell and Mick Bodley's steadiness in the middle of the back line and the exciting skills of Paul Showler and Kenny Lowe. The cups brought goals but no lasting success, but the play-offs were reached in the club's first season in the Football League. You would think everyone would be extremely happy and satisfied but, according to the media, all is not well at the Underhill Stadium. No one outside the club can really comment on internal matters, but it is a terrible shame that a club so admired for its style and attitude on the field cannot enjoy similar success off the park. Only one club can win the championship and three others can win promotion from the Fourth Division, but there is more to football than instant success. The club has proved its worth in the Football League. It has also impressed with its playing style and attitude so that Barnet now have more friends than ever throughout football. Barnet have laid the foundations for a very successful life in the League and hopefully Barry Fry, their very popular manager, will be able to enjoy the club's development along with the chairman and a very talented squad of players.'

CHAPTER EIGHT

'You won't be alive to pick the team'

One minute Stan Flashman was the most generous person in the world, the next he was a monster. He always thought that Barnet should win every match, but he particularly liked to beat Enfield whose ground, as the crow flies, is four miles away. The players, too, looked forward to this fixture because it was Stan's habit to put £2,000 in readies on the dressing-room table as an incentive for victory, to be shared among the squad. He would shuffle the money like a croupier with a pack of cards and if you were quick enough to go round the table three times, you'd get paid three times.

His dark side emerged one day after we had played out a goalless draw at home to Boston, where Howard Wilkinson and Jim Smith started their great careers. We needed to win to go to the top of the league. The Boston secretary, John Blackwell, is one of the most efficient in that capacity in the game and has been there for years.

He is a lovely man and after the match he went up to Stan and said what a good game it had been.

'You dirty load of bastards,' Stan stormed. 'You're a filthy team, now f**k off out of my boardroom.'

Their chairman, Pat Malkeson, said that if John was being asked to leave then he and the directors would have to follow suit.

'Well f**k off then,' Stan said.

He was a rotten loser. He couldn't handle it. Joe Vine, a scout from Newcastle, came to see me in the dressing-room and related what had happened. Stan may not have known it, but scouts used to descend on Barnet from all over the country just to get into our boardroom to watch our chairman's antics. He was a freak show, ranting and raving and totally unpredictable in his actions. After the game he had a real go at one of our players, Harry Willis.

'You'll never play for this football club again. You are f***ing hopeless.'

Harry, a coloured bloke, went white. The way Stan stormed at him was frightening.

'I'm going to rip up your contract,' he continued.

'Stan,' I intervened, 'you can't do that. Get out of it.'

I told Harry not to take any notice, but five minutes later the door flew off its hinges and Stan walked in with Harry's contract.

'Can't do it, eh?' he said. 'Can't rip up his contract? Watch me.'

With greatly exaggerated actions, he tore it into

shreds. Of course the FA holds the main contract and all Stan is destroying is the club copy.

'Don't you ever come near this ground again or my boys will break your f***ing legs and you will never play for anybody ever again,' he told poor Harry.

This, the chairman, at one of his own players. I had had many barneys with Stan like that and I knew that within a couple of days it would all be forgotten, but Harry, one of the loveliest men you will ever meet, was mortified. We were facing a Hertfordshire Senior Cup match against Watford the following weekend and that night Garry Bull and Harry drove back together to Nottingham, where they lived. At half past one in the morning I was on the phone to Bully, asking how Harry was. I said I couldn't raise him on the telephone and he said there was no way he would answer it, he was distraught. Bully said he did not think Harry would turn up for the Watford match and I replied that he had to. 'Go round now and tell him to ring me tomorrow.' Half an hour later, at 2 am, I was on the phone to John and Pat at Boston, apologising for Stan's behaviour. I constantly found myself doing that. Pat, whose father had preceded him as chairman, was brilliant.

'Baz, my dad was just like that, blowing hot and cold. One day he'd be the salt of the earth and give you anything and then he'd be hard as nails and deny you. It's not a problem.'

I was having a hell of a job with Harry. Two days later Stan brought up the subject again.

'Has Willis got fixed up yet?'

'Stan, Willis is playing tomorrow against Watford, mate.'

'He f***ing ain't. If he turns up I will have my boys there with baseball bats and they'll f***ing hammer him.'

'Stan, he's f***ing playing.'

Now it's a game of poker. With Stan, you never really know what he is going to do. I phoned Harry, who was still showing some reluctance to come and play, and told him to come into the club by the rear entrance, via the cricket pitch.

'Park your car up,' I told him. 'I'll open the gates and Gordon, my kit man, will get you in. If there is anybody at the front entrance waiting for you, I will know and I will deal with it.'

That is what he did. Kick-off time was approaching and there's no Stan in sight. We beat Watford 5–2 – and Harry gets a hat-trick. The dressing-room is like a carnival after the game and Bryan Ayres, the secretary, walks in with a message that Stan is on the phone and wants to speak to Harry. I looked at the player, and the player looked at me and I said: 'Go on then.' Harry goes and all the lads are speculating about whether that might be the last we ever see of him. Ten minutes later he comes back along the corridor beaming from ear to ear. Apparently Flashman told him: 'See how I geed you up, Harry? I'm a better f***ing motivator than that Barry Fry will ever be.'

What a man. Television cameras would arrive at the

ground to cover a match or a news item or some little cameo and the cameramen would film him as he drove into the ground. He would get out of his car and demand to know where they were from. Having identified themselves as the BBC or ITV he would ask why they were there.

'Barry Fry said ...'

'Barry Fry doesn't own this club,' he would jump down their throats. 'I do,' and proceeded to pick up their camera and smash it on the ground.

If things were going well he would offer whoever had made the biggest contribution two complimentary tickets to a top London show. Kirstine and I could not be classed as avid theatregoers, but in all my time with Stan we were always going to shows. We saw all the big stars like Dean Martin, Michael Jackson and Johnny Mathis. Then, one day, Stan said that he had Frank Sinatra coming over. Now I have always been a great fan of Sinatra and I asked Stan if there was any chance of a couple of tickets. 'They're £750 each,' he said. There was no way I could have afforded that, but my heart leapt one afternoon when I was sitting at home and he rang to say that there were two tickets for me for that night's show, which was starting in a couple of hours' time. We were ready in the blinking of an eye, went round to Stan's house to pick up the tickets and thoroughly enjoyed Sinatra, who was at his best.

My routine was that every Friday I would go to the chairman's house to pick up my wage. He would ask about the team, which was always something of a joke conversation from where I sat, and various club matters and he would hand over the money. This particular week I had been there for about three and a half hours and drunk 14 cups of tea before I brought up the subject of my wages.

'Stan, I've got to go now. Where's my wage?'

'Wages? You haven't got any wages for three weeks. You've got to pay for those Frank Sinatra tickets.'

I reminded him of the conversation in which I said that I couldn't afford them.

'You've got to pay your way, mate,' was his curt response.

No money was forthcoming for three weeks. His wife told me subsequently that he had got the tickets for two people who paid for them and didn't turn up to collect them, so they were spare on the day. Now he had sold them twice. Well, I suppose once a businessman always a businessman is one way of looking at it.

The rows I had with him were violent. One day he phoned up to inquire if everything was all right and I told him what had been happening, just as people do normally. He was nice as pie and then it was just like the shutters had come down.

'What are you playing him for? Why is he on the payroll? He's f***ing useless ...'

I'd say: 'Stan, you're the chairman, I'm the manager. I'll get the sack for picking my team but I'm certainly not going to get the sack for picking your bloody team.

I'd heard about you and I told you when I came here that I was picking the team and that's final.'

He exploded: 'You won't be alive to pick the team. You'll be in the cement under the motorway on the M25, you c**t.'

'Yeah? Well, you come near here and I'll do you in.'

'You haven't got enough money for that.'

'No, but my friends will do it for nothing, so f**k off.'

You were his best mate and his worst enemy. That's how he was with the players and everyone else. Utterly impossible. When I came off the telephone I was livid. The colour of beetroot.

My centre-half Mick Bodley was another at the club he managed to upset. Like every other club, Barnet received an allocation of FA Cup Final tickets. These are stamped 'Barnet' and Stan doesn't distribute them, he keeps them himself and sells them on the black market. When Mick inquired of Stan if it was possible for him to have a pair the chairman said: 'Yes. They are £350 each. That will be £700.' So he gives him two poxy tickets stamped 'Barnet' for £700. After the following Saturday's match Bods is busy telling everybody at the bar that he's handed over a fortune for these tickets, which were only worth three tenners. Unfortunately a local reporter was in on the conversation and in a Sunday newspaper it made headlines. I hadn't seen the paper, so when Bods rang me that morning in a blind panic I told him to take no notice of it.

'But I've had Stan on,' Bods said. 'He's told me that I am finished at Barnet. He said he was sending the boys round to blow my legs off.'

I told him not to worry.

'Don't worry? I've got my wife and kids here, Baz.'

I phoned Stan who said: 'The bastard's sold the story. I know what he's done. He's sold the story for £700 just so he can get the tickets for nothing.'

To be fair to Stan, he would always go into the bar after a victory – he never drank himself – to buy the opposition a drink. Never us. It was though they had done us a favour by losing, and this was his reward.

When he had calmed down over the Cup Final tickets he said I was to tell Bods that if there was an FA investigation, the player was to say that he had handed over the face value of £30.

There was another occasion on which the Bodley family had cause to worry. The players received their wages in cash from Stan every Saturday and Mick handed over his £250, all in £5 notes, to his wife, who took them to the bank on the Monday. Our training at the ground was interrupted by a phone call from Mrs Bodley, who said that she was being held at her local Barclays branch because she had deposited £250 of counterfeit money. Now it was Mick's turn to be furious with the chairman. He contacted Stan and related his tale of woe. Stan's reply was not very helpful.

'Well, it isn't my counterfeit money. All my counterfeit money is here on the table in front of me. I haven't used it yet. I reckon what you've got must have been among the gate receipts on Saturday. How unlucky can you get?'

Mick didn't know whether to laugh or cry.

'What am I going to do? Those are my wages.'

'I take money in good faith and you take money in good faith,' Stan replied. 'Take it to the bookies and try to get rid of it in that way.'

Kevin Durham, whom we signed from Wycombe, was one of the players who helped to get Barnet into the Football League. He was such a lovely lad that when it came time for contract negotiations he said that I should just pay him what I thought he was worth; simply playing league football was reward enough for him. He explained that he was taking a holiday with a couple of the lads from Wycombe and would then be going away with his wife and eight-month-old baby and he would see me in time for pre-season training. While he was away I got a phone call to tell me that he had died. He was 27. He had apparently had a few drinks on the beach and the lads had left him to sleep it off in the hotel room while they went out. They returned to find him dead. It was a terrible shock for everybody and I decided to stage a testimonial match for his dependants. The obvious choice of opponents was Wycombe and the fixture drew a full house to Barnet.

A few weeks went by before I received a phone call from a Sunday newspaper saying that they were running a story that Stan had not handed over the Kevin Durham testimonial money. I immediately contacted Stan and asked if the money had been paid.

'What does he want money for?' Stan boomed. 'He's f***ing dead isn't he?'

Then he slammed the phone down. I called him back and said that the story would be in the paper but he just said: 'Leave that to me.' In the end he had to cough up, but that was pure evil.

The man was unbelievable. I even witnessed him getting people the sack in the cosy environment of a restaurant. After that Clubcall Cup Final in Telford, we stayed overnight in a hotel in West Bromwich. We had played Sutton in the league the previous day and got beaten. Afterwards we picked up Stan and he joined the coach party on the way to our big match in the Midlands. Here again he showed his true colours. Sitting at the front, he barked at the driver: 'That's the last time you ever drive a coach for us. You don't know where you're f***ing going.' He would have the driver quaking in his boots, yet at the end of the journey, he would give him a £100 tip. Often his generosity knew no boundaries. He always laid on food for the lads, and if we travelled by train he would take the whole catering car over. There would be a pre-match meal on the way up and a slap-up four-course feast on the way back, all at his own expense. He even used to allow me to hire the England team coach for some away trips. We would stay in the best hotels and, overall, the five-star treatment received by Barnet players when we were still a non-league side could not be matched by Manchester United, Arsenal and Tottenham. That is why we were successful. It made the players feel good and important.

The sad thing about Stan is that he will be generally remembered for almost taking Barnet out of existence. With us leading the Fourth Division by a mile, a situation I had been forced to live with at various stages of my time in football again reared its ugly head. The lads were not being paid. They were owed a fortune in wages; I was owed £162,000 in pay, commission and the proceeds of a second testimonial against Arsenal. When I left Barnet, the fans called me Judas. If only they had ever known a grain of the truth. Stan took the unsound advice from his solicitor that there was no way in which the players would walk out on the club. What should have been done is that they should have been paid some money on account to restore something of their faith, but this did not happen. Instead, the Professional Footballers' Association stepped in to meet the wage bill, the FA intervened and a squad of players which would have climbed into the First Division in successive seasons – they were that good – all left to join other clubs for nothing. Unknown to anybody, Stan was in financial ruin. There were never any wage slips at Barnet. His method of payment was to deduct 'tax' so that a player on a basic of £150 a week would receive a cheque for £112, to be topped up by a cash payment on Saturdays. When the supplementary cash stopped I had a represen-tation from the lads who wanted to know why they were being short-changed. I asked Stan what was happening.

'They're not getting wages any more. They have been paid their basics and that's all they are getting from now on. I'm not paying them any more.'

I was on the lads' side then. My loyalty was to them. I contacted Gordon Taylor, whom I knew from my Bolton days, at the PFA and he came back after speaking to Stan to say there would be no further problem. But there was. It went on for weeks and months and the lads really started to get worried. There was the prospect of them getting behind with their mortgages and hire purchase agreements and now I'm fighting World War III with Stan. If, at any point, he had stepped forward to say that he had big money worries, the probable outcome would have been that we would all have taken a pay cut. As it was, he was sacking me almost on a daily basis. I just used to take no notice and go in the next day. Then, a week before Christmas, he sacked me by registered letter. Three weeks later he gave me my job back. That's how he was. He said that he had seen me on television and took pity on me because he thought I looked ill. I should have told him to stick his job up his arse, but there were 20 players at Barnet who were there because of Barry Fry.

What happened in the end is that we were training one day when four cars drove into the car park. Their occupants got out and the first of them introduced himself to me as being from the fraud squad. Another represented the Inland Revenue and a third was concerned with VAT. One of these gentlemen padlocked the gates.

They said that Stan and Helen Flashman had been arrested at seven o'clock that morning and that, at nine o'clock, they had taken all the paperwork from the club. They said they were not pursuing me or any of the lads but that the players must each give sworn statements about how much they were paid and by what means. If we played ball with them, they said, there would be no trouble. If we did not play ball, we would have to accept the consequences.

I called all the players together and told them the gravity of the situation, emphasising that they must co-operate with the investigators and tell them the whole truth. We had a big meeting at a country club just round the corner from Stan's house, this having been the venue in previous years for the lavish Christmas parties hosted by him. Gordon Taylor arrived at the club later and phoned Stan to try to arrange a meeting. He was told: 'I have sold the club. The new owners should be round there.' Well, we did have a geezer round at the club who was legally represented. I asked how much money he was putting into the club. It needed to be a substantial amount to compensate the PFA for looking after players who had not been paid for eight weeks and for the debt owed to me to be settled. It was clear to me that Stan Flashman still owned the club and that someone had been put up by him to make it appear that everything was above board and I let these views be known to them.

'It's a joke,' I ventured. 'If it is not, then how much are you putting into the club? It's a simple question.'

I repeated it many times and they could never give me an answer until they weakly conceded.

'We have a fixture against Halifax on Saturday. Out of the gate receipts we will pay the players a percentage of their wages.'

I asked them for how many weeks this method would be used and they said the Halifax game would be a one-off.

'I ask you again,' I said. 'How much money are you putting into the club? You are obviously going to put in no money whatsoever. It follows that you are not taking over this football club. You are front men for Stan, who is still running the club from his armchair at home.'

The players wondered what they should do and were advised by Gordon that, as the PFA had paid their wages, they should go ahead with the fixture against Halifax. On the day of this meeting we had a reserve game at Brentford. What was not known to anybody at the club was that, two days previously, I had taken a phone call from the Southend chairman, Vic Jobson, who wanted to know how things stood at Barnet. I told him it was in grave danger of going bust and he said: 'Do you fancy the job here?' I was now in a strong position with the Flashman front men and before we set off for Brentford I took them aside.

'Right. The lads are sorted out. What about me? You owe me £162,000.'

I was told: 'You are just a creditor. You will have to get in line.'

Flashman, summoned to appear at Barnet Crown Court to answer charges brought by the Inland Revenue, was pronounced unfit to plead on physical and mental health grounds and declared bankrupt. We had held a creditors' meeting at which I was advised to register a claim for the outstanding amount, but I realised the possible conseqeunces and there was no way that I was going to be party to the folding of the club I held so dear. I never received a penny; others recovered a small percentage of their dues.

Had Stan Flashman not come into the club in the first place it would never have known the success it enjoyed. That is why he should really be remembered for his positive contribution. He had been my hero when I went back there because he had saved my beloved Barnet, the club at which I was chief cook and head bottlewasher and in charge of all the other aspects of a football club. How I have lived long enough to tell the tale is a miracle, because in my 14 years at Barnet I suffered not one but two heart attacks.

The first of these happened on the day of our fixture at Gateshead. We had stayed overnight at a hotel, had our pre-match meal and boarded the bus to take us to the ground. I sat in the front and sighed heavily when the driver turned the keys and there was no response. It just would not start. I told the lads to get out and that we would give it a push start. I must have thought I was Superman. I moved a bit quicker than they did and started to push from the back on my own. I felt a twinge and perspiration began running down my face, but when I was joined by the lads we soon got the bus going. When I took my seat again for the journey, I felt numb and very uneasy, but I didn't take much notice of it. The game didn't help matters. We played hopelessly and were 2–0 down almost before we'd kicked off and, as usual in these circumstances, I was in a bit of a state. I went into the dressing-room at half time and went bananas. Suddenly, as I prepared to shout something, I could not talk. It was as though someone had tipped a bucket of water over my head. The sweat was pouring off me, my arm ached and, in panic, I made for the door and shut it behind me. I could hear the lads saying: 'F***ing hell. I've never seen him like that.' I tried to gather myself together and walked out into this giant stadium, with its running track surrounding the pitch. I took my place in the dugout and sat there alone as I waited for the team to come out for the restart. I felt terrible. An indescribable pain had manifested in my chest, but the lads' second-half performance diverted my attention. They were magnificent and we won the match 3–2. I wasn't my usual self and instead of jumping up and down and running along the touchline to celebrate a goal, I wasn't at all animated. I just congratulated them afterwards and got on the coach. I couldn't eat any of Kirstine's sandwiches, nor did I feel like a drink. I just sat there, staring into space, until we were dropped off at Sandy, where I had left the car. The lads thought I still had the hump because of our first-half performance. I had taken off my tie and my shirt to try to get a little more comfortable but the journey was endless. As far as Kirstine was concerned, she would not suspect anything was wrong. She had known me long enough to know that I get in moods about football and her tendency when that happens, rightly, is just to leave me alone. When we got into the car I told her that we had better drive straight to hospital because I had been in a lot of pain all afternoon.

By this time it was 11 o'clock at night. Gateshead is a long way from Bedfordshire. The nurse who met me at Bedford Hospital, where my mum had died, could see straightaway that I was in a lot of distress and arranged for me to be seen immediately. I was wired up for an ECG before the doctor arrived. He took one look at the printout and said that I would have to remain there. 'You have had a heart attack,' he said. Kirstine went to tell my father what had happened and spent the night with her parents. They all came to see me the following day, but the whole thing was horrible. I was in a ward with a lot of old people in a lot worse condition than I was. The man in the bed next to me had his wife and daughter visiting and they left for a cup of tea in the canteen because he was sleeping. They had been gone for barely a minute when the alarm sounded and a whole medical team arrived to try to revive him. He was dead. All the nurses were crying and the curtain was pulled round him and when the two ladies returned they were crying and screaming and chastising themselves for not staying with him. All this was happening within touching distance of where I was. I couldn't handle it. I was in a different world, one which you never think about in your everyday life. I could not sleep for the fear that I might not wake up again.

We had a game on the Tuesday night and a cup match was scheduled for the following Saturday, for which tickets had to be sold. I discharged myself on the Tuesday morning, having been told that they wanted to keep me in for a week. I was being constantly monitored but I just said: 'Look, I'm not being funny but I've got to go.' They protested that I must stay because I wasn't well enough to leave, but I told them that all those poor people on the ward were more in need of care and attention and they should concentrate on them. Kirstine tried to persuade me to stay but I was having none of it. I signed a form and scarpered. Mum had always had this thing about hospitals – she hated the very thought or mention of them – and now I understood why. I was overcome by the same feeling.

I relied on the club doctor and my own GP for regular check-ups because I was aware now of a blood disorder which, going back as far as one of those international tournaments in Switzerland when I was with Manchester United, had made my mouth bleed for four days when I got two teeth kicked out, combined with a dodgy ticker. It frightens you at first. Then you examine a lifestyle in which you don't eat all day, endure the stress of a match, buy fish and chips on the way home and stuff them into rolls which you eat while driving along. Then you'd be analysing the match, thinking about the personnel and end up eating four cheese sandwiches at two in the morning. I've never smoked a cigarette in my life, but I do enjoy cigars. It's all too much. The chest pains returned spasmodically and then, two years later, I got the same symptoms during training which I had suffered at Gateshead. I went to Barnet Hospital, where ECG tests were again taken. They wanted to keep me in but I told them there was no way I was staying there. They were adamant that something was wrong with my health and insisted that I should go to Harley Street in London. I had all the tests, but the doctor said further exploration was necessary. This involved me lying flat on my back, looking up at a row of monitors, with my arms and legs shackled. The specialist cut my arm on the inside of the elbow joint to insert a worm-like micro camera and blood flew everywhere. As this camera made its way through my arteries I watched its progress on the screens and he inserted a dye which, he said, would identify the problem. As this was in progress, I started to have one of my attacks. Blind panic set in as perspiration drenched me. I was unable to move because of the shackles and I shouted out that something was happening to me. 'That's lovely,' he said. 'I've never seen that before. That's wonderful.' A strange sense of humour pervades the medical profession. He revealed that one of my arteries was 60 per cent shut but could be cured by the thinning of my blood. I wasn't going to drop down dead, he assured me, and this, I must admit, came as a great relief.

I was to wait a short while, he said, before they would give me a meal and then I could go home. I looked forward to something to eat but then, just as the trays of food arrived, it started again. I panicked again and lashed out, upsetting everything on the trays. The doctor came rushing in and said it might be prudent for me to stay the night, again assuring me that I would not suffer these spasms in the future. 'You told me that half an hour ago and look what's happened,' was all I could say.

Touch wood, from that day 15 years ago to this, I have been fine with the help of four-pills-a-day medication.

CHAPTER NINE

Fry in, Collymore out

It is said that there is no fool like an old fool and so it was perhaps with something less than a coincidental element that, on April Fool's Day 1992, I joined forces with Southend United. This was my brand new dawn and the immediate task in hand bore much resemblance to my previous situations in that I was charged with rescuing the club from the heavy spectre of relegation. I had heard a lot about Vic Jobson, the vast majority of it very positive, in the decade during which he had been at the club's helm. Every year he had improved things in one way or another and was totally football-orientated. After a long discussion about future plans he offered me a contract, an unfamiliar document to me because in 14 years at Barnet, and in the previous six years with other clubs, I never had one.

One aspect of this gave me a percentage of outgoing transfer fees, Vic's theory being that I would be disinclined to sell my best players because a deterioration in performance could well eventually lead me to the sack. I was on 10 per cent, an arrangement which I previously had with other clubs. It is normal in football management. The time of year at which I joined Southend meant that the transfer deadline had passed. Nor could I take along my trusted backroom staff. My assistant at Barnet, Ed Stein, was given my old job and my player-coach, David Howell, was made number two to Ed. On the face of it my task was hopeless. Southend were seven points adrift at the foot of the First Division and I somehow had to motivate the exisiting squad into playing out of their skins in the remaining nine matches to avoid the dreaded drop. I was given a big incentive by Vic to achieve this and he also entered me into a pension scheme for the first time in my life. 'With a wife and four kids,' he said, 'it is about time you started looking after your family.' I have much to be grateful to Vic for. He ensured I was given the wisest of financial advice and this enabled me to buy the property in which we still live in Bedford. I thought I couldn't afford it and he persuaded me that I could. Along with Colin Murphy, whom I was replacing and who was to take a position on the board, and Danny Greaves, the youth-team coach, we talked into the early hours. It was the most positive of meetings and much of the optimism engendered must have rubbed off on the players because of those remaining games we won six, drew two, lost one – and survived.

I had one big asset in Stan Collymore who, at that level, was different class, as well as Brett Angell and

Spencer Prior. My other jewel was Danny Greaves, who stepped up from the youths to help me and did a magnificent job. I first met the players when Kirstine dropped me off at a local Autogrill to meet the team coach on the way to my first fixture at Terry Butcher's Sunderland. As I went through the coach to shake hands with everybody I was looking at the tops of heads. They all had their eyes to the floor. I called over Stan Collymore, who was being touted around transfer deadline time as a £1.5 million target for Brian Clough at Nottingham Forest.

'I've looked at your contract,' I said to Stan, 'which shows that there are still two and a half years to run. I realise it must be awkward for you, but if you do it for me, I will help you all I can in the summer.'

I asked him where he wanted to go and he replied that his ideal club would be Aston Villa.

'No problem,' I told him. 'My mate Ron Atkinson is there and I will do a deal with him. But I must have 100 per cent commitment from you in these last few games.'

We had dinner on arrival at Sunderland and I spoke to the players about the challenge ahead.

'Tomorrow, you must just express yourselves. I know what it is like being at the bottom of the league scrapping for results, but you are under no pressure because you have been written off by everybody anyway. Just relax, and if anybody is in bed before two in the morning I will fine them a week's wages.'

They took me at my word, went to a night club, slept well and played superbly, winning 4–2. Our next match, the following Tuesday, was against top-of-the-league West Ham. A marvellous run and cross by Collymore, bundled in by Angell, gave us an unexpected 1–0 victory in front of a full house at Roots Hall. All of a sudden we were on a roll. Our only defeat came at Cambridge United. I had recommended Collymore to Manchester United, who duly sent a scout to this game. I praised the player to high heaven to this scout, telling him there was nothing Stan could not do and how brilliant he was. He proceeded to have a dreadful game. He just had one of those days when nothing went right, we lost 3–1 and it should have been more and the scout was away and out of the ground within 20 minutes. After the game I told Stan that I had gone to the trouble of getting a scout down from Manchester United and that he had been f***ing hopeless. He just held up his hands and said: 'I know.' At the time he was having terrible family problems in that his sister in Cannock was dying of cancer. I used to urge him to take long weekends on his home patch so that he could be close to her and he never once took a liberty. He would be back for training sharp on a Monday morning and I never had a moment's trouble with him. He scored five goals in those nine games, despite all the pressure he was under.

Angell scored five as well and the whole team was magnificent. Vic thought I could walk on water. I had achieved the impossible and he was constantly praising me. This, of course, was music to my ears because I had spent a long time in football receiving tongue-lashings from men at the top and crossing swords with them. He loved the club, putting his heart and soul into it, and he was so genuinely grateful for my contribution. This was reciprocal. He would say things to me like: 'You're a born winner,' or 'You can achieve anything.' As a football manager you don't have any friends. You have got to pick everybody up ... the chairman, the directors, the fans, the players. Nobody picks you up. You are on your own. But Vic, in whom I found a friend and ally, was fantastic.

The summer saw the break-up of the team which had defied all the odds. Glenn Hoddle of Chelsea, Howard Wilkinson from Leeds, Trevor Francis from Sheffield Wednesday and Ron Atkinson at Aston Villa were all chasing Stan, with Ron appearing to be the most anxious to buy. However, he could offer only £1.2 million, although he pledged three players as part of the package. They were all good players but, unfortunately, I could not afford their wages. At the time the highest-paid player at Southend was on £550 a week – and it wasn't Stan Collymore. He was on £525, with a £10,000 signing-on fee at £3,333 a year for three years. It wasn't the best contract in the world, but Stan played with a smile on his face. He was awesome. He would get the ball with his back to goal, turn and beat opponents with his pace, power and skill and smack the ball into the net, with no backlift, from 25 yards with his right foot and 30 yards with his left. He also made a lot of goals down both left and right channels, spinning off his marker and delivering lethal curling crosses which left goalkeepers wondering whether to stay put or go for the ball. He was one of that rare breed of player who had the fans on the edge of their seats, anticipating something marvellous, whenever he was in possession. Everybody loved him.

I played it cool over his transfer, despite the rush for his signature. Frank Clark, who helped me a lot at Barnet when he was at Leyton Orient, and is a good friend, was taking over from Cloughie at Nottingham Forest. Whenever I needed advice I would always turn first to Frank. Where I am a hothead, he looks carefully at situations and weighs up things in a calm, level-headed manner. He said that he wanted Collymore, for whom Forest had already struck a deal of £1.5 million, but I told him that could not have been the case because, otherwise, he would already be there and, anyway, Southend's valuation was now £2.5 million. The competition for his signature was intense, but Frank's determination to get him was such that when he flew into Gatwick from a family holiday he had arranged for Colin Murphy and Stan to meet him there. We settled at £2.1 million, plus £250,000 if Forest gained promotion, £250,000 if he scored 25 goals in a season and £250,000 if he won an England cap. There was also a 15 per cent share of any sell-on from Forest, who eventually transferred him to Liverpool for £8.5 million. All these subsidiary elements were achieved, the promotion and goalscoring in his first season, bringing a lottery jackpot to Roots Hall for a player bought by Colin Murphy from Crystal Palace for

£100,000. Brett Angell, who was out of contract and unhappy about one or two things, joined Everton for £500,000 and Spencer Prior, also out of contract, teamed up with Norwich for £300,000. These departures, particularly those of Collymore, Angell and Prior, led the bookmakers to chalking up Southend as odds-on favourites to be relegated the following season.

It was an interesting summer. Over at Barnet, automatic promotion had been achieved by virtue of their finishing third in the Fourth Division and I received an invitation from the mayor to join an open-top coach parade through the town. Predictably, I suppose, I received a letter from Barnet in which it was stated that if I were to turn up, Stan Flashman would not like it. But because it was not a football club function per se, and because Stan was supposed to have nothing to do with them at that point – it was also clear that all the players wanted me to be present – I decided to accept. I have always been pleased that I did. It was a lovely day. Those outgoings at Southend meant that I needed replacements and from that team bus on which the players proudly showed off the trophy as it made its way through the streets of Barnet I acquired Jonathan Hunt, Mick Bodley, Gary Poole and Derek Payne, all for nothing. I would gladly have paid good money for them, but the affairs at Barnet were in such disarray that they were all free agents. Of course, they were immediately relegated again. It is a wonder that they could even raise a team. I also had Chris Powell, whom I thought the best left-back in the First Division, and he was eventually sold to Derby for £850,000. Tommy Mooney, whom I bought for £25,000 from Scarborough, was to move to Watford for £250,000 and it was rewarding for me to see him help the club so loved by Elton John and Graham Taylor into the Premiership for the 1999/2000 season. I had bought Jason Lee, who picked up the unfortunate nickname 'Pineapplehead', from Lincoln for next to nothing and he later joined Forest for £300,000. Ricky Otto, at £100,000 from Leyton Orient, was another buy. Ed Stein and Dave Howell left Barnet as they were going bust and joined me as assistant manager and player-coach.

So Southend faced a new season with a sea of new faces. The football world, meanwhile, had been shocked by the death of Bobby Moore, who was once manager at Roots Hall. He was, of course, one of football's greatest ambassadors and it was a very moving experience to attend his memorial service in London. Afterwards Vic told me: 'You have made so much money for us that you have got to spend £400,000, otherwise I shall become liable for corporation tax.' I have often wondered how many managers have been told by their chairmen that they must spend what, to me, was a large amount of money. I'll wager that there aren't many.

The Anglo-Italian tournament provided the perfect dress rehearsal for the new campaign and in the course of a 2–1 victory against an Italian side I was forced to substitute Ricky Otto. He had been taking the piss out of them so much that all his marker wanted to do was to kick him up in the air and I feared for his welfare in a seething cauldron of a match. As Ricky took his place on the bench Colin Hill, my good friend, warned me that the home fans, who were in a frenzy of hatred, would exact their revenge in the tunnel and that I would have to play things very carefully on the way off at the end of the match. It was a long walk to the dressing-room from the pitch, through an eerie dark tunnel. We had almost made it when, all of a sudden, this Italian jumped out of one of the rooms wielding a hammer. He made to smash it into Otto's head and I dread to think what would have become of him had Dave Howell, who is as strong as an ox, not waded in, grabbed the Italian's raised arm and twisted it until he dropped the weapon. It was a frightening experience for everybody, but we tried to put it behind us with a laugh and a joke in the bath. A local official escorted us out of the ground and into the team coach by a back route, which again took us through a long dark tunnel. The boys were winding each other up and the nervousness decreased with every step nearer to the safety of the coach. Out of nowhere I felt a sharp prod in my back and I instantly thought that a local Mafiosi had me hostage to a gun. My worst fear was confirmed when a voice said: 'Senor, you are going to be shot.' My heart sank. Then a chorus of tittering broke out, I turned round and realised that it was one of the lads turning the situation into a joke. I can't decide which emotion, relief or anger, was uppermost but we all had a good laugh about it afterwards.

Come the big kick-off on the following Saturday, with all the fans having read about our Italian experience, we thought we would start the season in light-hearted fashion. One player came into the dressing-room with a massive blow-up hammer and suggested that Ricky would be last in line as the team came out, with me hiding in the dugout brandishing this plaything. That is what we did, and I chased Ricky into the centre circle, bopping him over the head to the great merriment of the crowd. A great team spirit had been formed and by Christmas we were in second spot and looking certs for promotion to the top tier. At the turn of the year, however, the papers were full of a speculative story that I was about to become manager of Birmingham. They were soon to be our opponents in a league match, as were Nottingham Forest, and as is usual with imminently opposing teams I took the opportunity of seeing them play each other at Forest. Frank Clark looked after me in the directors' box but after the match the Forest chairman, Fred Reacher, said that he would like to invite me into the boardroom but had read about the Birmingham link and was embarrassed to do so because Vic Jobson was on his way up to the match.

Vic arrived a bit late and at half time he went into the boardroom while I went into the guest room. We took our seats for the second half and he leaned over and whispered in my ear that Karren Brady, David Sullivan's managing director at Birmingham City, had asked permission to speak to me and that he had flatly refused.

'Why did you do that, Vic?' I asked mischievously.

'She's not speaking to you. It's not on.'

Frank had said that he would see me in the boardroom after the game and wanting to keep this arrangement, I was pleased when Reacher said that it was all right to go in there now because Vic had left. Just as I was walking in there, who should be walking out but David Sullivan and Karren Brady. They were being followed by people who, I was unaware, were press men and I shouted after them.

'Karren, I believe you wanted to talk to me and that my chairman has not given you permission. You can talk to me any time you like.'

Also in the boardroom I saw Jack Wiseman who, at the time, was chairman of Birmingham.

'I'm not sure you should be in here,' Jack said.

'Well, Jack, it isn't your boardroom.'

When I got home that night I had a close look at my contract. Even though Vic had intimated I had a job for life, I discovered that I had to take his word for it – I did not have the protection of a legal document. This showed that if he wanted to get rid of me, he could give me six months' notice or six months' money in lieu. I must admit that when I signed the contract I had never even looked at it. Plainly, now, it wasn't a life contract or even a five-year contract. It was a six-month contract at best. Yet I have never held much store by contracts. I believe that, as a manager, if I am doing my job then the club will not want to get rid of me. I also believe that if I have a five-year contract and the club want to get rid of me, they won't do that because it would cost them too much in compensation. Anyway, I have never wanted to stay anywhere that I am not really wanted. I was angry when I discovered Vic's clause and I went to see him on the Monday.

'Vic, about this Birmingham situation ...'

'You are not speaking to them,' he countered, 'and that is the end of it.'

In between, on the Sunday, we played Leicester in a televised game and although both of us were in the promotion stakes it was a horribly dull 0–0 draw. I said to Derek Payne before the game that he should at all costs avoid being wound up by David Speedie, who was very adept at that. Of course, Speedie was his usual self and the pair were right on the touchline as I shouted: 'Payney, don't let him get to you,' with my timing so immaculate that it coincided with my player drawing his fist back. He was sent off and, in the circumstances, we did well to get a point out of the match. Afterwards all the broadcasters wanted a few words and they wanted to know more about the Birmingham business than my views on the match.

'I would like to talk to them,' I said to the interviewer. 'They have asked permission, but my chairman won't allow it.'

With that, Vic jumped in front of the cameras. 'Over my dead body will Barry Fry talk to Birmingham. He is here. He is our manager.'

I have never been comfortable with people telling me what I can and cannot do and that gave me the hump. At Barnet, Stan Flashman would ban me from talking to the press and I would talk to the press. I have always felt it a necessary part of my job. If we have played crap, they are entitled to say that. They are just doing their jobs, although Stan never saw it that way.

Back in Vic's office, I had developed an overwhelming curiosity about Birmingham and I wanted to pursue the matter. Southend was a small club; Birmingham a sleeping giant with massive potential. I knew them when Gil Merrick was in goal and Trevor Francis played for them. The chairman could see how pumped up I was and, though he was sighing with resignation, eventually he gave me a letter, which he made me sign, saying that I had his permission to talk to Birmingham but that, under no circumstances, was I to become their manager. It made no sense to me.

When I arrived at Birmingham City, I discovered one big toilet. It hadn't had a coat of paint for 20 years and looked a total shambles. I saw David and Karren, whom I had originally not taken seriously in a football context. But I could not have been more impressed. They showed me a scale model of plans for ground renovations, stated that money would be available to strengthen the team and left me in no doubt about their ambition to see their club in the Premiership. I asked why they wanted me and Sullivan said that, at his Essex mansion, he had read about me at Barnet and Southend and was impressed by how I had operated on shoestring budgets. Although there was plenty of money, he said, he wanted to invest it in the stadium while I was to wheel and deal in players in the only way I knew. Most of all, he said, he wanted me to put bums on seats, as I had done at my previous and current clubs. For people known on the football circuit as Porn King and Bimbo, they came across as highly educated and very knowledgeable.

'What's your role, love?' I asked Karren.

'My role is to bring in the finance to enable David to achieve all his aims here at the football club.'

It was her baby, really. She always wanted to go into football. A dyed-in-the-wool Arsenal fan, she has been a football nut ever since she left school. She is a clever woman and made untold millions for Sullivan in his sex empire. What she told me is right. Everybody needs sex in one way and another and if you have the monopoly on fulfilling their fantasies then you are bound to make a lot of money. David is the first to admit that she is responsible for much of his fortune. And Karren Brady is one hard bastard. She had to be to survive and prosper in the man's world that is football. The single most impressive element of this entire meeting was that when I asked what I would be given to achieve their ambitions – a figure of £6,000 a week had been mentioned in Sullivan's own paper, *The Sport*, although he insisted this was just paper talk – he said that he would not allow me 10 per cent of transfer fees, a practice I had enjoyed for 10 years. 'That would only encourage you to sell our best players,' he reasoned, and even though it would limit my earning potential I liked his commitment. The offer wasn't any great shakes, but I was impressed by their passion for the club.

The Southend board was meeting that evening and I had a terrible journey down the M6 on my way to Roots Hall, not only because of the stop-start traffic but also because I was in inner turmoil. Nobody had given us a cat in hell's chance of survival at Southend, yet here we were lying in an automatic promotion slot to the Premiership. On the other hand, though Birmingham were in the bottom three and facing relegation, I felt excited that this sleeping giant wanted me to awaken it. Vic, as usual, chaired the meeting. I said that I had seen Birmingham and wished to join them. He argued that I had a job for life at Southend, adding that Birmingham was not being run by football people and that I would be sacked within three months if I didn't deliver. I countered that the reality of the situation at Southend was that I did not have a long-term contract, however much he wished to argue to the contrary. One of the directors, John Adams, asked how much it would take to persuade me to stay, pledging £15,000 personally and his weight behind a more secure contract. I was on a basic of only £55,000 and had done so well for the club that I felt justified in seeking more, but a visibly angry Vic rose to his feet.

'Barry, I will give you not one penny more than you are on now. I will look at it again at the end of the season but, for now, there is nothing.'

Adding that it was a matter for the other board members if they wished to do something to keep me, he then stormed out. It was turning into an emotional meeting and Colin Murphy left to bring Vic back before saying: 'Gentlemen, we cannot allow Barry to leave this meeting without a new contract because, in just six months, he has made such a difference to this old club.' Vic, a man of principle, would not budge. John Adams, now resigned to the situation, said that he could stay no longer because he was heartbroken. He went home. The meeting ended with a few of the directors saying that the decision did not have to made there and then, but it had, in effect, already been made. I stood up, wrote a cheque for £27,500 and handed it to Vic.

'There's my notice. I'm leaving.'

He protested that a parting of the ways could not be orchestrated in that way.

'A contract is two ways,' I said. 'If you can get rid of me with six months' notice, then I can do the same to you.'

I told him that I had checked this with the League Managers' Association. I said I was sorry that it had come to this and the atmosphere lifted.

'You can't afford this,' Vic said. 'I don't want your money.'

He handed back the cheque, but I just threw it on the floor and passed over a pre-written notice letter. Vic asked for five minutes with me. We went into his office, where he reiterated that he did not want me to go.

'I love you, Baz,' he said. He then went on to wish me all the success in the world but said that he would sue in respect of Birmingham's approach to me.

He thanked me for what I had done and I bawled my eyes out. I couldn't handle it. Vic was a friend. He cared for me and I really felt that I was letting him down. I asked if he would make Ed Stein manager and Dave Howell his assistant and he said: 'No, I won't. They're not good enough. They will stay here until such a time as I find a new manager and then they will go.' In fact they were sitting in their cars outside, waiting for me. I told them what had happened and they walked out on the club there and then. My feeling of guilt lifted when I subsequently learned that Vic had made an official approach to Hendon for the services of their manager, Peter Taylor, who lived in Southend. His 'Not A Penny More' boardroom speech was suddenly in sharp focus.

CHAPTER TEN

Brady blues

Breakfast with Karren Brady was at the Birmingham Hyatt Hotel. There were more participants than she had anticipated, for although she knew I would be taking along Ed Stein as my assistant she had not been expecting Dave Howell to arrive as player-coach. It had been a long night. The three of us drove north to meet her, our Southend days over, and the first call I received the next day interrupted breakfast. The caller was John Adams, who said that although he was aware I had left they were in a pickle because Stein and Howell had not arrived for training. 'I know,' I told him. 'They are with me in Birmingham.'

This played into Southend's hands. They kept Howell's registration so that I was never able to play him and a big hearing followed in which Birmingham were made to pay £125,000 for their illegal approach to me. It was all rather bitter and twisted. Birmingham had been left high and dry when Terry Cooper let it be known

171

that he wished to resign as manager to pursue other interests. It was no secret that the club made several attempts to persuade him otherwise, but he was determined on his chosen course of action. Life in football can sometimes be very cruel, and after a noon press conference to announce our arrival my first task was to call in Cooper's coach, Trevor Morgan.

'You know what it is like in this game, Trevor. When a manager goes, his replacement wants his own team around him and I am no different. You have done nothing wrong and you may be the greatest coach in the country but, sadly, you have to go.'

My new arrivals and the impending departures created a lot of paperwork for Karren, but I could not fail to be struck by her alacrity. Trevor was paid off on the spot. Instead of managers, coaches and other staff being made to fight through the courts for compensation for month after month, here was someone showing a touch of class. No negotiation, no arguments. Job done. The following day, a Friday, we set off for our away fixture at Crystal Palace, my first match in charge. I got off to a bad start. When we arrived in London I addressed the players regarding the team selection.

'Right lads, this is the team,' and proceeded to reel off the names of players and substitutes.

'Er, boss …' Danny Wallace tried to interrupt but I ignored him and went on to tell them how I expected them to play.

I was unfamiliar with some of the players' names and

when I said that I wanted Graham Potter to man-mark Palace's danger man, John Salako, Wallace piped up again.

'Potter can't do that, boss.'

'Why not?'

'Because he ain't here.'

I had been told that everybody was travelling but here I was, picking a man who was still back in Birmingham, to play. This caused much amusement. The mood, however, was to swing the other way when Karren unexpectedly joined us. She told me: 'We haven't let you know, but we have been battling all day because Southend have obtained an injunction preventing you from being the manager for this game.' I was temporarily in no-man's land, but once again she showed her skills by getting the injunction lifted in the nick of time.

We went into the match on the back of an appalling run which had seen Birmingham lose their previous six games without scoring a goal. It didn't help matters that the guy I wanted to play left-back had been left behind in Birmingham but George Parris, a great old pro who had previously done well with West Ham, said he would step into the breach. It wasn't ideal, because he was a right-footed player and was marking Salako, who scored the winner from 30 yards as we lost 2–1. My first home game was against Charlton and drew a crowd of 14,000, whereas the attendance for the previous game at St Andrews had attracted 4,600. I walked round the ground, greeting the crowd, and the response was fantastic. We turned the tide with a 1–0 victory and Christmas was now upon us. Our big holiday fixture was a local derby at home to Birmingham's fiercest rivals, West Bromwich Albion, and I was disappointed to find on my arrival at the ground that the pitch was blanketed in snow. I said to the secretary, Alan Jones, that regrettably there would be no chance of playing and he said: 'You watch.' His intention, he said, was to have an announcement made by the local radio station that help was required to clear the pitch. I thought there was no chance because it required an army to clear it, not just a handful of fans.

Within half an hour I was watching in astonishment as, indeed, a veritable army arrived. With a burning desire to get the match on they used every implement they could bring to hand to clear every flake of snow. The match kicked off at the scheduled time of three o'clock in front of a giant crowd of 28,228, the biggest First Division attendance of the season. I was aware then of the partisan passion and foaming fervour of The Blues fans. Despite having Dave Barnett sent off we won 2–0 with goals by Andy Saville from the penalty spot and Paul Peschisolido, who suffered a bad leg injury, and after this game I knew why I had gone to Birmingham. The whole big-crowd, local-derby, deafening-roar experience was magical. The fates would have it that, a few short weeks after joining Birmingham from Southend in circumstances which were not the happiest from the seaside club's viewpoint, we were to play each other in a New Year's Day league match. It was a 12,000 sellout.

I was warned by the police that it might be in my better interest to stay away, but their advice was pointless and misguided. How could I avoid being there? And, more to the point, why should I avoid it? Sometimes in life you have got to face the music. David Sullivan took more than a passing interest and this was very welcome. He inquired about the New Year's Eve arrangements, where we were staying and whether or not I would allow the lads a celebratory drink, and when I told him that we would be at the Swallow Hotel in Waltham Abbey, close to his Essex home, he invited us all round to his place for dinner. 'F***ing hell, David,' I said. 'I'm taking the whole squad. There will be about 28 of us.' He just smiled and said that would be fine. We went by coach on the short journey to his £7 million mansion and, judging by the expressions on some of the players' faces, you would have thought they had just entered paradise through the imposing iron gateway which swept open to allow us entry. He had arranged for a band playing 60s and 70s music to entertain us through dinner and afterwards he asked if anybody would like to play tenpin bowling. He just happened to have an alley! When the players said they would like that, but had no shoes, he opened a few cupboards displaying every size of appropriate footwear and the game commenced to the accompaniment of a jukebox. We were in a different world and everybody had a wonderful evening, rounded off nicely when he allowed each member of the assembled party to make a telephone call to greet their nearest and dearest. If they had not so far been impressed by their chairman, they were now. Dave Sullivan is a rich man who likes to indulge his passion and I was interested to learn that he made his first £500 from selling bundles of football programmes. To be fair, he would talk sensibly about football to me almost every day. I didn't necessarily agree with some of the things he had to say, but at least I felt that he was making an input. He certainly wanted the best for Birmingham City Football Club.

Southend, on the other hand, harboured no such glad tidings on the day Birmingham were the visitors. I have never seen so many people in the Roots Hall car park an hour before kick-off. 'Judas,' said some banners; 'We Hate Fry' others. As I got off the coach I was greeted by a hail of missiles of every description. I knew that I would be in for a hot reception, but never in my worst nightmares did I anticipate such venomous hatred. It was so ferocious and threatening that the police had to form a gangway so that I could get into the dressing room in one piece. Everybody on the Southend staff, the receptionists, secretaries, board members and players, were fine, but it was obvious right from the kick-off that the fans wanted to put one over on me. Their cause was hardly hindered when, after just 10 minutes, our centre-forward Andy Saville was sent off. The crowd abuse continued unabated for every second of the 90 minutes and, perhaps spurred on by this, Southend won 3–0. After the game, Vic Jobson apologised on behalf of his club's fans and I told him: 'Vic, I'm a football supporter at heart. All supporters want to be managers, or play at being managers, and I just consider myself lucky to have achieved that.' The whole experience demonstrated to me the amount of upset and grief I had caused. I could see it in their eyes.

It was not the first time I had been on the receiving end of such disaffection. When I joined Southend from Barnet – who, that summer, had been the subject of a Football League inquiry which resulted in all their players leaving for different clubs – there was further evidence of the uncanny knack that the game has of bringing together two clubs with a score to settle. The draw for the first round of the Coca Cola Cup paired Southend and Barnet, at Underhill, in the second game of the season. We were expected to win, and win well, because Barnet were down and out. All the players had left on free transfers and they were starting from scratch. Everybody in the game, and nobody more so than I, felt very sorry for them. We walked out to a scene behind the goal which made my heart sink. It was wall-to-wall with hundreds of banners which said 'Judas' and 'Rape' and, for the first time in my life, I was badly affected by the impact of abuse. It was like a kick in the bollocks. Those fans did not know the truth. I departed from the club with them owing me £162,000. I had not been paid for eight weeks. I had suffered two heart attacks while there. I had been arrested on Christmas Eve while trying to prepare their pitch. I took out a second mortgage to help them. I had two testimonials there, giving away the proceeds of one to foot the wage bill and not receiving anything from the other. For 14 years I had put them before my family and that is terribly wrong. The 2–0 defeat hurt big time, but the game itself was a non-event for me from first whistle to last because of the constant abuse. I had many letters afterwards recognising that what had happened had been totally out of order.

In few other walks of life do passions run so high. While at Southend we played in a televised match at Millwall and won 4–1. I don't know what happens to me emotionally when my teams score a goal but, as usual, I set off running down the cinder track in celebration and obviously upset one of the home supporters so much that he landed a right hook before running off into the distance. I don't mean to offend opposing supporters, nor am I taking the piss, but being a supporter at heart makes me react in the way I do.

Southend's result against Birmingham was a turning point for them because under their new manager, Peter Taylor, they had been struggling. Now it was our turn. The whole thing went horribly pear-shaped. We went three months without winning a game. We had so many injuries that I kept having to bring in new faces. There was never the time, nor even the opportunity, to mould them into a unit and things just staggered from bad to worse. I learned then of a gypsy curse which was said to have been put on the ground. I set about relieving St Andrews of this millstone by relieving myself – in all four corners of the pitch. We even lost to Kidderminster, from the Vauxhall Conference, in the third round of the FA Cup. When the draw paired us together, David Sullivan was confident.

'Well, that's us through to the next round.'

'David,' I warned, 'I've just come from non-league football. These are hard games.'

I was alone at St Andrews in taking this game seriously. We missed a penalty and should have won easily but Graham Allner had been doing a brilliant job at Kidderminster for years and years, insisting on them playing football, and again it was a local derby with passions running high. They got the breaks and won 2–1 – and jolly good luck to them was my reaction.

At the time we could not win an argument. Several football forums organised by the local radio station were being held in pubs across the city, giving the fanatical Bluenoses the opportunity to voice their opinions. I was often invited along and though I knew it was inevitable that I would take some stick I felt it my duty to appear. I would walk in to a chorus of booing and then the taunts would start. A geezer with a pint in each hand once came up to me and said: 'Why don't you f**k off back to the smoke, you cockney bastard. We don't want you here. You're f***ing useless,' to which I replied, 'I ain't going back until I've finished what I started.' They soon learned that I was as passionate as they were and I never ducked a question. What these forums taught me was that Birmingham City Football Club constitutes the entire lives of these fans. They live and breathe the football club, with everything that happens in the days between matches one massive void in their existences. If we lost, they were shattered for a whole week. I would go back to the players and say: 'Lads, if we had the passion and commitment shown by the supporters we would be certainties for the Premiership.' Birmingham is a massive place with some dodgy areas and even dodgier characters, but the Bluenoses all have this one thing in common. Their football club.

All through this bad spell it became increasingly apparent that Karren Brady did not like me. In her book, *Brady Sings The Blues*, and more recently face-to-face, she admitted that not a single day passed by in my first year at the club without her wishing to sack me. She thought I was the wrong man for the job. I was taking over from Terry Cooper, who was such a gentleman and so professional. I was my usual uncouth self but, having said that, Karren could swear better than me when she was stirred. She didn't have a clue where I was coming from and thought I was a little boy in a toy shop, wanting to buy everything on the shelves. She could not fathom what I was trying to put together. The relationship wasn't usually a problem for me. At times I felt that she did not appreciate how important it was to sign a particular player. There was sometimes a clash between my wish as a manager to obtain the best players reasonably available, and her wish as Chief Executive Officer to make the best business deal. For instance I wanted to sign two non-league players and offered them three-year contracts at £350, £400 and £450 a year. The players signed and the contracts were countersigned by Alan Jones, but after having taken them into Karren and emerged from her office, he nodded me to one side.

'She'll only give them two years,' he said.

As you can imagine, I was not best pleased. I marched in and said that she was undermining my authority.

'That's all they are getting, Barry,' she said. 'Take it or leave it.'

Of course, the players took it and as they made their way out she looked at me smugly.

'There you are. What are you talking about? I've just saved this club money. That's my job.'

It is at times such as that lose-or-draw run – we never won – that you discover who your friends are. The Gold brothers, David and Ralph, who co-owned the club with Sullivan, gave me great support when I was at my lowest ebb and I was very grateful for that. They did a lot for me and had faith that I would get it right. I am not sure that Sullivan did and I know for sure that Karren did not. She thought I was clueless.

Towards the end of the season I told Karren that I thought a three-day break at a health farm would do everybody the world of good. I had a lot of injuries in the squad, several new players, many individuals, but no team. I had a lot of knitting-together and building of team spirit to do. Togetherness was the keyword. Just as we were about to set off I got a phone call from Karren.

'I've got some bad news,' she said. 'Pesch's knee has

blown up. He won't be able to make your trip. It has happened before and I have to take him for a cortisone injection, then he needs to rest at home for a couple of days.'

We started to have a good time from the moment we arrived. Frank Bruno was there sparring as he trained for a forthcoming fight and was good company. The lads worked hard in the gym and had facials and massages, each looking forward to a nice blonde masseuse only for some to be disappointed and opting out when a bloke emerged to perform the task. We were having a drink together in the evening when I said what a pity it had been that Peschisolido was unable to be with us, relating Karren's telephone call. As if a brass band were striking up, they all burst out laughing. Bemused, and obviously not in on the joke, I asked what was going on.

'Don't you know, boss? Karren and Pesch. They're an item.'

'No,' I said. 'I don't believe that.'

We had been back at the club a couple of days when Karren rang me.

'You have got problems in your dressing room.'

'How do you know what problems exist in my dressing room?' I asked.

'It has been brought to my attention,' she said.

'Well, young lady, the only f***ing problem I have in my dressing room is you f***ing around with one of my players!'

Oops! Behind her closed door I told her: 'Listen,

Karren. You are single, Pesch is single. I don't care. You can do what you like. It's nothing to do with me. But when I take my players away I expect all of them to be there.'

She protested that it was genuine and, to be fair, it was. It wasn't as though they were having an affair. Despite the tremendous difficulties that they must have had to endure in building a romance within the club, their relationship grew stronger and they got married and now have two lovely kids. It was a problem at the club at the time because we were not doing well and, in those situations, everybody points at little insignificant things as possible reasons for lack of success.

Our visit to the health farm seemed to do the trick. We all got our acts together and in our last 10 games we won seven, drew two and lost just one. It helped that, because of ground rebuilding, we had to play the majority of these run-in fixtures away from home, a venue at which we had completely lost our way. That is promotion form by any standard, yet we were relegated, of all things, on goals scored. And that was hard to swallow for a guy who was used to managing teams which banged in over a century of goals in a season and it was even harder to swallow for the fans to be survived by West Brom. Our last match of the season was at Tranmere, with West Brom at Portsmouth. We had to win. Jim Smith, the Pompey manager, rang me up.

'Baz, you are not going to like what I have to say, but I have eight players out of the team on Sunday.'

'What did you tell me that for? I'm depressed enough already. Do you want me to shoot my brains out?'

Jim said that he did not want me to be under any impression that he had fielded a weakened side, while reiterating that there was nothing he could do about it. Things looked promising at Tranmere. All the travelling Bluenoses – 5,000 inside the ground and a further 5,000 outside – were dressed up for their big day out and were ecstatic when we went one-up. They equalised and then we plundered the winner, but we had heard that West Brom were a goal up and, in view of what I had been told by Jim Smith, I knew there was no way back. Everybody was gutted by the reality of relegation in the dressing room, but such was the Bluenose commotion around the ground and on the pitch that I was told I would have to take the team out to meet the fans because they did not look as though they were anything like ready to leave. They were fantastic. I was chaired sky-high and carried round the entire stadium – and we had just been relegated! I half-expected a throttling, but by now I had come to know the fans better than that. The average crowd had risen from 4,000 to 14,000 and while dropping into Division Two was the downside, the positive side of things was that the sleeping giant was blinking open its eyes.

CHAPTER ELEVEN

'How many caps does that woman wear here?'

David Sullivan doubted the wisdom of Birmigham City's sights being set on the Premiership, arguing that St Andrews would need to attract a full house to every home match and there had been no sign of that happening for a long time. It was my view that he would not be able to build a stadium big enough to accommodate a Bluenose crowd in the elite division, drawing the parallel of Middlesbrough who, when they won the First Division, had an average gate of 14,000 and had since gone into orbit. People cannot get a ticket to watch them for love nor money.

Season ticket sales went well during the summer, even though Division Two football was about to be served up, and I set about bringing in some new faces. I bought Liam Daish for £50,000 from Cambridge, though Karren Brady had not been happy with the results of his medical and sent him for further scans on his back, and I brought in Steve Claridge, who took a cut in wages to join us for

£200,000, also from Cambridge. I wanted to sign Chris Powell from Southend, but the £1.5 million valuation I had put upon him when I was there backfired on me and Vic Jobson would not let me have him for less, so no deal was struck.

One player I did get from Vic, though I had to go to £800,000 for him, was Ricky Otto. We were desperate for a centre-forward and I became determined to buy the 6ft 7in giant Kevin Francis, whose goalscoring record at Stockport was phenomenal. I was happy enough that we were playing good football, but we were lacking in presence in the box. The deal was to be £400,000, with another £400,000 becoming due after a number of appearances, but it could not be struck at the time because he failed a medical. So Otto, a natural outside-left, was signed, with me having persuaded Karren that he could play at centre-forward, and he scored twice on his debut against Leyton Orient. Unfortunately one was at the wrong end and we drew 1–1. Now I was able to argue that it was vital that we sign Francis. It was a con really. I knew that if I asked to sign two players, an outside-left and a centre-forward, I would be pilloried, but to pursue the matter in that fashion, arguing that my experiment with Otto had not succeeded, might work. It did.

On the eve of this opening fixture in London I had my first hint that all was not well in our little world. I picked up the local Birmingham paper to find a big article on Sullivan in which he was apparently quoted as saying: 'If Fry hasn't got us in the top three at Christmas, I am going to sack him.' This was wonderful encouragement, just the tonic you need as you take the first step into a new campaign. We haven't kicked a ball yet and, here I am, apparently being threatened with the boot. I was well and truly pissed off by that. Later, one of the newspaper's reporters rang me to enquire whether I had seen the piece and I told him that I had been fortunate enough to have read it on the team coach. He asked for my reaction and then, of course, he had another story for the following day. In my time at Birmingham I cannot remember a single face-to-face row with Sullivan, but this was the first of many exchanges through the columns of newspapers. Because he, Karren and I had a high profile in and around the city it was easy for the press to get a ruck going. This particular season the structure of the league was that only the champions would be automatically promoted, so everything was at stake. It had not been a good start and a peculiar atmosphere pervaded the boardroom after the game. Our directors had read the exchange in the newspaper, we hadn't played at all well and we had only drawn. Much more had been expected after that good end to the previous season and there was a general feeling of discontent. In the run-up to the big kick-off, a local bookmaker was offering 10–1 that Birmingham would win the league and I could not wait to impart this information to Sullivan.

'David, you're a betting man. Put your shirt on us winning the league.'

Shrewd man that he is, he replied: 'I wouldn't touch it. The odds are too generous.'

Most of the lads struck the bet and so did I. A Bedford bookie was quoting the same odds and I steamed in there, too, but things looked distinctly unpromising when, after four games, we were still seeking a first victory. Bearing in mind the apparent quotes in the press, I began to feel under some pressure. People were already beginning to speculate on a weekly basis whether I would still be in charge for the next match, but I knew there were mitigating circumstances in that, in these early stages, we were missing half a dozen players through injury. I told everybody to reserve their judgement until we were able to field our strongest side. We slowly began to find our feet, as I expected, and although I had not engineered a top three position by Christmas, Sullivan expressed the opinion that he was satisfied with our progress. So was I. The fans were fantastic, the redevelopment of the stadium was taking shape and I was convinced that we would soon find the rich seam of form that would strengthen our challenge. There existed, though, a niggling undercurrent ... the odd bit of negative gossip here and bits of newspaper criticism there. When I picked up on these I would call David and ask if I should go to see him at his home, but he would always say that there was nothing in these stories or that he had been misquoted or a matter had been taken out of context. Then there were the constant calls from Karren to see her in her office. Usually you had to hand it to her, she would act as peacemaker.

'You and David must stop bickering and fighting publicly. Don't you understand the harm that causes the club? If the owner of the club wants to say something, just let him say it. Don't get back at him through the papers.'

She would get her knickers in a twist, but always in the club's interests. David would say some disloyal things at times and it wasn't in my nature or experience simply to take these things lying down. At the same time, he could be very supportive. I would make out a case to Karren for buying or bringing in a player, such as when I wanted Peter Shearer from Bournemouth in a deal which involved us paying no money until he had played a certain number of games, and she would often reject it. When she did, I would go to David and point out that I felt we had a bargain and he would overrule her and rubber-stamp it. He made me aware of the ownership structure of the club from the outset, explaining that he owned *The Sport* newspaper, which owned 50 per cent of Birmingham City, with the other 50 per cent owned by the Gold brothers, so that if a £2 million injection was needed he would put in £1 million and the Golds £1 million between them. The public perception when I arrived was that Sullivan was the top man. The Golds were virtually unknown. I always let it be known when the fans had reason to be grateful for something or other that as well as thanking Sullivan they should also thank the Golds, who matched his money. I would make a point of praising them for their contributions. I felt this was only fair. Sullivan told me that if he wanted something, then nine times out of 10 he would be backed by David Gold. Ralph, on the other hand, was rarely so accommodating. The trio have umpteen businesses between them these days and Sullivan has a most impressive stud farm, with over 100 horses, in Stansted. My love of horses meant that I gleefully accepted his invitation to visit this wonderful establishment and it was then that I learned that David had once owned racehorses. The Golds were not interested in either the stud or in racehorse ownership, but the usual form was that whichever business the Golds and Sullivans were considering getting into, a half share would be offered to the other. Contract negotiations, whenever there was a danger that they might be persuaded into paying too much money, were usually left to Ralph, the thrifty one of the threesome. It's always best to know your strengths and weaknesses and it was a very successful liaison.

There are occasions on which my football business brain ticks into overdrive, too, and I manage to achieve something which is beneficial to all parties. This was never better demonstrated than my signing for Birmingham of the diminutive Portuguese winger Jose Dominguez. My chief scout, Lil Fuchillo, told me that one of his acquaintances, David Hodgson, the former Liverpool player, was the agent for a foreign kid whom he had seen on tape and was deeply impressed by. He wanted me to view the tape, but I have never done business that way and I told him to tell Hodgson to get the player over to

Birmingham, where I could see him in the flesh among all the muck and bullets. At the time Dominguez was with Benfica and out on loan to Faro. Benfica were looking for £80,000, with a further £80,000 after a number of appearances, and when I first told Karren that I wanted to get him over she said that no more players were to be signed. She refused to pay his flight and accommodation. I told Hodgson of the situation and he said: 'Baz, if you see this bloke you will sign him. He is your type of player.' I went to David Sullivan who, again, demonstrated his fairness by promising to meet these expenses if a transfer was concluded. Hodgie was so confident that he forked out for the boy, so this little dwarf, speaking broken English, arrived on the scene. We got him set up for training and when he started to play I rubbed my eyes in disbelief. He was brilliant ... so quick, so agile, so deceptive. And that was in spite of Birmingham having the single worst training facilities it has been my misfortune to encounter in a lifetime in football. We didn't even have a training ground in the first 12 months that I was there, and everywhere we turned – corporation pitches and the like – it was too wet or churned up. I would spend all morning seeking out a suitable place to train and it became a hugely frustrating exercise. The club had sold off its training ground and during my first six months we had seven different centres. There was no stability and no pattern and this must have contributed to our downfall. Dominguez, however, conjured such tricks that you would have thought he had trained in such circumstances all his life. I had to have him. I told Sullivan that I could obtain international clearance for him to play in the reserves the day after he arrived and he agreed that I should proceed. There were only 500 people at this reserve game, but how privileged they were to have seen such a performance. He was excitement personified and they gave him a standing ovation. I was really sold on him and I told Karren that we must sign him.

'He's money in the bank,' I said.

Both Karren and David were loathe to take action. I turned to David.

'If I said to you that if you gave me £100,000 now and in 12 months' time I would give you back £1 million, what would you do?'

He said that he would give me £100,000.

'Well, f***ing give me £80,000 now!'

He still wasn't convinced and I kept beating on about how we could have a hugely talented kid who was far from the finished article and who would delight the crowd. On top of that, we could have him for wages of just £450 a week. He still would not have it, so I arranged for Dominguez to play another game that week before he went home. During all this I had the player in a room with Karren, Hodgie and Ed Stein.

'This boy could go to Liverpool, you know,' says Hodgie.

'Well f***ing take him to Liverpool then,' replies Karren.

'Hold on,' I say, 'I don't want that boy to walk out of the door until he has signed for us.'

The boy couldn't comprehend anything of the proceedings, least of all a woman being involved in transfer negotiations, and at this point I got hold of David again. He asked to speak to Karren and told her to watch him in action and if, in her view, he was any good she should just pay the money. She left the room and Hodgie turned to me.

'This is a Mickey Mouse club. How many caps does that woman wear here?'

In the end she didn't watch the reserve game but told David anyway that she felt they should go along with me and my judgement. When David first saw Dominguez in action after we had signed the player, he wasn't at all convinced about him. Two days later Karren told me that David thought I should sack Lil Fuchillo. He was the one who brought Dominguez over in the first place, he reasoned, and because Sullivan didn't think he was any good he felt that a head should roll.

'Hold on,' I told Karren. 'If you're sacking Lil, then you have got to sack me. I saw him with my own eyes and wanted him to play for the club. Further, if you sack me, then you have got to sack yourself because you were the last one to give the nod on signing him.'

'We'll leave it in abeyance for a little while, shall we?' she said.

On the following Sunday we faced Peterborough in a televised match. We won 4–0, despite Claridge missing a penalty, and the goal of the game, if not the season, was scored by Dominguez, who got the ball in his own half, set off on a mazy run which took him past four or five players, cut inside and smashed it into the net off the far post. Fantastic! Straight after the game the television crew wanted me in front of the camera and the interviewer was positively drooling over our new signing.

'Barry, it looks like you have unearthed another gem in this boy Dominguez. What a find! How did you come by him? What's the story behind that?'

'Well the story behind that is that this week David Sullivan wanted Lil Fuchillo and me sacked over bringing him here. But you know David, he doesn't know a goal line from a clothes line.'

David is, in fact, very knowledgeable about the game and I said this half in jest. Unfortunately, unknown to me, he was in the boardroom sipping a cup of tea and watching this interview on television along with all the directors of both clubs. Apparently, on hearing the words 'he doesn't know a goal line from a clothes line', his jaw dropped and he let slip his cup and saucer, making a right mess of the carpet.

I jumped into the shower and was interrupted by one of the staff with the message that Karren was at the dressing-room door and wanted a word with me. I told him to say that I was in the middle of a shower and would see her later, but he insisted that she wanted to talk to me straightaway. I got out and, dripping wet, put a towel round me. She gestured me towards the boot room.

Above: The mercurial Stan Flashman and me with Barnet's Alliance Premier League championship trophy.

Barnet
FC LTD   souvenir programme 30p

Friendly Match

BARNET
v
MANCHESTER UNITED

Monday March 29th 1982
K.O. 7.45 p.m.

Above: The programme for Barnet's friendly against Ron Atkinson's Manchester United at Underhill in March 1982.

Left: A young Stan Collymore in action for Southend during an FA Cup fifth round clash at Sheffield Wednesday in 1993. As his manager, I never had a problem with him.

Above: It s February 1994, and my arrival as manager of Birmingham City is announced by the club s managing director, Karren Brady.

Below: Anxious moments in Birmingham s last game of the season at Huddersfield. We won 2-1, clinching the Second Division title in 1994/95.

Left: Proud Birmingham figureheads David Sullivan and Karren Brady after the Auto Windscreens Final success over Carlisle at Wembley in 1995.

Right: Paul Tait scores the match-winner to send 50,000 Bluenose fans in a crowd of 78,000 wild with delight.

Below: My salute in front of the media on a truly memorable occasion.

Left: A winning team. West Ham manager Harry Redknapp, Scottish football hero Ally McCoist and myself on BBC television s *A Question Of Sport*.

Right: Sir Alex Ferguson, who has done so much for Manchester United and the League Managers Association.

Left: One ball I didn t fancy heading, delivered by boxing legend Frank Bruno.

What more could a manager want? An early bath at home with a nice drink and a big cigar.

Left: Newly-installed at Peterborough in August 1996, with pot-hunting firmly on my mind.

Right: Taking a dip at home with three of my children: Frank, Amber and Anna-Marie.

Left: The Fry entourage pays a visit to the Peterborough club shop.

Left: Jason Lee tussles with Barnet s Mark Arber during the 1999/2000 Third Division first leg semi-final play-off. My old team were well beaten.

Right: Andy Clarke slots home the winning goal against Darlington at Wembley and our promotion to Division Two is secured.

Left: It didn t do my ticker any good but it all came right in the end – a Posh manager with a posh trophy.

'Bloody hell,' I thought, 'my luck's changing here. She's going to say "Well done, Baz, brilliant 4–0 win, great crowd … how about it?"'

Instead she slammed the door shut and shouted at me in no uncertain terms.

'Don't you *ever* embarrass David like that again, saying he doesn't know a goal line from a clothes line and making him spill his drink in front of all those people. Do you understand?!'

David had already left – he always went early – and when I said that I had better have it out with him she cut me short

'Stop this bickering and fighting, you two. Stop it. me in my office tomorrow morning.' Then she stor off.

During the course of my drive home, I su developed the greatest respect for her. I had re huge roasting, but her loyalty to David was unquestionable, it was also demonstrable. I th I would be like that with my players. In th room I would tear a player off a strip and t in front of directors who might criticise th I would defend him to the hilt. I would p that is what Karren did to David. She moon in my estimation that day.

Yet here was another example of which was to greatly flaw that sea and it was unnecessary. Just when chugging along nicely some daft

195

along to temporarily derail you. Where we should have been united as one, and embracing each other, it was as though we were rival factions. Something Karren would do or say would wind me up and I would respond; David would antagonise me and I'd hit back; then I would say something which upset the pair of them. Where was the harmony? We all wanted the same thing, the best for the club, but the fact was that we were on different wavelengths. I got off to a bad start with Karren. She asked which company car I wanted and where, to some people, this would be an important issue I could not have cared less. I'm not a car man. As long as they get me from A to B I'm happy, so it could have been a BMW, a Rover or a pushbike. I wasn't bothered.

This was not the case with Ed Stein, however. He wanted the latest super-duper machine with alloy wheels and more trimmings than a Christmas tree and Karren, who could be different class in these matters, gave him the money and off he went to London to purchase his pride and joy. He was soon to witness the dark side of the moon. Karren called me one day and ordered that I sack Ed.

'Why?' I asked.

She said that she had just been on the phone to the and heard him calling her a c**t.

'Karren,' I said, 'if I sacked everybody who called me that we would never get a team out.'

What had happened was that Stein was in the office with Day, who had spent 14 years at Tottenham, so

Left: Posh chairman Peter Boizot and me after the management structure of the club had been finalised.

Right: Our lovely dog Basil sporting a Peterborough United shirt.

Simon Davies (above) and Matthew Etherington, the two youngsters who came through The Posh Youth Academy and joined Tottenham in 1999/2000. Both made their first-team debuts in the Premiership that season.

was a vastly experienced man, and was at this time assistant to Karren. She was on her way in and was constantly being frustrated in her efforts to speak to her secretary because the phone was engaged. So she rang Peter's direct line. When he answered he put the phone to one side as he went between offices to Angela, Karren's secretary. Just then Alan Jones, the club secretary, walked by the door and inquired of Ed how he was getting on.

'I'm alright,' he said, 'and so will you be because it looks as if that c**t isn't coming in today.'

Karren, of course, could hear every word. I was driving off to training as this was taking place and afterwards she came to see me.

'I'm not having that,' she said. 'It's disrespectful. He's got to go.'

Too many times I stuck my neck out for Stein and Howell and maybe I should have heeded the warning signs earlier than I did. By the time I realised that, it was too late. However, in this instance, the compromise was that she would take Ed's prized car away from him and replace it with an inferior model. That was clever. Now she had undermined him and there was no doubt as to who was really in the driving seat. Not for the first time, she had demonstrated her power.

After a short time of staying in hotels when I took over, I began to think that I needed a more permanent base for occasions such as Kirstine bringing the family to stay. I told Karren this and that I didn't mind paying for it. Better than that, the club then bought Karren's house in Solihull and allowed me to live there rent-free. 'That's how much we all think of you,' Karren said. Howell and Stein both said when they were appointed that they would move to the Midlands, but Stein never did and spent his time travelling backwards and forwards. I got a couple of house keys cut and told them that, to save on hotel bills, they could use the house when it was not needed for family gatherings. Karren, meanwhile, had moved within the locality and it was her practice to walk her dogs in the woods. On one of these outings she heard a commotion coming from the house, went to investigate and discovered that there were all sorts of comings and goings with women and players as well as Ed and Dave. They were obviously holding parties there without my knowledge. After speaking to me she called them both in and demanded the return of the keys.

'You have abused the manager's hospitality,' she told them. 'Your behaviour has been disgusting and you are banned from going there.'

Not being in possession of the full facts, they foolishly told her that it was my house and what went on there had nothing to do with her.

'That is where you are wrong,' she said.

Ed, unfortunately, could do no right. We had two reserve sides at Birmingham, one in the Avon Insurance League and the other in the Pontins League. Both did well, and when people criticised the size of the playing staff at the club they should have realised that, with three teams, you need 42 players to put on the team sheet for a start. I went to all the games, in whichever league they were played, because I saw it as part of my job. Karren would sometimes check with Alan Jones which of the managerial team had been to which game and she discovered that Ed had not attended a game that he was supposed to.

'No disrespect,' she told me 'but how can your assistant manager coach players he has not seen in their match the previous night?'

David, too, was very adept at flexing his muscles. When, that season, we reached the final of the Auto Windscreens Trophy at Wembley I put it to him that I would like us to spend two days at The Swallow Hotel and he refused point-blank, reasoning that we were due to play in a more important league match against Brentford three days after the Cup Final. In retrospect he was right, being thorough and professional, but I was persistent.

'Look, no matter where you are in football, as a player, manager, supporter, director or, as you are, an owner, your big dream is to play at Wembley. I'm not taking my lads to such an occasion and then f***ing off back directly to Birmingham.'

He would not budge. Another issue here was the ties which were to be worn on the day. The captain Liam Daish – they don't make players like him any more – was stunned to discover that Karren was going to make us pay for sporting club ties, having forked out for very smart blazers and trousers. He made a stand and said that, as a matter of principle, the players were going to go along to Marks & Spencers and buy twenty of the same ties. Again, more petty squabbling. We were going to make a quarter of a million by going to Wembley and here there's a dispute about twenty £5 notes for ties. Stupid. My long-time friend in football, Colin Hill, was so horrified about all of this that he promised that if I wanted to take the players to the hotel, then he would foot the bill. And he did. In the end, Sullivan wavered and paid for the stay himself, but so much friction had been caused through an unnecessary and petty stand-off.

It was a long way from the perfect day. Leading up to the Final there had been the usual sideswipe in the papers, but this time between Karren and myself. I remember seeing her, looking quite stunning, and David on the pitch at Wembley and sensed their pride as they gazed upon 55,000 Bluenoses in a 78,000 crowd at the mecca of football. A Paul Tait golden goal gave us the trophy and yet, would you believe, there was still aggro that night. In celebratory mood we all had a lovely meal at The Swallow and this was interrupted for me by a late-night telephone call from a newspaper. The reporter asked if I knew that when Tait scored he had pulled up his shirt to reveal a T-shirt with the imprint 'Shit On The Villa'. I was not aware of it. This is supposed to be one of the happiest days of my life and, suddenly, I am not looking forward to a sleep which will be constantly interrupted by visions of what will appear in the following day's newspapers. Villa, of course, have always been one of Birmingham's big rivals and I could visualise all hell breaking loose. World War III in Birmingham had been ignited. I confronted Tait, who said: 'It was only a bit of fun, boss.'

I did not like going into extra-time in this game because, as David had made plain, the importance of our midweek clash could not be overestimated. Brentford were top and we lay second with two games in hand. A win would do us a power of good and the last thing you want is for injuries and exhaustion to be stacking up. We had already beaten Brentford at their place with Peter Shearer, not for the first time, scoring the winner from midfield. He was making his comeback from injury at Wembley but faltered and I had to take him off. However Mark Ward, whom I had signed from Everton, was playing out of his skin. It was a pity we would not have them operating together because they made a fantastic midfield partnership. It was a 25,000 sellout at St Andrews and, even then, I had trouble. Ron Atkinson and Dave Bassett, two of the biggest names in the game, wanted to come to the match but had been told by Karren Brady's office that there were no seats available. I considered this to be shoddy treatment and promised them that I would get them accommodated by one or other of the sponsors. It was against this background that I learned that Trevor Francis also wanted to attend and had been told that there was no problem; he was always welcome at St Andrews. Further, it was reported back to me that Karren had told Trevor that whenever he was ready for a job – *the* job – at Birmingham he only had to say the word. Again, not that I had anything against Trevor, I was seriously pissed off by this. Anyway, in a game in which he was to completely shatter his knee, brave-as-a-lion Kevin Francis, who really should not have played at Wembley, scored a terrific opening goal for us. Big clumsy bugger that he was, he was a Bluenose through and through and would demolish brick walls by running through them on the club's behalf. Such was the commitment and determination of the players in pursuit of the championship at that stage that, in successive matches, Francis, Shearer and then Dave Barnett, who had been excellent at the back, all suffered long-term bad injuries.

We have just won a cup final at Wembley, triumphed in the biggest league match of the season, are set fair for promotion and the information coming back to me is that Trevor Francis is in the boardroom and the directors are looking as though they have lost a pound and found a penny. How could they be unhappy? I arrived home that night not in a state of euphoria, as I should have been, but in a pall of paranoia.

Now there were three games to go and, in the first of these against Brighton, a win would have brought the championship. We were 2–0 up and coasting until we had Gary Cooper sent off. Before we knew it we were trailing 2–3 and then we were awarded a penalty in the last minute. Mark Ward took it and hit it straight at the keeper but, fortunately, was able to tuck away the rebound. At least we had a point. Our penultimate game was at home to Lennie Lawrence's Bradford and they played as though their lives depended on it. I asked him afterwards what had been the reason for their exceptional performance in a 0–0 draw and he revealed that when the tannoy announcer said that we only needed to win to take the title his boys grew ten feet tall and determined that they would spoil our big day. The final-day scenario was that we needed a point from our trip to Huddersfield and Brentford had to win to possibly deny us. We played magnificently and won 2–1. Again, the Blues fans were unbelievable, completely taking over one end and giving deafening vocal support.

It was that kind of season. We played Liverpool at home in the third round of the FA Cup and held them to 0–0 in front of a capacity crowd. When we went to Anfield for the replay, the omens looked good when Otto equalised their early goal. With the full-time whistle imminent he was through on his own and should have scored the winner, but he made a mess of it and the game went into extra-time. When there had been no decider, and with a penalty shootout looming, the Kop gave us a standing ovation which I shall never forget. They were wonderful. We lost heavily with the spot kicks – 4–0 – and in my usual way I was protective in front of the press afterwards, telling them that at least we had been consistent. They all felt bad about the first penalty miss and, not wishing the player to be embarrassed, they all decided to miss on purpose. Afterwards David Moores, the Liverpool chairman, and Roy Evans asked me about my views on Stan Collymore and, intriguingly, Jose Dominguez and my goalkeeper, Ian Bennett. I told them that I thought the world of Collymore; that he could score great goals, create goals for other players in sensational ways and was a crowd-pleaser. They asked about his troubles, specifically his rumoured propensity for missing training sessions, and I said that I had never experienced any form of inappropriate behaviour from him. The message from them came through loud and clear that I was the only person in the football world to have a good word to say about him. I have always lived by the rule that you should speak as you find and I always found Stan to be utterly reliable. They, the mighty Liverpool, signed him on the strength of that conversation.

Another highlight in that memorable year was that we played – and looked like beating until Chris Sutton popped up with an equaliser – Kenny Dalglish's Blackburn in the first leg of the Coca Cola Cup at St Andrews. The Scottish blood in Kirstine sometimes makes her passions run high and from the moment the draw was made she relished the prospect of meeting Kenny. Her normal interest in football is best illustrated by the fact that, during the course of matches, she knits or listens to music, but he is the one person she has ever put on a pedestal. She likes his clean-cut image and the fact that there has never been any dirt dished on him. She thinks he is lovely. It may have been beyond her wildest dream, but Kenny came up to the St Andrews boardroom after the game and had his photograph taken both with my son, Adam, and with her. In the second of these you can distinctly see her tongue hanging out. He made the offer to Adam that if he fancied going up to Blackburn he would show him all the facilities and then left for the team coach. Kirstine was busily admitting to all and sundry after Kenny's departure that she should have made more of the conversation, such as volunteering to accompany Adam north for a guided tour of Ewood Park, but that she had been somewhat tongue-tied. Right on cue, Kenny walked back in through the door with the announcement that the coach had broken down and that he would be spending some more time with us. Kirstine went a kind of beetroot colour!

We lost 2–0 in the second leg at Blackburn, but we were far from disgraced against Kenny's multi-million pound outfit. Just rubbing shoulders with such elite company gave everybody a taste of what life might be like in the Premiership and, with that possibility now looming large, we went into the summer break on the crest of a wave.

CHAPTER TWELVE

Over to you, Trevor

I began to have nightmares about Trevor Francis. Niggling and nagging away at the back of my mind was the thought that he only had to say the word and the Birmingham job – my job – was his for the taking. Now I hate board meetings, and would never attend one given half an excuse, but at the conclusion of our very successful season I made the unprecedented move of calling a meeting of the board on my own account. A sixth sense was telling me that Francis was not only wanted by the board but that he, too, craved the managership. I didn't beat about the bush.

'Right, gentlemen, I believe that you want me out. What is the position?'

Sullivan accused me of being paranoid and said that he did not know what I was talking about. I told Karren that an informant had said he heard her assuring Francis that the job was ready for him to walk into any time he wished, but she refuted this.

'That is not true, Barry. Yes, I have invited him to the club, but purely on the basis that he is a legend here.'

'Listen,' I addressed the board. 'I'm a man of the world and accept most of what goes on. If you want Trevor Francis, terrific. If you think the club is ready to be moved on a stage, great. Let's just say it has been a great time, shake hands and I'll pack up and leave.'

David repeated his accusation of paranoia, adding that the club would never do what I was suggesting was afoot.

The papers were full of my suggestion that the club was ready to sack me to make way for Francis and, as the board meeting disbanded with an assurance from them that I was their unanimous choice of manager for the following season, I faced the night feeling only slightly more comfortable and still far from convinced. The league title ... the cup ... bumper crowds ... the healthiest balance sheet from transfer wheeling and dealing they had ever seen. Exactly what did they want? Maybe I had delivered too much in too short a time. Twelve months later, it emerged that Francis had rejected my job at the time, leading me to suspect that my assumptions had been correct.

I was in such a state that Colin Hill insisted on taking me away to Portugal for a few days to chill out. The way with most people of my age is that as they have got older and wiser they are more philosophical about life's nuances, yet I have never got out of the habit of challenging derogatory statements and attitudes. Maybe I have just never grown up, but I will never take things lying down, nor would I be comfortable in doing so.

I received a call from Karren, who said that we had received an offer of £500,000 for Jose Dominguez from Sporting Lisbon. She thought this a good price but I disagreed and said: 'Karren, there's no way we are selling a player like Dominguez for half a million.' In the summer I had negotiated for him a new three-year contract, but while I was away Sporting told Karren that the player was homesick and craved a move home to Portugal. I told Karren to do nothing until I returned; that I was in Portugal anyway and would go to see him.

I told the player that I had gone to the ends of the earth to sign him, what a great player he was and how highly I valued him. He said much of his problem was down to his girlfriend, who could never settle in Birmingham.

'Then don't change your club,' I told him. 'Change your bloody girlfriend.'

I related to him that at one of the forums a couple of weeks previously, one fan had said that if he returned from the pub one night to find Jose in bed with his wife, he would simply turn round, go back to the pub and allow Jose to finish the job that he had started.

'That's how much they love you in Birmingham,' I told the little fellow.

It didn't work.

'Barry,' he said, 'I am not coming back. I am staying here.'

'This makes me look a right c**t. You have no sooner signed a contract than you are walking out on it.'

His response negated every aspect of my argument.

'At Birmingham, I am to get £500 a week,' he said. 'At Sporting I will get £25,000 a month in my hand, an apartment and a Mercedes sports car.'

'I understand,' I said. 'But please don't tell me lies. It's nothing to do with your girlfriend and everything to do with the f***ing money.'

I told him he would have to sign a waiver and I would have to negotiate a sensible transfer fee, but that there were no hard feelings. I was only sorry to be losing such a great talent. Apart from the Dominguez interruption – and it eventually took the most complex of negotiations to arrive at a £1.3 million transfer fee – this break did me a power of good and I was looking forward to Euro 96 on my return. England and Sweden had scheduled fixtures at Villa Park and the agent Dennis Roach, whom I used to play alongside at Bedford, asked if I would be interested in signing the Swede Kennet Andersson. The asking price was £1.3 million and, of course, I viewed him as potentially a great asset to Birmingham. I alerted David Sullivan both to his availability and my desire to sign him, but he said that was too much money to spend. I did my best salesman job on David, who relented when I said that season ticket sales would go through the roof if we were to sign this boy. He asked that all the details of his personal terms and so forth be faxed to the club and I got really excited about it, particularly as I had been on to John Ward at Bristol Rovers about Marcus Stewart and viewed an Andersson-Stewart partnership as our passport to the Premiership, all for a £2 million package.

Alongside this issue, there arose a question over a new contract for Steve Claridge who, in our promotion season, had scored 25 goals. Steve is one of those guys who has got to be embraced and loved and he did not take kindly to Sullivan's prevarications. When he came to the club he had been promised that if he did well, he would be looked after and he did not want to be short-changed. I have been criticised by Steve, whose view it is that I am the worst tactician in the game. To have got 25 goals out of him must have been some feat, then. I bought him for £200,000 and sold him to Leicester for £1.3 million. Not bad tactics, eh? No matter what he thinks about my managerial ability, it is indisputable that I got him a good move.

At this exciting time of the European Championships, Derby County were looking for a manager. I knew their chairman, Lionel Pickering, through encounters with Derby while I was at Southend and when I bumped into him at a function he congratulated me on how well I had done at Birmingham and let it be known that they were looking for a manager to replace Roy McFarland. I volunteered to him the information that Birmingham were not happy with me, and wanted me out, and he said that if ever a situation developed in which I might leave them, I should give him a call. Within 24 hours the football world was buzzing with rumour that I was about to join Derby. A Sunday newspaper had it as a stone cold fact. I had spent the previous evening at a London Hotels League dinner, having been president of that organisation ever since they found me Andy Clarke. He was a washer-up in one of the kitchens, and because he was a Barnet supporter a couple of their officials brought him along so that I could have a look at him. Andy went on to enjoy great success as a member of the Crazy Gang at Wimbledon and later joined me again at Peterborough.

This bout of socialising in the capital had put me largely out of circulation. On the Sunday, without having laid eyes on a newspaper, I dropped Kirstine off at home and drove to Villa Park, where I wanted to see Andersson in action for Sweden. Immediately I set foot in the place I was besieged by a posse of reporters wanting to know when the deal to join Derby would be done. Sullivan, they said, had told them that I had been uncontactable and in hiding for a few days. I thought it might be diplomatic to phone him.

'Where are you?' he snapped.

I told him that I was pursuing the Andersson transfer at Villa Park.

'But everybody says you are going to Derby.'

'Do you want me to go to Derby?' I asked.

'Well, I suppose that if you want to go to Derby, you had better go to Derby,' he responded.

He took some convincing that I had been overnight

in London, despite my naming the hotel and assuring him that 300 people were present who could bear witness and, once again, I felt horribly destabilised. I called Lionel Pickering and told him I would like to take up his offer of a chat. He invited me to his home and we had an immensely enjoyable discussion which showed that we thought pretty much along the same lines. He said he admired the teams I assembled at Southend and Birmingham, had been keeping an eye on my progress and viewed me as the right man to take Derby forward. He, in turn, struck me as the kind of chairman that I would be comfortable with. The reality of the situation, though, was that I was the manager of one club and speaking to the chairman of another. I spent that evening at The Hyatt in Birmingham and, out of the blue, I received a telephone call from David Gold.

'What's going on?' he asked.

I told him. 'I really do have the impression, from speaking to David Sullivan, that he doesn't give a damn whether I stay or go.'

He said that David probably felt a little let down and I said that, if that were the case, how did he think I felt? Some people, I told him, owned football clubs for years without enjoying a fraction of the success that Birmingham had achieved in the previous 12 months. The future could not have been brighter.

'I don't stay where I am not wanted,' I told David. 'You will owe me some money if I go, but just forget about it. It's not a financial issue.'

Next on the telephone was Karren Brady. She was very curt.

'I want to see you in my office at nine o'clock tomorrow,' she said, before smashing the phone down.

At the appointed time she said that she had a call in to Lionel Pickering.

'Have you spoken to him?' she asked

'Er ...'

'You have,' she asserted. 'And I'm going to do them for making an illegal approach.'

I told her that no approach had been made and she became extremely aggressive.

'You are staying here,' she said. 'We are not letting you go. You've done a good job here. What's your problem? Do you want more money? I ask again ... what is your problem?'

I told her she knew full well what was bothering me.

'You could at least have the bollocks to tell me the truth about Trevor Francis,' I said.

She reiterated earlier assurances that there was no truth in that and, right on cue, Lionel's call came through.

'Have you been speaking to Barry Fry?' Karren boomed. 'If you have, I will sue you.'

She slammed down the phone. I called Lionel soon after and apologised for the possibility of my having got him into trouble. He just said that he was pleased I was fixed up but I said: 'Look, I don't know whether I'm fixed up or not. I am, but in my own mind I am not.'

The silly thing was that the whole picture could have dovetailed nicely. Trevor Francis could have taken over at Birmingham and I could have gone to Derby, who were managerless. Life rarely works out so simply, does it? I would have loved to have gone to Derby but, in the end, my old friend Jim Smith was installed and what a magnificent job he has done. When they were promoted to the Premiership I sent a congratulatory telegram to both Lionel and Jim. I have wished ever since that I had pursued the matter to a conclusion but I was between the devil and the deep blue sea. Karren went on to say that she would give me more security by writing into my contract a clause which would give me more money if they dismissed me. 'That,' she explained, 'will ensure that we don't sack you.' Now, at least, I had signed a new contract and everybody was set for an attack on the First Division in a positive frame of mind. We had a very good start and, by Christmas, we were lying second in the league. Then our goalkeeper, Ian Bennett, broke two fingers. It looked like he would be out of action for up to six weeks and I had to bring in the reserve keeper, Bart Grimmett, long before he was ready for first-team action. Bennett never played again all season and we dropped from second to below halfway. Besides Bennett, there were other contributory factors. We had lost Dominguez, a player who had the fans lifting the roof as he simply ran onto the pitch; Liam Daish, my captain marvel, had been playing out of his skin but left for Coventry in a £1.6 million deal; and at Christmas Steve Claridge, a renowned big gambler, was determined on a new contract. Every time he did his bollocks, his answer was to seek a new club, or a new contract with his existing club so that he could get a signing-on fee, to pay his debts. Here we were again.

In turn Karren, then David, rejected the request out of hand. 'Once a gambler...,' David said. 'This is the third new contract he has sought.' My pleas that this one would be for life, that he had taken a pay cut to join us and that he was a hero to the fans, fell on deaf ears. Claridge owed me a fortune. We would have bets with him, such as the day one of Sullivan's horses was running and we had the inside track on how strongly it was fancied to win. Claridge stood bets for Mark Ward and myself and, after the horse had duly romped home, he owed us a fortune. He paid out Wardie eventually but with me the outstanding amount was so much that the only way he was ever going to be able to repay the debt was through me promising him £250 every time he scored a goal. As with all gamblers, desperation often crept in and at Portsmouth one day he laid claim to some recompense for laying on – but not scoring – two goals.

'Go on, Baz, I made two,' he said.

'So what. You get nothing for assists.'

Then I weakened and told him that he had earned a monkey, betting parlance for £500. Claridge was lovely; the scruffiest bastard I ever laid eyes upon and totally unorthodox. He lived in his car for goodness knows how long, forced onto the street by his latest disastrous crossing of swords with the bookies. But on the field of play he was something else. Great player. With the way he ran he always brought to mind Forest Gump. Once he started he couldn't stop. You loved him, but his gambling got him into so much trouble. Every now and then you had to bale him out and I just accepted this as one of life's little peccadillos. I told him after training the following day that he had no chance of getting a new contract and he asked if I minded his seeing Karren personally. Of course I did not mind at all, but I held out little hope for him, particularly in view of a letter he had received from her after my little meeting in which she virtually said that he wasn't worth what he was then being paid, never mind harbouring ambitions for a rise. He emerged from his tête-à-tête shaking his head and, his pride bruised, told me that he had to get away.

'I can't play for this club again,' he said.

In the second half of the season I got a call from Ron Atkinson, who said that he was desperate for a centre-half. I told him there was no one better than Daish, but Ron felt he was too slow. I could not have disagreed more. 'No one gets past him, Ron,' I said. 'He's brilliant.' Sensing an imminent deal, I agreed to leave him out of the first team at Stoke and field him instead in a reserve game in which Ron plotted to play Peter Ndlovu among a few other talented players and to throw the kitchen sink at Daish who, at this stage, was thoroughly disaffected. He had had several run-ins over

217

all kinds of issues, such as his views that the club's ambitions did not match his own as club captain, and just wanted away. He was the salt of the earth in my book. He would head away 707s and 747s. We played this match at St Andrews on the Saturday morning, with me already having marked Daish's card that he was being watched. Big Ron stood next to me on the touchline and every time Ndlovu got the ball his manager screamed: 'Go on, Peter. Piss all over him!' He was to be disappointed in one respect and delighted in another. Every time Ndlovu made to go by him, Daish would kick him a mile in the air and emerge with the ball. By lunchtime Coventry's chairman Brian Richardson, Big Ron and I were all huddled over a contract in the boot room where I had once thought that my luck was in with Karren.

Also missing at Stoke was Claridge. Gutted by his fruitless negotiation with Karren, he wanted to go to see Leicester manager Martin O'Neill, who had been showing more than a passing interest. I had no objection to that. We were still in the semi-final of the Coca-Cola Cup and it was clear that my two best players would not be involved in that. Great business, for sure, to reap £3 million for two players who cost £250,000 between them, but nobody could say that our name was on the trophy. I fell out with Claridge after his away-day. Martin told me that he had made the player a far better offer than the one he was on, but Claridge said that he was not going. I could not for the life of me understand this. I told him that, on this Monday evening, he was in the reserves at Wolves. When I arrived there I told him to put on the No 9 shirt and he said that he was not prepared to do that; he had done a deal and was a Leicester player. I told him that he had had all day to tell me of that and that he must now run out with the reserves.

'You c**t,' he said. 'You can't do that.'

I wanted to show him whether I could or not.

'You have f***ed me about, I've given you time off that really I should not have done, he's offered you a blinding deal that you have rejected and I'm pissed off with you. Now get that shirt on.'

He did ... and proceeded to turn in the worst perform-ance of his life. He was f***ing hopeless and badly let the team down. At half time I told him to piss off. I had the right hump with him and him with me. He could be a bit like that. He had a bad time with us, going 26 games and scoring only two goals, which was most unlike him. Then he went to Leicester and took ages to open his account there. Of course, we still had to face Leicester in the league and when the fixture came around, near the end of the season, he was on fire. He scored the first goal and could not resist running by my dugout and making gesticulations, bless him. Claridge certainly did the business for Leicester, scoring the goal at Wembley which took them into the Premiership and, in the final analysis, his move was a good deal all round. I was sad-dened to receive a real going-over from him in newspaper articles in which he said that he had never been treated as badly by anybody as he had by me.

At Wembley for their big game, however, I was in the Royal box and when he ascended the steps for his medal I shouted over to him.

'Hey, Claridge. I'm that w**ker you keep moaning about!'

He came over to give me the loveliest hug.

'Baz, it's paper talk,' he said.

'It's f***ing you,' I said, 'but no hard feelings.'

He smiled the kind of smile which probably only football people know. It meant that bygones are bygones.

We faced Leeds at home in the first leg of the Coca-Cola Cup semi-final in the nightmare situation of not only having lost Dominguez, Daish and Claridge but also having three players suspended. We lost 1–2, despite a great Kevin Francis goal, and we also lost in the second leg at Elland Road. Despite those reversals, it had again been a good season with big revenues, gates of over 18,000 and, at one stage, a lofty position of second in the league. There was no escaping the fact, though, that our last ten games, with a severely weakened squad, were pretty disastrous. Frankly, we were shit.

A recent incident on our travels to Tranmere didn't help matters. It was one o'clock in the morning and I was enjoying a nightcap in the hotel's small lounge bar with David Gold as the players, so I thought, were nicely tucked up in bed. His route to the gents took him through the main bar and he returned with a look of horror on his face.

'F***ing hell, Baz,' he said. 'Dave Howell and Ed

Stein are conducting a card school with a couple of the players.'

Now it was my turn to go to the loo, despite Gold's protest that he did not wish to be known as a grass. Not only was this card game in full swing, it was being witnessed by several supporters who were sitting on bar stools. I gave the culprits a long, disapproving stare. They knew what action to take. This could have caused a major embarrassment. We won the game as it happened, but if we had lost their irresponsibility would have left us wide open to justified criticism. I got a monstering from Karren, who rightly wanted to know what my assistant and coach were doing playing cards with players at that time in the morning. I passed on her sentiments, telling them they could play until dawn as far as I was concerned, as long as it was in the privacy of their rooms. Their time, unfortunately, was up. A combination of card schools, missing games, misdemeanours and house parties – they were the straw which broke the camel's back – led to their dismissals. I could do nothing more for them. I got Ed in and told him.

'There's your money.'

He refused to take it, saying that he was entitled to much more and would take the case to court. He asked who was responsible for his sacking and I told him.

'Me. Karren has warned you and warned you ...'

'She has always been after me because I'm black,' he interrupted.

Nothing could have been further from the truth. He just did not help himself. Dave, I think, was very unfortunate. He managed to keep his nose clean for most of the time, but got rolled into the picture.

All along the line, Sullivan had told me that he would never sack me. If the time came to call it a day, he said, he would alert me to the fact that I had one more month, in which he would fund the purchase of new players, to have one final hit and I always responded that he could not have been fairer than that. He did not keep his word. Going back to the Southend days, I was called a greedy bastard for going to Birmingham because, they said, I went for the money. What nobody realises is that it cost me nearly £300,000 in commission on Collymore alone, money that I could never have got back at Birmingham. Much was made of the number of transfer deals I was involved in at Birmingham, but what is incontrovertible is that I made them £11 million. There is not a manager in the country who can point to that scale of profit. Gary Breen is an example. He cost £150,000 from Peterborough and was sold to Coventry for £2.5 million. Even my bad players made money for the club most of the time. Okay, I made a couple of boobs. Kevin Francis cost £800,000 and was sold for £200,000 and Ricky Otto, who also cost £800,000, went for nothing. It's the bottom line which counts, though, on balance sheets.

Our last game of the season was against Aston Villa in the Birmingham Senior Cup, a competition which Birmingham had not won for more than a decade.

Despite having two players sent off we won 2–0 and received a magnificent trophy. There was an awards dinner that evening and the club was represented by the Gold brothers while Doug Ellis, the chairman, was there for Villa. There is a traditional and deep-seated historical hatred between the clubs, or at least the supporters of the two clubs, which, thankfully, I was never drawn into. In fact I have always liked Aston Villa. I like what Doug has done at Villa Park and I admire the way their teams always play. I placed the trophy on the top table, between Doug and the Golds, and said to the Golds that here was something to be proud of – a trophy long coveted by them. I had always had a great relationship with the Golds, particularly David, who on the eve of matches would often ring to say that I should not have dinner with the team but with him. We would talk into the early hours about the club, football, life in general and, whatever the topic, we would always get on. He was a friend. I was shocked by his reaction when I placed the trophy in front of him. I looked into his eyes and there was nothing there. Something was amiss.

In the hotel foyer the Gold brothers and I met a broadcaster of our acquaintance, Gary Newbon, and he spoke to them in fulsome praise about my achievements. I chipped in that I already had four players lined up for the following season, including the free-scoring Marcus Stewart of Bristol Rovers, and was looking forward with relish to the announcement of these signings so that, once again, season ticket sales would go through the roof.

The Golds could not have been more disinterested if I had been talking about opal mining in Coober Pedy. They could not wait to get away.

I did not know until the following day that they knew my fate had been sealed. It would have been nice for one or both of them to have invited me to their room, cracked open a bottle of champagne and behaved like gentlemen over our parting of company. There is no good way to be sacked, but that is as good a way as I know. I would have liked them to have done that, because their failure to do so has left me wondering what they were trying to gain by not telling me, or what they were hiding. I always felt and said that if I were ever to get the sack from Birmingham City there was only one person with the bollocks to do it. That person is Karren Brady, and even she did not do it.

The cutting of ties was done in a peculiar way. The following day there was a league managers' dinner and golfing event. Old Jack Wiseman, the FA councillor who had been through all the hard times, could easily have been dispensed with as chairman when Sullivan and the Golds took over Birmingham, but was kept on board in an almost honorary capacity so that he could enjoy the position without the flak. I invited him to this social day, because he loves all the rubbing of shoulders with hierarchical figures, but when I arrived at the club, really only to take him along, he uncharacteristically ignored my morning greeting. Ten minutes later, Alan Jones informed me that Jack wished to see me in Karren's office. When I walked in he was pacing up and down like a cat on the prowl.

'It's about today's events,' he said.

I could tell from his demeanour that he was not going to be present.

'Don't worry,' I said. 'I just thought you would like a game of golf, a dinner, a cigar and putting your feet up and then back to the club tomorrow.'

'I can't do it,' he said.

I insisted that it was okay but he said: 'Yes, but you don't realise the reason I can't do it. They're getting rid of you.'

'Who's getting rid of me?'

'We are.'

'What? And they've f***ing sent you down to tell me?'

He began to cry. I said: 'Listen, Jack. It isn't your fault. Don't worry.'

He replied: 'The decision has been made. There's no way I can come to the league managers' dinner, play golf, be in your company and have a drink in the knowledge that you are going to get sacked.'

He was absolutely distraught. I called Alan Jones in and asked if he was aware that I was facing the sack.

'Yes. I can't say anything, Barry.'

I asked him to get Sullivan on the phone. He could not make contact. Nor could he contact the Golds. Karren could not be tracked down. I went downstairs to the dressing-room area, where Kevin Francis was receiving treatment from the physio Neil McDiarmid, affectionately known as the Road Runner and one of the best signings I ever made in my life. A brilliant man. I was in something of a daze and just blurted out to them that I had been sacked. I walked out and got into my car, heading for the function in Hertfordshire. So much had been going on that it took until halfway through the journey for me to think about contacting Kirstine. Just as I was about to, driving down the M6, the midday sport bulletin on Radio Five said that there was some shock news from St Andrews: manager Barry Fry had been sacked and they had David Sullivan speaking to them. That was good. Radio Five had contacted him all right. Funny that I could not. I listened in total disbelief as, very short and not so sweet, he explained that I had taken the club as far as I could. I felt like a mile-high pile of shit.

I arrived home and sat down with Kirstine.

'You ain't going to believe this ...'

'You've got the sack.'

I asked how she knew. 'The telephone has never stopped ringing.'

I felt terrible that she had learned the news in that way, but my wife is nothing if not a realist.

'Well, it doesn't surprise you does it?'

The fact was that, despite all my doubts and suspicions over the previous 12 months, it still came as a shock. What board of directors would encourage and allow you to name and pursue four players in the knowledge that they were going to sack you? Also, after the departures of Stein and Howell, they agreed to my making Lil Fuchillo assistant manager until the end of the season. I wanted to bring in Dave Sexton, who was then the England Under-21 supremo, as head of coaching. He was delighted by my approach, saying that his contract with the FA expired on 30 June and that he would join us the following day, an arrangement – and something of a coup – which appeared to thrill the board. Kirstine asked if I could pick up Adam from school. 'He will be devastated,' she said. And she was right. Adam, who was 11 at the time, came to every game with me. His bedroom was plastered with Bluenose scarves, rosettes, posters and pictures and his little world revolved around them. I could feel anger welling up inside me as I prepared to tell him what had happened and I thought I had better ring David Sullivan. Despite many attempts I was unable to contact him. I knew that every Monday night he went to Stringfellows in London and he had always made it clear that if ever I needed to speak to him after dark on Mondays that is where I would find him. I could reach him anytime, anyplace, night or day, 999 times out of 1,000. But could I this time? Not a chance.

Outside Adam's school gates I put my arm around him and told him I had been fired. Here was a little boy who had been looked after wonderfully at the club, an ever-present in the boardroom, where he was fed and watered and asked about his football progress, after games, whose world was about to cave in.

'I thought you were doing all right,' he said, tears welling in his eyes.

'So did I, son,' I said, 'but it happens.'

We ambled home – I purposely wanted to walk – and when we got there I saw the television cameras waiting for us. Adam made straight for his bedroom and I faced the same questions from interviewers which I had been unable to answer to my son. My mind was in turmoil. That evening I was going to another League Managers' Association dinner. I spent an hour with the television crews and before I left for the function I went upstairs to see Adam. What I saw made me cry like a baby. In the short time he had been home from school he had torn down from his bedroom walls every scrap of Birmingham City memorabilia. The walls were bare and he was on his knees, sobbing his little heart out. 'I've got to go love,' was all I could say to him. In retrospect, it was an education to see the way all the kids reacted. Little Anna-Marie was hopping around the house chanting, in that childish sing-song way: 'My dad's got the sack ... my dad's got the sack.'

'I'm glad you're sacked,' she smiled. 'I'll see more of you.' Jane, my eldest daughter, was devastated.

My arrival at the dinner was greeted warmly. John Barnwell, the president, said: 'Brilliant. Lovely to see you. You could have stayed at home and sulked but you haven't.' Martin O'Neill thought my dismissal a scandal. Others concurred and it made me feel a lot better being among professional football people who knew what they were talking about. Also present at this function was Trevor Francis. He came over to me for a word.

'Well done. Unlucky.'

I told him: 'I thought you were getting the job at this time last year?'

'They've asked me,' he said, 'but I have always turned it down.'

'Perhaps you won't this time,' I said.

Everything I had suspected was confirmed from the horse's mouth. They had approached him not once, but several times. I have no animosity towards Trevor. When he was appointed he phoned me at home.

'You can tell me to f**k off if you like,' he said, 'but I would appreciate a card-marking about one or two things.'

I went through every single player and then gave him some advice.

'They have got to get some Premiership players and pay £3,000 or £4,000 a week. You must make that point. I did not. There has got to be plenty of money in there from my wheeler-dealings. Make sure they put it at your disposal.'

I told him that I had done a deal to sign Marcus Stewart, but he said he wasn't interested in the player. Stewart joined Huddersfield and only scored 20-odd goals for them in 1998/99! In this 40-minute conversation I told him my opinion of David, Karren, the Golds and everybody at the club.

The next morning I drove to Birmingham. Karren, who was pregnant at the time, said she had been taking some time off because she had previously miscarried and did not want to lose this baby. She was embarrassed. She said that she had not seen my departure coming and was unsure whether or not she could have changed the course of events if she had been present.

'We had an agreement, here's your money,' she said. 'Do we owe you any more? What about your expenses? You can keep the car for three months and the house here for another month. Just drop the keys in to me.'

The general pattern of events in football is that when a club wants you they will give you anything and everything; when they want you to go they keep you waiting for your dues. Not this time, though. Karren's parting shot was that I had been good for the club. She was unaware, she said, of the reasons for my sacking and I said: 'What grieves me is that I cannot get to speak to anybody.' She gave me another number for David Sullivan and my call was answered by a secretary. She confirmed that he was there and that I could speak to him before correcting herself.

'He is not available,' she said.

'Listen,' I said. 'I don't know why he doesn't want to talk to me. I don't want to fall out. Just tell him thanks very much for giving me the opportunity to manage a club like Birmingham for the last two and a half years.'

One minute later our phone rang. Kirstine picked it up and said: 'It's David Sullivan for you.'

'Hello, David.'

'I got your message,' he said. 'That's very nice.'

'Yes,' I said, 'and I meant it. I can't understand why

I've been sacked and it's pointless arguing about it because it is done.'

He did not know what to say and the conversation trailed off.

The following day I came in to a message on my answerphone. It was from Ralph Gold and went: 'I must speak to you, Barry. I'm going on holiday to Portugal and I will not enjoy it unless we have spoken.'

When I called him he said: 'I cannot tell you how bad I feel. I couldn't speak to you at that awards dinner, but I want you to know that I was totally against your dismissal. I feel so bad that I'm thinking of cancelling my holiday.'

'Ralph,' I said, 'I've been in football a long time. These things happen for whatever reason. We will never fall out. Go and enjoy yourself.'

He said that on his return he and his wife Di would like to take Kirstine and myself to dinner at The Ritz in London. Unlike some people I know, he was true to his word.

CHAPTER THIRTEEN

Posh but pricey

One consolation of my sacking at Birmingham was the severance cheque and I took this home to Kirstine, handed it over and told her to put it into the building society. She deserved it for having put up with me. I then went into my home office and played back the 74 calls on my answerphone. No fewer than eight of these calls were from Chris Turner, a long-time friend of mine then running Peterborough United, saying that he urgently wanted to speak to me.

Chris is a former Posh player and manager and he and his best mate, Alf Hand, owned the club. We went back a long way to my days at Barnet, when he was the successful manager of Cambridge United. He did me a lot of favours by loaning to me such players as Gary Poole, whom I eventually bought off him for the best five grand I ever spent.

He also loaned me Liam Daish, whom I later bought for Birmingham for £50,000 and sold for £1.6 million,

Dion Dublin and Chris Leadbetter. When he got the sack at Cambridge it not only came as a shock to him but to the whole of football. I immediately invited him down two nights a week to help with our training just to keep him involved in the game. He got the shock of his life when he asked what we did at dead-ball situations at Barnet.

'I order them to get it over here … get it over there … and somebody just heads it in.'

He asked if I thought we should be a little more organised than that.

'That's your job, mate. We are already brilliant and if you improve us by five per cent we'll be bloody marvellous.'

He did. He enjoyed it, he had a smile on his face and we had lots of laughs. He could not understand my approach to the game, nor that of my players, but what he could not find an argument for were the fantastic results we got at Barnet.

When the call came to Chris from John Devaney, the chairman of Peterborough, to go and manage them again he sought my advice and I told him: 'That club is your heart and soul. Go and do it. I know you will make a success of it.'

And he did. We kept in touch along the way and I remember one particular transfer deadline day he wanted to bring in a big centre-forward and a left-sided player and I told him to get Ken Charley and Gary Cooper from Maidstone. He said that he had only seen Charley play wide on the right, but I told him he was a far better centre-forward. Chris took my word for it and signed that pair along with four other players and this new influx eventually brought him promotion.

They enjoyed great success together and the following season they had the honour of a Wembley appearance in the play-off final. Chris invited me into the Royal Box, where I sat beside him for the whole of the game, and it was a fantastic occasion with Peterborough winning courtesy of two Charlery goals. I think I was more excited than Chris, or at least it would have appeared that way to the casual observer because Chris tends to keep a severe check on his emotions and I, of course, do not. Despite my privileged seating, I was dancing and flinging myself about like a two-year-old while Chris sat cool, calm and collected throughout. Almost regal, in fact.

Whenever I was without a game, and whenever I could, I would go and watch Peterborough because of Chris. I had spent many hours there when Noel Cantwell, my old Manchester United mentor, was there as manager. It was one of those grounds ... not far from where I lived, very welcoming and offering the opportunity to meet up with friends. When Chris was manager my mate Lil Fuchillo was his assistant and he took over the reins when Chris was moved upstairs. It was good to have some banter with people I respected in the game.

It was against this background that Chris tried so hard to get hold of me. I steeled myself to return all the calls, the first of these being to him. He said he could not believe that I had been dispensed with by Birmingham.

'Neither can I,' I told him.

He invited me to go to Peterborough. I knew he had been ill because I had visited him in hospital, but reaffirming this he said that all the worries associated with the club had led to his illness and his wife, Lynn, was very worried about him. With Chris, although he always gives the outward impression of being untroubled, he stores everything up inside and allows it all to get on top of him. Now he had to go back into hospital and he would appreciate a chat about my joining The Posh. I told him that it was too early for me to make a decision, but that I would seriously think about it. I was about to have a holiday with my pal Colin Hill on his yacht in Monaco, tying this in with watching the grand prix.

Curiously Colin, who has become my best friend, was first introduced to me by Chris when I was at Southend. He is a football nut, like myself, whereas Chris is more golf, the horses and football now and then! Consequently I got on better with Colin, because I have never known anything about golf, horses have only ever meant one thing – losing money – and football is my passion, my hobby, my life.

I popped over to see Chris in hospital and my heart went out to him. He was in a bad way. He told me he needed help and it was an ideal opportunity for me. He no longer wished to be involved in the football side of things at the club and it was his wish that I completely take that over from him. I asked him what Alf, who was the majority shareholder with over 50 per cent in the club with Chris having the minority stake, might think of that and he told me that when I returned from holiday he would be at home in convalescence and I should go and see him.

We enjoyed the wonderful occasion of the grand prix and, to be honest, I needed the break. When you get the sack, as I had done at a few clubs, you feel you have no friends, you are alone in the world, you are a failure. You question, not really believing it, why it happened and you become sad and depressed. It is very easy to get down in the dumps, and although I tried to put a brave face on it I was hurting like hell inside. In quiet moments you experience every emotion known to mankind. Frustration. Anger. Hurt. Unloved. Unwanted. Humiliation.

For every person who puts his arm around your shoulders there are a million who laugh in your face. I don't know what it is about English people. They love to build you up but they enjoy even more the dismantling. It is at times such as these that you have to be strong, determined and hold a belief in yourself and your abilities. Colin was good for me. I always enjoy his company, and although I am not a motor-racing fan the occasion is quite splendid and takes place in a charming, relaxing location.

At the end of the day, though, you are out of work. I had many offers from the likes of TV and radio but none of them particularly interested me. I wanted to be in football because this was the one thing which gave me a buzz in life. Colin got straight to the point and asked what I would like to do.

'Col, I am fed up of getting the f***ing sack. I have been at Barnet and made them £3 million profit as a part-time outfit and got them into the league; I've been at Southend and made them £6 million and taken them from the bottom of the Second Division to second in the First Division in eight months; and I've been at Birmingham, where I took the crowd from 4,600 to 18,500. I've since made them £11 million. Say what you want, I made them £11 million. What I really want, Col, is to own my own club, where I can back my own judgement and stand or fall on my own ability. If I see a player I want, I can go and get him without asking an owner or a chairman or a board of directors. F**k the lot of them. On my past record I can't fail.'

Colin, a man who had fulfilled his ambition of being a millionaire by the time he reached the age of 40, made his fortune in property. We never talked about his business when we were together. The sole topic of conversation was football and he was great for me. He said to me that he and his partner Sean, who had joined us, would give me £1 million to do that. Colin left the room and Sean said: 'You don't believe him, do you?' I said that we had all had a bit to drink and no, I did not. 'He will give you every penny of £1 million,' he said, 'but he will not give you a penny more.'

When he returned I brought up the topic again.

'Colin, are you serious?'

'When we get back, Baz, you have got £1 million. Do it. Just do it. But if you come back for two bob more, you will not get it. You stand or fall on the back of £1 million and your own ability.'

This really got me going. I was really excited, thinking 'Peterborough ... just down the road ... tremendous potential.' We went from Monaco to the airport by helicopter and I remember thinking how much I hoped it didn't crash. I just wanted to get home and get stuck into this venture. When I got back I could not wait to ring Chris, who invited me round that afternoon to meet himself and Alf. Chris was in bed and Alf and I sat round him with Lynn bringing us tea and biscuits. Chris said: 'You can see the state of me, Baz. I just want to get out of the club, it's killing me.'

Excitedly, I told them of Colin's offer and was somewhat deflated when they immediately said no. Peterborough hold the freehold, a great asset in itself, and they both felt it was worth more than I was offering. They said they were already in negotiations with a few people and wanted to take the club forward with a new 25,000-seater stadium on the outskirts of town while selling London Road. Chris instead persisted with his line that he needed someone to take over the football, but that I could have the combined total of Alf's 51 per cent of the shares and his own 24 per cent, giving me 75 per cent of the club, for nothing as long as I took on the debts of £650,000.

This overdraft sounded peanuts to me and I told them

that this looked very good. They had just built a new stand which was looking absolutely magnificent. There were some bits and pieces to finish but the deal sounded promising. I asked if there were club accounts and I was shown the current state of the books and ledgers for the previous two years. I asked if I could take them away and they agreed with the rider that their chief executive was someone called Iain Russell. 'He is just what you need – someone who won't let you spend money.'

The next day, armed with all these accounts, we went to Colin's home in Ipswich. This is a magnificent £7 million dwelling with water fountains all over the place, a football pitch and space for a five-mile run in the back garden, a fitness gym, squash court, swimming pool ... the lot. When I was at Barnet he invited all the boys there and played six of them in turn at squash and beat the lot of them!

I will never forget what he said.

'I told you on the boat that I would not give you a penny more. Tell Alf and Chris that I will give them £1 million for the freehold. I will give you £250,000 to get the overdraft down to £400,000. There will be no more. If I get the freehold I will put it in Switzerland so that you will not be able to borrow any money against it.'

Fair enough, I thought.

Excitedly, Iain and I put the proposal to Alf and Chris but again they would have none of it. When I called Hilly to relay their refusal to budge, he stiffened his manner.

'Baz, I have never given you a bum steer, have I?' to which I had to affirm that he had not and had always been spot on with his advice.

'Don't touch that club with a bargepole,' he said.

'F**k off Colin, it's the greatest opportunity I will ever have in my life.'

'I'm telling you,' he said, 'don't touch it. Promise me you won't touch it.'

He then promptly departed for Portugal, where he owns a lot of properties, and in his absence I could not resist speaking to Chris once again. I really, really fancied it and when I mentioned it to Kirstine she looked at me blankly.

'Do you know what you are doing?'

I said that of course I did.

'You say that every time and we've finished up with four kids!'

'Trust me,' I said. 'Just trust me.'

'Like I did when you got me to sign a piece of paper and I thought we were going to have an extension to the house and instead you paid off the covenant at Barnet. Do you really, really know what you are doing?'

She knew it was what I wanted. I got together with Chris and Alf and we basically did a deal in which Alf and Chris kept the freehold and they would form a Posh holding company. They were to keep the bars and run the night club which was at the ground at the time. I was just going to have the football side, paying the wages from central funds, the gate money and the overdraft. I was quite happy with that arrangement. I didn't think it was a big thing. Although nothing was agreed legally and bindingly, we were all happy enough to proceed down that path.

Although nothing had been done to legalise the deal we decided to jump the gun a little to generate interest among the fans. Besides, I was going away on holiday and there was much to be done. We contacted all the relevant media people with an announcement that I was going to be the new owner and soon the club had a battery of television cameras around it. I said I was going to bring in certain players, break the transfer record and really go for it because I thought the club had great potential. I had already had long conversations, I said, with the chief executive Iain Russell about what savings could be made. One board member had resigned and Alf no longer wished to be the chairman although, with over £400,000 worth of director's loans in there he was to remain on the board. He had done more than enough for the club and didn't really want the hassle any longer.

Chris asked if I wanted to bring anyone else in as members of the board, but I knew the existing people, and the club, well enough to be comfortable as things were while electing a chairman from their numbers. Chris suggested the local solicitor Roger Terrell, who is a football nut, for involvement at board level but, to be honest, I didn't give a toss who was on the board.

I have only ever wanted to be involved with football, not agendas.

The press statement read as follows:

BARRY FRY IS THE NEW OWNER OF PETERBOROUGH UNITED

As of 10am today, Friday, May 31, 1996, Barry Fry is the new owner of Peterborough United Football Club.

One of the modern game's most colourful personalities, Mr Fry has acquired the shareholdings of club chairman Alf Hand and chief executive Chris Turner, who have both tendered their resignations.

Mr Fry comes to London Road as Director of Football and intends devoting all his energies to the day-to-day management of the playing side of the club, with present financial controller Iain Russell becoming the new chief executive and Roger Terrell the new club chairman.

All parties have decided that financial aspects of the change of control will remain confidential.

For Chris Turner and Alf Hand, today's momentous changes represent the culmination of considerable personal efforts over a number of years to safeguard the long-term future of the club.

Commented Chris: 'It was always the intention of Alf and myself to stand aside should the right person come forward and now this moment has arrived we have given every assistance to enable this to take place. We wish Barry Fry all the success in the world and feel confident the public of Peterborough and the surrounding area will respond just as positively. Barry has asked both of us to stay on as directors and we will be giving this invitation a lot of thought over the next few weeks.'

Chris, who holds a unique position in football having been a player, captain, manager, chairman and chief executive of Peterborough United, has recently been in hospital again and admits his health has been a contributory factor in reaching the decision that this is the time to go.

As the new owner of Peterborough United, Barry Fry pledges himself unhesitatingly to the club, commenting: 'The potential is enormous but things on the field have slipped a bit and the results of the last two seasons were simply not good enough. I want to assure the supporters of my total commitment and ask for their 100 per cent backing as we set about making the most of a tremendous opportunity to take the club forward once again.'

He added: 'Chris and Alf have done a wonderful job improving the club's facilities beyond recognition with the impressive new Freemans Family Stand, a training ground second to none and an outstanding youth scheme, which is an area that impresses me greatly. Now I will utilise all my resources to staff the senior squad in a manner that will bring the success the club so richly deserves.'

The proposal documents which went before the board are the subject of a confidentiality agreement and I am unable to reproduce them here.

Now I had got it, done the business and it was time to go on holiday for a fortnight with Kirstine, the four kids, Lil Fuchillo, his missus Jackie and their two kids. It was obvious to myself and all the assembled company that it took as long as boarding the aircraft on the outbound flight for me to get ants in my pants. As soon as we arrived I was on the phone to inquire how the season ticket sales were progressing and this became a daily routine. 'How have the season tickets gone?' was always my opening gambit and as they got better with every passing day I was getting really excited.

Well, I was the owner now!

But instead of lying on the beach and playing with the kids and generally unwinding I was very pent up. It got to the stage where I was on the phone for this, on the phone for that and I really was hopeless. After five days my head was going round and round and it actually reached the point where I was feeling unfaithful being away from the club. My next call was to discover whether I could get a flight home. I could. And when I told Kirstine, Lil and Jackie that I was flying back the next day, they thought I had lost my marbles. They could not fathom the logistics, reasoning that our homeward flight would not be available for another eight days.

But I said that I had managed to make alternative arrangements and that even though our car was parked at Heathrow I would be landing in Birmingham and planned to get a taxi, sorting out the rest as best I could. I was determined and nothing was going to stop me.

They said: 'Well if you're going, we're going.' So when I told the kids that night they thought, and desperately hoped, that I was joking. I think, looking back, it was the worst thing I have ever done in my life. The kids cried all the way home on that plane. They had enjoyed every minute of their much-curtailed holiday in the sunshine and here was their horrible dad dragging them away in the name of football and looking very pleased with himself because he was on his way back. I don't know how I could have been so selfish, spoiling that holiday not only for the kids but also my wife and good friends and their kids.

By this time I had asked Lil to come and help me out at Peterborough and Mickey Halsall, who had played for the club for a decade and whom I knew well, was delighted to accept my invitation to stay on as a coach. The football side had been sorted out and I just could not wait to get my teeth into it. I'm very embarrassed about it, I really am. I'm not being funny about football but really your wife and kids should come first, second, third and fourth and I had put them last, last, last and last. I treated them like shit. It just shows that, along with a lot of other men, I am very selfish and even though that's the way most of us are it does not make me feel good. It's cruel.

Once in place I talked to a couple of players who were

out of contract about coming to join us and the position with them was that their fees would be fixed by a tribunal. Walsall's Martin O'Connor, and Paul Shaw from Arsenal, whom I desperately tried to sign but couldn't, were the players involved and I did manage to get hold of O'Connor for £350,000, which was a club record. I met Shaw, who had been at Peterborough on loan and was outstanding, on two occasions. The second of these was at South Mimms service station on the M25 and I was sure that I had persuaded him to sign. But after seeing me he went to Ken Friar, the Arsenal managing director, who promised him that although there would be no more money he would get a better chance of first-team football.

That swayed him and, being a whisker away from signing a player I really wanted and believed would help us to establish a strong league position, I was gutted.

Subsequent events were to put such a disappointment in true perspective.

CHAPTER FOURTEEN

A small matter of £3.1 million

Strange things began to happen around Peterborough United. I talked to Iain Russell, who said that things were looking rosy and that I had around £600,000 to spend because of the run on season tickets. In that first month of June they had been snapped up in record numbers. I had got Ben Hallam, whom I knew at Birmingham, in on the commercial side and Mickey Vincent, who was in charge of the commercial affairs of the club, was away on holiday at the time in Florida. By the time he returned Ben had done much of the work. Mickey already had in place shirt deals and the like and, in the knowledge that I could have done much better than that, I simply tore them up.

You would not believe the shirt sponsorships I got. It was all money, money, money and the fans showed such faith in me, not only with season-ticket sales but every match, every individual kit and every match ball was sponsored before we even kicked a ball. It was phenomenal. The hype in the city was just amazing.

One or two things which didn't bother me at the time perhaps should have done so. Iain would say: 'Hold on, the bank needs £20,000.' He hinted at a cashflow problem which I simply could not understand because we suddenly seemed to have money coming out of our ears. I told Kirstine I needed £20,000 but that it was only a director's loan and we would soon get it back. Again she asked if I knew what I was doing and I reassured her that I did. Then, at a later date, I wanted £10,000 and then £4,600 and again £8,400 and things were not looking as rosy as I thought they should.

In three pre-season games I just charged a fiver at the gate and this brought in terrific crowds. It was a thank-you gesture to the fans and something I had picked up from Karren Brady at Birmingham, where she used this concessionary admission for games like the Auto Wind-screens Trophy. Then, once the season got underway, we had signed eight or nine players, which cost a lot of money, but things were coming out of the woodwork about which I knew nothing.

Iain dealt with the banks but I wasn't really happy and suggested that the £650,000 overdraft should be turned into a loan so that it would at least create some breathing space. What I had put in, even though I was not a shareholder and had no place on the board, amounted to quite a substantial amount of money and I was now getting quite a lot of hassle at home from Kirstine, who had taken me at my word when I told her that my involvement with the club would cost nothing.

I would shrug off these protests by saying that in life you had to speculate to accumulate.

On my way to a meeting I tried without success to contact Iain and instead phoned the bank. I asked to speak to the manager, Geoff Cooper, and when we were put in touch I asked what he thought about my proposal regarding the overdraft becoming a loan.

'What proposal?' he asked.

I told him that it had been sent to him by Iain.

'I don't take any notice of what he says.'

I found this strange considering that he had been there along with Chris for some years and asked Geoff to send me a letter to the effect of what he had just told me. He did.

Difficulties had arisen about the plan to change the freehold of the ground into a holding company because of tax implications and my 75 per cent shares had not been forthcoming. Now I wondered what the hell I had let myself in for, but I felt highly responsible because we had had all the publicity scene and so forth.

When I received Geoff's letter I called an emergency board meeting and I opened proceedings by telling them of the unsavoury and unwelcome discoveries about sums of money owed by the club and that it was all pay out and little coming in. They said that by and large they were directors in name only, with businesses of their own and little time or inclination to concern themselves, and these were matters best left to Chris and Iain.

I showed them the letter and told them that something was drastically wrong.

They did not have an answer to any of my questions and, of course, Chris had resigned as soon as I took over. So I said he would have to come back because he was the only one who knew the answers.

'Sorry, gentlemen,' I said. 'I am going to do what I should have done in the first place and get an accountant in here to go through all the books.'

They not only agreed, but offered to bring in auditors to work alongside the accountant. My man was in there for a few months, uncovering all sorts of debts. And whichever way you looked at it, the football club owed the princely sum of £3.1 million.

You could argue that £420,000 was Alf Hand's director's loans; that another £300,000 was an interest-free loan from the Football League for the new stand. There was no immediacy or urgency about them because they were always going to be long-term financings. Nevertheless, they had to be repaid sooner or later. Now I was getting all these sets of figures and I was absolutely horrified. I was in such a state that I was going to the training ground and hadn't a clue who was training or what they were doing. Me. At the training ground. With a briefcase. All that was on my mind were figures, figures, figures. Budgets. Gate receipts. And more figures.

It actually taught me a lot, not least to appreciate other clubs and boards of directors. When you look at the gate receipts from 6,000 people, they look fine until sundry items are taken out of them. By the time the police bill has gone, the stewards' bill has gone, the VAT is gone, the ambulance bill is gone along with everything else, you are left with sod all to last you a fortnight between home games. Not to mention the players' wages.

You look at that and wonder how on earth any club survives, not just Peterborough. It's mission impossible. Then you have the bank ringing and saying we have no assets and we simply cannot spend any money.

'Hold on,' I said. 'You've got to be joking. We own the freehold.'

'Ah, but it's green-belt land,' the bank manager said. 'You can't sell it.'

'What about the players? They are assets.'

'They don't appear on the balance sheet, so as far as we are concerned they are worth nothing.'

'But I can sell "x" for that amount and "y" for any amount ...'

The next call from the bank was to inform us that our account was to be frozen. Our wage bill for the coming month was £110,000 and now we had no facility to put our hands on the money. Another board meeting is convened and I say: 'Well, there's seven of us, lads. We've got to put £30,000 in each to pay the wages.'

Alf quite rightly said that he had already put in over £400,000 and was putting in no more. The others said they were not prepared to do it. The common consensus among them was that the players would have to go without and I found this totally outrageous. I could not have the stigma of having taken over a football club and within five minutes deprived the players of their income. I certainly could not allow this dire situation to become public knowledge. One word breathed in the wrong direction would have had all our creditors panicking and jumping up and down and we would have been liquidated overnight.

I was shitting myself big time. I tried every source I knew to borrow the money and those who did not refuse outright quoted horrendous interest rates. It was time to turn once again to my mate Colin Hill, but he said: 'Baz, I told you not to go in there. That I would not give you a penny. You would not listen. You are on your own. Your wife and kids will never go without, but you, you c**t, you think you're Jack the Lad ...'

It was really what you wanted to hear when you're down and out but I had to admit it. He was right.

Chris said he had some interest from a group of Norwegians in purchasing the club and then Keith Cheeseman resurfaced with his own interest. But the fact was that I needed £110,000 there and then. And not just £110,000. Some of this included signing-on fees and there were the following month's wages to think about, meaning that I really needed £210,000 to create a little bit of breathing space.

I knew I could sell some players but I said to the bank manager: 'If you put me under pressure, I've got to sell someone for three bob and he's worth twenty-three bob.'

'I'm sorry,' he said. 'Business is business.'

The pension with which Vic Jobson saw me all right at Southend, my house, my car was all there was for it.

I put all my eggs into one basket and, there you are, £210,000. I didn't have £210 in reality and now I knew that before long I could be living by the river in a tent. Kirstine always said she'd share a wigwam with me and, boy, she doesn't know how close she came to playing Little Whitefeather opposite her Hiawatha. It was the most frightening, horrific experience to be made to endure and the main reason is the responsibility you feel to a whole lot of people – your family, the fans who a very short time previously thought their Messiah had arrived, the players and the rest of the staff.

Our results were up and down like a yo-yo but I could not concentrate on matters on the pitch and the fact that we were crap. I was taking so much on board and the penny suddenly dropped that I didn't even have a share in the place. I could have walked out with my head held high and not given a stuff. It was all on trust, a case of 'I want to come here because I'm a lunatic football manager. Go on, I'll take your debt off you.' They must have thought they had won the Pools.

In a very short time the whole caboodle turned upside down and inside out. I could understand how it had made Chris ill. It was making me ill. I couldn't sleep – I was up all night looking at these blasted figures – and there was this constant churning of the stomach. You'd go for a pee and you'd have these bits of paper full of budgetary items. There wasn't a five-minute period in any day when I wasn't reaching for a pen and scribbling down things.

I gathered the necessary money together and we re-opened our bank account. Then I sold Martin O'Connor to Birmingham for £528,000 up front and everybody said what a great deal it was. Oh yeah? It was a shit deal. I would have got a million for him if I had not been put under pressure. Trevor Francis had me by the short and curlies. But once again to be fair to the Golds, they had heard that I was in trouble and came to the club for dinner and to watch a game. Before the kick-off they asked how they could help.

'Unless you give me lots of money, you can't,' I said. 'I have got myself right in the shit.'

They made inquiries about whether they were allowed to put some money into Peterborough, but it is not permissible for directors of one club to operate in the same capacity at another club. Yet in my hour of need they were there, sitting at a table and talking as constructively as they could about it. And just talking about it was a help.

Transfer fees are normally spread over a period of time and nobody gives you the money up front, but Birmingham did because they knew I was struggling. It was £528,000 in one cheque, bosh, thanks to David Sullivan.

Still more things were being uncovered by the accountant and the auditors and I am bound by a confidentiality document as to the recourse taken. Suffice it to say that when the Peterborough public became aware of the extent of the club's problems, they thought that in view of all the money I had spent on bringing in players I must be the one to blame.

It is simply not the case.

What I hold my hands up to is being no financial expert, possessing no expertise at all in business matters. All this had been a salutary lesson and the misery of it did not end with sets of figures upon bits of paper. Although it broke my heart, I had to sack both Lil Fuchillo and Mickey Halsall. Both had enjoyed long and distinguished careers at the club. But with the bank foreclosing I could not allow sentiment to interfere with my judgement. That really was hard, but it is a fact of life that the club is bigger than any individual. I had to sell whichever player I could just to bring in some funds, however small and undervalued.

Each board meeting had cost-cutting at the top of the agenda and the question of the continued employment of the youth development officer, Kit Carson. He had been at the club for three years before I arrived and, so far as I could see, had brought in a lot of very talented youngsters. It was suggested that we dispense with this very important aspect of life at the club and I was totally against it. Given the situation in which we found ourselves, it made more sense in my mind to keep the youngsters, develop them and turn them into the players of tomorrow.

It was only an exercise to unload the more senior players who were earning around £600 a week apiece and pin our hopes on the kids earning a quarter of that.

Thankfully, my philosophy became the saviour of the club. Those kids were never assets appearing on a stupid balance sheet – but they became invaluable to Peterborough United.

CHAPTER FIFTEEN

Saved by the Pizzaman

I was so intent upon nurturing the youth development within the club that we organised a dinner specifically to raise funds for their benefit. All the tables were taken by local businessmen and alongside me on the top table was Kit Carson. Just as Martin Peters was as a player, Kit is ten years ahead of his time and the methods deployed by Howard Wilkinson, who won a championship with Leeds United before going on to high-powered roles within the Football Association, might well have been copied from my colleague.

When we are talking Academy we're talking Under-9s right through to under-19s from all over the world and, at this dinner, over in a corner would be little Johnny, who is 10 and hails from Wales. He stands up, introduces himself and tells the entire room all about himself and his ambitions and why he wants to play for Peterborough United.

Next to him is a 12-year-old who does the same and

he is followed by a 14-year-old. They are all polite, well-mannered and articulate and a lovely collection of fine young gentlemen. I sat there with a lump in my throat and a tear in my eye as I considered how proud their parents must be.

Kit delivered a marvellous speech and the evening, to which my contribution was £1,000 out of the fees I was paid by the local paper for writing a weekly column, was a great success. It ended with an invitation from Kit to the gathered businessmen to become involved in the youth development of Peterborough by forming a committee and continuing to help to raise funds.

Proceedings ended with several people showing interest in taking part and it was decided that a meeting would be held at a date to be decided. The diners were just dispersing when I was pointed in the direction of a tall, imposing man who had apparently donated £1,000. He was picking at the buffet and I left my place at the top table to approach him.

'Excuse me, mate, I would just like to thank you very much for your kind donation.'

'Oh, yes. Who are you?'

I told him I was Barry Fry, the manager of Peterborough, and he told me his name was Peter Boizot and that he owned the Great Northern Hotel in the city, opposite the railway station.

He offered its facilities for the planned youth development committee meeting and when I expressed my gratitude he said he was doing so because he had been so impressed by all the youngsters and, in particular, the lad who had been seated at his table.

'Are you interested in football?' I asked him.

'No, not really. I play hockey and I love my jazz, but my father used to bring me here to London Road. It would be one week at Leicester and the next at Peterborough, but I was born in Peterborough and my parents were here for a long time.'

He added that he had an interest in, and did quite a bit for, the cathedral in the city and when he asked if I knew much about this place of worship I had to admit that my knowledge was strictly limited.

Kit began to receive a lot of correspondence in connection with the youth academy and the donations were surprisingly and reassuringly in the region of £15,000. A month after the fund-raising dinner we duly assembled at the Great Northern Hotel, where Peter Boizot welcomed us and said that there would be free drinks from the bar all night, as well as a complimentary buffet, for the two dozen or so people sitting round the table. In an adjoining room he was indulging another one of his interests in the form of a train exhibition, to which he invited me to take a peep and asked if it would be all right if he kept popping into our meeting from time to time.

He could not get to grips with the reason why we wanted to set up a different account for the youth development. I explained that the club had an awful lot of debts and was losing a stack of money and nobody in the world of finance trusted it. Therefore to keep the youth, and through it the future, going money had to be raised to allow it to stand as a separate entity. People, I ventured, would be happy to make donations to the youth cause but never to a lost cause.

'Is Alfred Hand still at Peterborough?' he queried. I told him Alf was still on the board, and when I reiterated that the club was on the verge of collapse he said: 'I used to go to school with Alfred. I shall give him a ring in the morning.'

We talked until 2 am until I said that I had better be on my way. He inquired where I lived and said: 'Good heavens, you can't drive to Bedford. You must take one of my rooms upstairs.'

Peter then started to pop into the club occasionally. One night we had a youth game which he watched and he was effusive in his praise.

'They're jolly good,' he said. 'I enjoyed that.'

'Well, I told you. We have some very talented youngsters here and they don't appear on any balance sheet. They're worth a lot of money, some of them.'

'Mmm,' he said. 'Very interesting.'

As time went by his visits became more frequent, although I did not take too much notice until one day Alf called a board meeting. Alf, Nigel and Peter came into my office before the business commenced and Nigel said: 'We have just had lunch and you will be pleased to know that Peter Boizot is going to help us to save the club. He is putting in £250,000.'

'What?' I was incredulous.

I looked at Peter and said: 'Mate, if you don't have £2 million don't bother coming in here.'

Alf and Nigel each shot me a look which said 'Shut up, you silly bugger' but I was unabashed and went on: 'I'm telling you. It's horrific.'

'Don't take any notice of him, Peter,' said Nigel. 'He exaggerates.'

'I am being very conservative when I tell you that it will cost you £2 million. I am not saying you won't get it back; it will be an investment. But don't come in here with your £250,000. It won't last two minutes, mate.'

When we sat down in the boardroom Peter kept looking at me a bit strange. There was the question of whether he would be welcome on the board and, to a man, with the exception of Chris Turner who, funnily enough, abstained, they were in agreement because here was a local man who does so much for the city in general.

Peter asked for co-operation with the lawyers and accountants, one of whom was his nephew Matthew, whom he wanted to bring in to go over all aspects of the running of the club and when, as I knew would be the case, there were many dark mutterings I was able to help them by reeling off the names of a host of individual players and my valuations of their worth. It was a bit like speaking to a brick wall, because they sought proof of their valuations and, of course, I was unable to provide any incontrovertible evidence. What I could offer, I said, was a lifetime's experience in football with the rider that if I did not know what I was talking about then they would have a long and futile search for the man who did.

'Anybody could say that,' was the attitude, but they had a job to do and I had a job to do and at this stage mine was to convince them that we had a lot bigger assets than ever were shown, that the potential was there and that we would grow and grow in a regime in which the right people were looking after the financial aspects and the right people were running the football side. In all honesty, I think I failed. But it was little wonder because it did look a hopeless case.

Out of the blue my telephone rang and it was Peter. 'I am with Matthew in Soho,' he said. 'Would you care to come to meet us to discuss the club?' The nominated venue was Kettners and the appointed time 6 pm. Getting through that area of London at that time of the day was a nightmare and I arrived 40 minutes late. Matthew had left and I rather hoped it had not been in disgust.

Although I had now met Peter a few times he remained something of a mystery figure to me. He was well-heeled and had an air about him and although I suspected he was very wealthy I had no idea in which area he had made his fortune. My best guess was that it was probably family money.

Kettners is a magnificent building and when I remarked upon this and the quality and quantity of bubbly in the exclusive champagne bar Peter led the way down to the cellar, which appeared as though it housed all the bubbly in the world under one roof.

He gave me a mini-tour, which included the stunning restaurant, and when we adjourned to his office he said, unsurprisingly, that his accountants had advised him not to become involved in Peterborough United but that he was considering flying in the face of such advice and was thinking about it. 'I'm a Peterborough man,' he reiterated, 'and I want to help people. They were going to knock down the cinema in the city and I bought it because I did not want this facility to be taken away.'

Peter is unique. Although I have no interests coinciding with his I always found him interesting to talk to about a variety of subjects because his passion for what he likes and enjoys matches mine for football. We talked about his businesses and I discovered that he ran a couple of magazines, employed more than 100 people at Kettners, owned the hotel and the cinema in Peterborough and sundry other small concerns. The sting in the tale was that he was the founder of Pizza Express. He explained that he had spent five years in Italy and that when he returned to England he discovered that nobody had seen the potential in his favourite snacks, pizzas. He borrowed £500 from his mother and launched what is now one of the world's most successful enterprises. He sold his major shareholding for many millions and is now its president.

Before I left him that evening he confided that he had made up his mind and was going to take over the football club. 'That remains between you and me,' he said. 'And there will be stipulations. I cannot take on that big debt and give you pots of money to spend on players. Also I cannot come into the club, have been there for a little while and then you go.'

'Believe it or not,' I said, 'despite the harrowing time I have had I retain a lot of love and affection for the club and I really want to make it work. I don't want to walk out of there with people pointing the finger and saying that I am a failure. Besides, you know that I think there is massive potential, that the game is changing and that Peterborough can be in the forefront of that change.'

Peter said: 'That is why I want you on board.'

We each became party to a private agreement. He also said that he thought me very foolish to have taken out the loan for £210,000 but stated that he would pay that off for me. Even though this took several months I never suffered a moment's anxiety because I knew it would be done. Peter is a man of his word. One evening we were sharing a glass of red wine and a cigar and he told me that the deed had been done. I shuddered to think what the interest might have been and could not resist the inquiry. He said that it had cost £289,000 to release me from the burden.

In football you never trust anybody. Ever. With Peter a handshake is good enough for me. He is different class.

The evening's business concluded in Soho, we decided it might be a good idea to take in some of the night air. Midnight was approaching and the streets were packed with seekers of fun. 'Do you come here often?' Peter inquired with what I hoped was nothing even approaching a chat-up line, nor a condemnation of my nocturnal habits. I said with astonishing good timing, in view of what happened next, that I had never been in the area.

'Hiya Baz, how are you doing?' shouted a group of revellers as though they had known me all their lives.

'Oh, they just know me through football,' I explained rather sheepishly. Then we turned the next corner.

'It's Barry Fry! How's it going?' roared another group.

'Are you sure you haven't been in Soho before?' questioned my companion.

Then we ventured into a pub for a drink and little did I know that this was a gay bar. Peter was busy telling the landlord that he was about to become involved in football, and I was to be his manager, and I was besieged by people wanting to talk about the game.

'Are there a lot of gays in football?' asked Peter as we made our exit. 'Didn't you know that this is one of their hang-outs?'

'I don't know,' I said.

Our next stop was at a famous purveyor of fine cigars and immediately we walked into the shop the man behind the counter said: 'Hello, Barry. How are you?' Peter's face was a picture. Of course, I had never seen the man before in my life but such is the high profile of football nowadays that you can barely go out of your own front door without being recognised.

Soho is one of Peter's stamping grounds and everybody knows him, not least because he runs the Soho jazz festival, which has a ten-day duration every year.

In an environment completely devoid of ethics, scruples and principles, Peter is a breath of fresh air. A gentleman. He entered the new millennium as a 70-year-old man with a new goal in life – taking Peterborough to hitherto unscaled heights – and that says much about him. He has a lovely voice and speaks several languages and has a great knowledge of the world and what makes it go round. Like myself, he is a workaholic and there are simply not enough hours in each day for him to do what he wants to do.

We are known in Peterborough as 'The Odd Couple' and I suppose there is some justification in this. I have known enough jailbirds in my time, yet Peter is so far removed from that kind of company that if you mentioned that word to him he might think it is something which flies. He's worth a conservative £50 million and I have an overdraft of £15,000. Yet we get on like a house on fire.

It was in 1997 that he took over the reins of Peterborough and his arrival was announced, of course, to the accompaniment of a jazz band. His acquisition had been engineered very thoroughly, with him acquiring all the shareholding, albeit with his customary generosity towards Alf Hand and Chris Turner.

What a relief it all was, and not least to the players who now had no worries about whether they would be paid their wages. Without Peter Boizot there would be no Peterborough United today. It would simply have slammed into a wall.

We did not have the most auspicious of starts under Peter. In fact it was a downright disaster because we were relegated from Division Two to Division Three. Despite this, Peter showed his colours when, with the fans in mind, he reduced admission prices and, having walked all round the ground and deemed the toilets to be disgusting, had them completely redone. There were puddles by the turnstiles and he had the whole area tarmacked and he would spend money on all kinds of facilities. He even had to fork out £250,000 on aspects of the new stand which had been neglected, while our pitch was in an awful state and he funded the improvement of the playing surface.

In truth, the supporters don't really care about those things. All they want is a winning team on the park, but there was a succession of so-near-yet-so-far situations which contrived our bad start. Because he is so genuine I desperately wanted things to happen quickly for Peter, but we lost out when we were one game away from a sellout at Old Trafford in the FA Cup; we lost out when we were one match away from Birmingham and another sellout in the League Cup; and we lost out at the area final stage and a trip to Wembley in the Auto Windscreens Trophy.

Many people have been chairmen of clubs who have never got near to Wembley over a period of many years and here, for the first time, I wanted that more for somebody else than I did for myself. But it was not to be.

The following season, 1998/99, started so well that we

were on top of the league at Christmas with just two defeats in 23 games, but the goals dried up as a succession of injuries took their toll. The fans began to take out their frustrations on me, amounting almost to a personal vendetta, and so did the local newspaper.

Of all the chairmen I have had, Peter Boizot has been the most supportive and he was the one picking me up when it should have been the other way round. He also showed immense support under almost intolerable pressure as 6,000 fans started to wave red cards at me at home matches. He had people going up to him, showing him their season tickets and saying that they would never go to Peterborough again as long as I was the manager, yet his reply was that as long as he was there then so would I be.

Yet I have such respect for him that if he were to say at any given time that it was time to call it a day, there would be no argument. I owe him everything.

I suspect that, one day, Peterborough United will have cause to recognise that same fact. Continuity is the key. I have never heard of a ten-year contract in football, but Kit Carson, who demonstrated his vast knowledge by taking the likes of Ruel Fox, Chris Sutton and Tim Sherwood to Norwich when he worked there, has one. Paul Ashworth, the youth-team manager at the time, was given a five-year contract. Appointing from within has become a club strategy. As our young players get better and take us up through the divisions, their values will soar and so will the long-term welfare of the club.

As a Third Division club in 1999/2000 we had 17 international players under the age of 21 and much of that is due to Peter's patience and long-term thinking. Just one moment of panic might have upset the apple cart, but he is smarter than that.

When I arrived at Peterborough I wanted to own it. I envisaged a situation where, when I wanted a player, I would get him when I wanted and how I wanted and for my valuation of his worth, without seeking permission. That soon went out of the window. And perhaps we should all be grateful for small mercies.

CHAPTER SIXTEEN

Play-offs, promotion and ponces

Peterborough United's journey into the new millennium was to feature an opening-day win for the first time in my four seasons there, promotion to the Second Division through the play-offs, the biggest transfer market mugging in the game's history, a vicious, evil hate campaign directed at me and, in the end, boardroom activities which erected a giant question mark over my future at the club.

On the evidence of the previous campaign, when we finished just two positions outside the play-off places, we needed to find only a five-point improvement in 1999/2000 and the omens were good right from the start when we beat Hartlepool 2–1, with 19-year-old Francis Green netting an 84th minute winner, and followed up with a single-goal victory at big rivals Northampton courtesy of Simon Davies' 25-yard strike.

We made it three wins on the trot with a 2–1 defeat of Leyton Orient at London Road, with Steve Castle's header in first half injury time against the club he had served for nine seasons proving decisive. A hiccup against Plymouth was followed by a magnificent Posh performance in beating promotion favourites Darlington 4–2 and we were set fair, though now in third spot we faced a home game against Chester with no fewer than six of our young players away on international duty. Once again with the help of David Sullivan, Karren Brady and David Gold, who allowed payment in stages over 36 months, I was able to introduce a new £250,000 signing for the club in Howard Forinton, who proceeded to score both goals in a 2–1 victory.

We assumed leadership of the division with a 4–1 hammering of Shrewsbury, but a home defeat by Barnet knocked us off our lofty perch and in the build-up to our next game at Hartlepool there was a lot of unrest in the camp which, in the wake of a lousy 1–0 defeat, began to boil over. Our scheduled next two games, at home to Hull and away to Rochdale, were postponed due to Hull's involvement in the FA Cup and a frozen pitch and a lot of incidents on and off the training pitch were coming to light.

I had been trying for three years to secure the services of Wayne Turner, who worked both for the FA and for Arsenal. He was the man who handed out the badges to newly-qualified coaches, so you would struggle to get much higher in that sphere of the game. He had also played at every level and been an assistant manager at Luton and Wycombe, so I felt Paul could learn a lot from that situation and would also be protected from the players.

I felt that with Wayne as my assistant manager and Paul Ashworth remaining as First-team coach, I would then have the management structure that I felt we needed. At the chairman's request we called a meeting and told Paul of our intentions. Paul felt uncomfortable with the new arrangement and he proposed that he became reserve team manager instead of First-team coach to which the chairman and I agreed.

While this was going on David Pleat, Director of Football at White Hart Lane, spoke at length to me three days before Christmas about possible transfers, but the kind of money he was mentioning was not acceptable. He concluded by saying that he would arrange for his chairman, Alan Sugar, to fax my chairman, Peter Boizot, with a £2 million joint offer, with stage-by-stage increments, the following morning but I told him that I would be recommending that this be rejected. Previously Peter, David and I had met at Kettners and we turned down David's offer of £1 million for Matthew Etherington.

Sugar's fax was not forthcoming and when Peter made contact with Pleat he was told that it would not be arriving at all because it was felt he would use it to alert other clubs to the players' availability and boost the price. A verbal offer of £1.5 million was then made by Pleat and when Peter relayed this information to me I said that I had turned down £2 million the previous evening, so how could he be prepared to accept £500,000 less?

Peter asked me to fax Pleat with my own demands, which were £3.5 million, with a further £2.5 million based on appearances for Spurs, Under-21 internationals and full internationals. Pleat replied that I was in cloud cuckooland and he did not want to do business with me, preferring a personal meeting with Boizot. At that stage in the negotiations, I dropped out of the discussions. For the first time in 25 years of football management, I did not conclude the deal.

Etherington and Davies had been delighted early in the season when they spent a week with Manchester United at the invitation of Sir Alex Ferguson, who had been made aware of their abilities. No bids followed, but instead of being dejected they were just grateful to have spent some time in the company of idols like Ryan Giggs and David Beckham. Now their chance to join a Premiership club was at hand and Peter Boizot, being the gentleman he is, called them to his side and said he had always told them that if their big opportunity came along he would not stand in their way. Now, if they wanted it, he would be true to his word. Both players said they felt they had gone as far as they could go at Peterborough and would dearly like to join Tottenham to further their careers.

Training on Christmas Eve, with our Boxing Day match at home to Rotherham looming large, proved a disaster, with our goalkeeper Mark Tyler hit by flu. Our youth-team keeper, Dan Connor, had gone home to Ireland and we were unable to contact him. I was overcome by a sense of panic, but we had a 15-year-old keeper called Luke Steel who had impressed me enormously when I watched the Academy games on a Sunday morning. Preparing a young lad for his first game is not as easy as it might seem. We needed to contact his headmaster for signed permission to play and this was bang in the middle of the school holidays; we had to register him with the Football League and he needed a club shirt with his name on from the Posh store. We arrived at London Road to find three of our players suffering from illness, so we had Tyler, Chapple, Shields, Castle and Hanlon missing, Etherington playing while feeling absolutely lousy and a 15-year-old keeper on the bench.

A holiday crowd of 10,793 saw Rotherham hammer us 5–0, a club record home defeat in the league, and our plummet to 10th in the league did nothing to lift the gloom over what was a thoroughly depressing Christmas.

The following morning I picked up Wayne Turner at the Post House Hotel in Yaxley and took him to meet the board of directors. It was a unanimous decision to appoint him as assistant manager commencing on 1 January, with Wayne having given an assurance that he had no problems with Paul Ashworth taking charge of the reserve team. Our coach was due to leave for Exeter and the chairman asked if I would send in Paul to the Great Northern Hotel to finalise his new role.

We were staying overnight in Bristol, with our London-based and Birmingham-based players having made their own way, and when we arrived I was met by Steve Castle who said that he had taken a phone call from Ashworth in which he insisted that he had been sacked. As soon as I got into the hotel I called all the players together and told them that as far as I was concerned the new set-up was that Wayne Turner was my assistant and Paul Ashworth was reserve team manager. Those were the circumstances in which I had left Peterborough just a few hours previously.

Minus the injured Davies and Etherington, the lads emerged for the pre-match kickabout at Exeter to a chorus of boos aimed at them and me which continued from that point right through to the final whistle in a 2–2 draw. Unknown to me, Ashworth had gone to the papers and they ran stories accusing me of sacking him. What a load of rubbish. As far as I am concerned, Ashworth should still be at the club in the role he wanted as reserve team manager. Now some of the fans had turned against me, believing that I'd sacked Ashworth and left Davies and Etherington out of the side because of the Tottenham situation. But their non-stop boos could not prevent a real battling display, despite having Castle sent off after 20 minutes, highlighted by two fine goals from Clarke, who was cock-a-hoop at the news of Ashworth's departure. He was on fire that day.

Yet instead of the players being applauded for their backs-to-the-wall effort, all they could hear were cries of 'Fry out . . . Fry out . . . Fry out.'

When I got home I took a call from a distraught Peter

Boizot, who had been listening to the match commentary on the radio. He said that if I was driven out by the fans then he, too, would go and this was a tremendous lift for me personally. I told him that I had never been a quitter, was not about to start quitting and that whatever shit came my way I would stand up and be counted.

I could easily have lived to regret those words, because the flak that followed was something you would not wish upon your worst enemy nor believe is capable of forming any part of the human psyche.

The venomous attacks by a handful of so-called supporters, were aimed specifically at getting me out and they tried anything and everything to achieve their goal. For many days the local papers were full of hatred for me and allegations that I had sold the club down the river, sacked Paul Ashworth and sold Davies and Etherington on the cheap. In the lead-up to our next game at home to Swansea on 3 January, Peter Boizot called me to his hotel to tell me that Pleat had been in touch to say that he could give him only £740,000 for Davies and £500,000 for Etherington. I said, 'Peter, it's the worst possible time to sell the players because we have just hit our worst patch and several of the players are injured. If you will just wait, you will get much more money.' I reminded him that six months previously we had turned down £1 million for Etherington and we were now considering half that amount.

When later he told me the details of the deal I was very angry, to put it mildly. I immediately phoned Pleat and called him all the names under the sun. We had a blazing row in which he said that he worked for Tottenham and had to get the best deal he could for them. I was not happy. I have had a lot of dealings with David since we played for England Schoolboys together in 1960 but it seems to have been one-way traffic. I did him many favours, but he has never loaned me a player and I told him in no uncertain terms how disappointed in him I was.

We began well against top-of-the-league Swansea, Matthew Gill scoring the opener and Steve Castle making it 2–0 on the stroke of half time. As Castle went to ram the ball home a section of the 6,439 crowd started chanting 'Fry out . . . Fry out . . . Fry out' in a quite disgusting display of antipathy which continued right through a second half in which the Welshmen scored the three needed to win the game. It was Wayne Turner's first match and I had brought in Jason Lee on loan from Chesterfield. Jason, Wayne and the rest of the players could not believe the scenes.

Their manager John Hollins said to me afterwards: 'Barry, thank your crowd from me for winning the game for us. If they had encouraged you, instead of getting on your backs, we would not have lived with you.'

After the game there were demonstrations outside the boardroom. Peter's view was the way the fans had turned against me was quite scandalous and we did not have to wait long for further evidence of this. That evening Adie Mowles, a so-called supporter, went on Radio Cambridgeshire to say that as a family club, with its academy and all that, it was disgusting that Peterborough should employ as its manager Barry Fry, who had left his wife and seven kids. (In fact, unless somebody knows differently and cares to identify themselves, I have six children. And I most certainly had not left my wife.) He further alleged that I had taken brown paper envelopes, bribes from David Pleat, in respect of the sales to Tottenham of Etherington and Davies and that I had prevented Paul Ashworth from acting as the players' agent in negotiations for their transfer.

Both of these players have their own agents, so why Paul Ashworth would want to negotiate their transfers was news to me.

He also went on to say that I ran the club from top to bottom and had sole responsibility for signing the cheques and added that as for Wayne Turner, he had got the sack as manager at Hitchin. The only time that Wayne Turner has been to Hitchin was to watch a game and Peter Boizot is the only one at the club who signs the cheques.

Shortly afterwards I went onto the same radio station and said it was disgraceful that people such as Mowles should be allowed to publicly slander people on air.

In between times Darren Peake and Mick Bratley, chairman and member of the supporters' club, had met with Peter Boizot to ask for a club museum and Peter, being the kind man that he is, bought them the lease on a shop in London Road in which they could set up this museum, promising help in every way, shape and form.

These so-called supporters saw Peter at his hotel after the parting of company with Paul Ashworth, taping the conversation and handing it over to Ashworth. How underhand can you get? I said on air that, in my opinion, people such as these were 'sponging ponces'.

Unfortunately my lack of vocabulary let me down on air and what I said was misinterpreted. The message I wanted to impart was that there was a small section of the supporters to blame (such as the ones that wait for free tickets when I get off the team coach on away matches and then slander me five minutes later) but, of course, Peake put out messages that I was calling all Peterborough fans sponging ponces. Much was made of this, and they took along a petition to Peter to have me removed despite a fulsome apology from me to the 99 per cent of Posh fans whom I believed then, and genuinely believe now, to be decent people. Peter said that they had had a go at me in a very personal way and I was simply having a go back and what was wrong with that? Nevertheless, Peake said that he was going to sue me after I named a few people in my programme notes. The real supporters would keep coming to me and say that they did not agree with what he was doing. It became apparent to Peake during a meeting of the supporters that he did not have the backing of the majority and he duly resigned as chairman. I believe that Peake and Bratley have now joined the newly formed Independent Supporter's Club whose motives were allegedly questionable.

Mick Bratley has his own website and I am told his

message board is totally anti Barry Fry. There are literally hundreds of messages with only about half a dozen of the same sad people talking all the time. It was not long before their activities were brought to my attention by a supporter who does not like me, does not think I've done a good job but who thought the whole tirade thoroughly unfair. He had found a 'secret' e-mail site, for which you had to be a fully vetted member, and had managed to infiltrate it. On this site people were leaving messages with their names thinking that no one outside the 'group' had access to it. Chillingly one of their messages read: 'Surely there is someone who can arrange a contract killing? It would solve so many problems.' The source of this message appeared to be the father of a boy who had recently been one of our mascots. I confronted him but he obviously denied it as they all do. In another message a letter allegedly written by Mick Bratley said that Kit Carson was running the show and that all their orders came from Kit. That might explain why Mick Bratley's website is constantly praising the Academy and Paul Ashworth and they are constantly having a go at me for not playing enough youth team players. There is probably not a manager in the country that plays as many youth players as I do so I cannot understand where they are coming from. As soon as they knew that this site had been infiltrated, surprisingly it was all deleted and they all denied knowledge of any of it. I still have the pages and pages of e-mails which were taken off before it was deleted and the police were informed.

Weeks later I had a letter from Mowles apologising for his behaviour and while that is all very well the damage, I'm afraid, had been done. Little did he know what damage he did to my family. I have not got a problem with supporters if they are talking about football . . . bad decisions, great goals and all that goes with the game. But what do they know of internal matters which gives them the office to pass opinions? It was clear there was an agenda. A dirty, filthy agenda.

After the Swansea defeat, which sent us down to 12th in the table with all talk of play-off places a distant memory, I had a meeting with the players in which I said that although the fans were after my head big-time the chairman had confidence in me and I, in turn, had confidence in them all as individuals and collectively. We had got to stop feeling sorry for ourselves and keep being aware that we had two games in hand, which nobody ever mentioned. We were still in a useful position and it was time for us, whether the crowd was nought or a million, to unite. They certainly took it all on board because we went to Hull next and after going two goals down produced a stunning comeback, with a last-minute winner from Clarke, after I made my famous substitutions. This really put the lads in buoyant mood in front of fans who also seemed to have got my message that no matter who was in charge of their football team they should at least support the players.

Our next game, at home to Northampton, attracted a crowd of 9,104 despite calls for the supporters to boycott the game and vote with their feet and Jason Lee ensured a famous double over the old enemy with his match-winning goal. It took Wayne Turner all of two minutes, with his consummate ball skills and dedication to training, to gain the respect of all the players and there was now renewed optimism in the camp. We had setbacks against Darlington and Cheltenham, where our keeper Mark Tyler dislocated his shoulder and had to have it pinned, but our 1–0 win at Shrewsbury courtesy of Andy Clarke took our recent record to eight wins in eleven games since the arrival of my number two, Wayne Turner.

There were, I'm afraid, many more casualties in this run and before our 2–0 win over York, Peter Boizot sanctioned a deal I had done with Neil Warnock at Sheffield United for the £30,000 transfer of their midfield man Jon Cullen at £1,250 a month for 24 months. We badly needed reinforcements and on transfer deadline day we brought in goalkeeper Andy Woodman on loan from Brentford, David Oldfield from Stoke, Jason Lee and Adam Tanner from Ipswich.

We now went six games without a win but managed to retain our interest in the play-offs by nicking a point here and there, and by the time the last match of the season at Chester came around our place was assured. The Chester game had deep significance in that they were fighting for their lives and in the lead-up to it I decided to take a gamble and held a private practise match at Cambridge solely for the benefit of Tyler, whom I really rate highly as a goalkeeper and felt would be the rock on which we could build our play-off foray. The Nationwide League rates Tyler, too, because he was picked, as a Division Three goalkeeper, to represent them at Under-21 level against Italy.

Although he started off shakily in this private game, conceding two early goals, Mark showed me enough to justify his selection and there is no doubt that my picking him, and his subsequent fine display in the 1-0 win at Chester, was a massive boost to everybody as we looked forward to the play-offs. My gamble had paid off bigtime, but for Chester there was no such luck. For the second season in succession we were to send a team tumbling into the Conference on the last day, having brought about Scarborough's demise a year previously. There is no joy in that. The place is like a morgue. All you see around you are fans crying and players on the pitch with their heads in their hands and when you go into the boardroom for a drink there are no hellos and goodbyes from people who are simply overcome with grief. You just pour yourself a glass of something, knock it back and get out of there. There is no consoling anybody.

Barnet home and away in the play-offs was a mouthwatering prospect for me, but I could not help thinking that there might be a twist in the tale. John Still had done marvellous things there, with them leading the table for a third of the season and holding a play-off place right to the wire. There was no doubt that, on their day, they were more than a match for anybody in the league and we would have our work cut out. It was the away leg first and when we arrived at Underhill I was told that this could be the very last match at the stadium because of the council's refusal to issue a license for 5,500 people, which is the Football League minimum. Before the kick-off for this Saturday match we had already sold 10,000 tickets for the return on the following Wednesday. Interest was sky-high and we put ourselves in the driving seat with a deserved 2-1 victory. The home leg featured the most stunning hat-trick it has ever been my privilege to witness, a real collectors' item from David Farrell with long-range shots from left and right and the most exquisite chip, also from distance, which if a Brazilian had scored would have been shown on television every five minutes. David felt that he had a point to prove from the first leg, when he touched in a Clarke shot that was going in anyway and was ruled offside. I gave him some stick and Still called him an idiot, but his protests that he had been onside were proven correct by television footage and he really had the bit between his teeth in the return.

We had ten days to wait before the final against Darlington and I took the players for a four-day break in Jersey which proved to be great preparation and, meanwhile, the ticket office was working overtime to meet demand. We had to play on a Friday night because of a scheduled England versus Brazil game at Wembley on the Saturday and, no disrespect, but that 33,303 gate would have been doubled if it had been played 24 hours later.

Five years previously, when I led out Birmingham City in the Auto Windscreens Shield final, my son Adam was the mascot and now my younger boy Frank, more excited even than I, performed the role. Before the big kick-off at a waterlogged Wembley I stood out in the rain and watched our Under-13s beat Darlington Under-13s and to see these little lads go up and get a bigger trophy than the one we were to receive later was lovely.

We thought Darlington would be very difficult opponents. I have the greatest respect for their manager, Dave Hodgson, whom I've known for ages, and their new flamboyant chairman George Reynolds. Dave was the agent for Jose Dominguez. I said to George before the game that it was a pity one of us must lose and it looked after 20 minutes as though only one team, ours, was heading that way. Darlo, with eight players who had 18 previous Wembley appearances between them to their credit, completely and utterly outplayed us to the extent that we could not get the ball. We never got a kick, but some great defending and a bit of luck saw us remain on level terms and we came a bit more into it until, at half time, I was relieved to get the players in with the score at 0–0. We had over 20,000 fans there and I said to the lads that we had to show the same passion as they were demonstrating. We had let ourselves down, in front of partners, mums, dads and friends and had not yet even started. 'For Christ's sake, play some football. Believe in yourselves. Stuff 'em!' I yelled.

Basically, that is what they did. I had felt when we walked into the home dressing room at Wembley that this would be our day because I had done that in 1960 with England and again with Birmingham in 1995. This, I felt, was to be my own hat-trick and I was right, thanks to Andy Clarke. He had been an inch wide of the far post with one effort before he played a one-two with their goalkeeper in the 74th minute and tucked it away. I thought I was a greyhound in trap six and just took off in a celebration which was frowned upon by the FA, who said they were going to report me. Never mind. They could not take away the wonderful feeling of seeing little Frank wearing a medal and, in the VIP area, my 78-year-old father, my wife Kirstine, my sons Mark and Adam, my daughter Jane and her husband Steve and my three grandchildren as well as my daughters Amber and Anna-Marie and friends from the club such as the groundsman Derek and his wife Margaret and all the office staff. I will never forget the joy on all of their faces. For some reason I was reminded that at one point in the preliminaries to a recent England game I had demonstrated my ignorance of events outside the game when Mark shouted over to me: 'Look dad. There's Caprice.' I responded: 'Who's he playing for these days?'

Matthew Etherington and Simon Davies were there cheering us on because they had played a big part in our promotion-winning season. They had by now made their debuts at Anfield and had started at Manchester United. You can't do much better than that considering it had been just three months since they'd left us, especially at the ages of 18 and 20.

I invited Peter Boizot onto the Wembley turf and he had a run with the trophy. There are chairmen who have been in the game 20, 30 and 40 years and never been to Wembley, let alone won something there. I felt so proud for him. My mate Colin Hill was on the bench with us as well. You know when you are down and out and you've got no job and a cheque drops through the letter box a week before Christmas – that's a real friend. He has helped me out behind the scenes at every club I have been connected with because he is a football nut and just to have him there, as part of the occasion, was lovely.

The stadium lights were going out as I sank into a hot bath and began to let it all soak in. The ups, the downs, the bitterness, the feuding and, ultimately, the triumph swam through my mind and I could have wept. I thought of the former club secretary and my PA Caroline Hand who, in June 1999, was admitted to hospital and spent the next four months fighting for her life. She suffered from cystic fibrosis, but this did not prevent her from being the shrewdest judge of people I have ever met. We formed a wonderful friendship and she was loved by everybody who knew her for her honesty and integrity and the way in which she called a spade a spade. She was a very brave lady. We would go to meetings up and down the country, staying in hotels and talking into the early hours of the morning, and never once did she complain about her condition. She was always immaculately dressed. Caroline passed away in late September 1999 while still in her thirties. At her funeral there was a representative from nearly every league in the country as well as all the Nationwide clubs, such was her popularity and respect throughout the game. I miss her.

While Caroline was in hospital Julie Etherington (Matthew's mum) temporarily took over the role as Club Secretary and my PA until she was officially appointed in October 1999. Julie has worked at the club for six years, the first two of which she worked voluntarily for the Youth Development department as secretary to Kit Carson. She helped to put together the Academy Business Plan which got us Academy status and has carried on Caroline's role in the same professional manner. Julie has supported me through all the traumatic events leading up to the play-offs, even though she has been the subject of abuse herself, and without her help and loyal support I don't think that I would have got through.

Thinking back, without Peter Boizot's total backing in allowing me to bring in a few players and Wayne Turner, none of this would have been possible. Since Wayne took over as assistant manager we had only lost four games out of 27. His contribution has been enormous and without him we would not have got promotion.

After the match, the team went to Peter Boizot's restaurant, Pizza on the Park, in London to enjoy a meal and celebrate our promotion until the early hours. The next morning the team enjoyed an open-top bus ride through the streets of Peterborough among thousands upon thousands of people, some of whom ran alongside us from London Road through to the end of our two-hour journey. It was incredible.

On the following day, Sunday, I had a phone call from Peter Boizot saying that Kit Carson had called a meeting with him and the Directors and did I know anything about it. I said that I didn't and that I certainly hadn't been invited. The meeting was held at the Great Northern Hotel while I was watching the Division Two play-off final between Gillingham and Wigan. Peter Boizot set up a more detailed meeting for the Tuesday. In between I was back at Wembley on the Monday to see Ipswich at last gain Premiership status. It had been a wonderful, wonderful weekend.

On Tuesday, four days after gaining promotion, I turned up as scheduled for the board meeting. Within an hour the world of Barry Fry had fallen apart and the promotion party was well and truly over ...

SEVENTEEN

Competing with the Big Boys

The first item on the agenda at that board meeting was the appointment of Nigel Hards, previously a director and very much a fan, as chief executive of Peterborough United Football Club. It was at the request of the board of directors that he returned to the club, bringing with him the financial expertise he had acquired as a well-respected local businessman who had once helped to build the Thomas Cook empire.

I thought it was a shrewd move by Peter Boizot to bring him back as chief executive, because this demonstrated a desire for the club to be run on a professional footing. But the convivial nature of the meeting soon shifted to acrimony, as I became upset at an allegation that during my tenure as manager I had failed to encourage the youth players. I pointed out that no other manager in the country had played so many teenagers, 14 in all, in the course of a league season; what's more, in the course of the last two reserve games against Ipswich and

Bristol City respectively, 14 and 15 of the 16 players, including substitutes, had all been Academy boys.

I felt grossly insulted. A blazing row ensued and when it was over I was convinced that I had been sacked. As I left the boardroom to go into the car park my phone rang. It was a journalist who wanted to come and interview me about the joys of the wonderful promotion we had achieved through the play-offs. I told him it was a waste of time as I had just been sacked.

Of course, by the time I got home every journalist in the country had been on the telephone or descended upon the Great Northern Hotel to seek out the directors. All hell broke loose.

But the next day, when I spoke to the chairman, he put it down to an almighty misunderstanding. Peter Boizot has never been less than supportive, and he said that he wanted me back at my desk pronto and at no time had he wanted me to go. There was uproar, because those supporters who had wanted to see the back of me for so long thought they had got their way and made their feelings known about this latest development in no uncertain terms.

The wonderful relationship that I enjoy with Peter gave me extra delight to be walking back into London Road the next day, albeit with my mind in total turmoil. The two of us do not argue very often, but when we do, we do so very passionately, fervently believing our own versions of the points at issue.

I have strongly-held views on many things and am

quite prepared to state differences of opinion not only with the chairman, but with the other directors, the players and the fans. It is often interpreted that I am a trouble-maker, but I think that airing your views is healthy for the club and the individuals concerned with it. I don't see any harm in it. Our beautiful game is all about opinions, and they are what make it so interesting.

We would all pick a different team and we all see individual games very differently. What is life without an opinion?

Kirstine could see the state I was in and immediately walked into a travel agent, booking a holiday in Spain for the family. Looking back, it's one of the best things she has ever done, because I was a volcano ready to explode at any moment. It didn't help matters when, on our flight out, I asked which hotel we were staying at and Kirstine said she didn't know; that it could be any one of three and that it would be allocated to us at the airport.

Oh no, I thought. This is going to be a Mickey Mouse adventure. But we settled into the most rewarding, most relaxing and most therapeutic family holiday that we have ever taken together. We took a couple of days out to visit Barcelona, showing Amber and Anna-Marie all the great sights of that wonderful city, and we couldn't miss the opportunity to take Frank and Adam to the Nou Camp, one of the world's greatest stadiums. Even though it was empty it was absolutely fantastic, although unfortunately they were like kids in a sweet store when we visited the club shop and my credit card took a right old hammering!

But I rested, and it was nice to spend some time in the bosom of my family. I miss that immensely through the season, when football becomes all-consuming. You learn a lot about your kids and you realise how much you're missing as they are all growing up at such a rapid rate. I'm not much of a holiday person but, I must admit, I needed that one.

Once I was back at work the sun, the relaxation and the odd glass of wine had recharged my batteries and I was raring to go. The mountains I had left behind were now molehills as I saw everything in a new light.

I knew from the board meeting that I would have to cut the squad strength and work to a budget – which until then I thought had something to do with car rentals – for the first time in my life. We brought in only one player in the summer and this was Blackpool's Richard Forsyth, who had previously played under me at Birmingham. A midfield player who is a great passer of the ball, he's also good for morale on the pitch, in the dressing room and in training – just the kind of guy some of my young players needed around them.

I said at the start of the season that if we retained our Second Division status then it could be considered a success, especially as we had one of the smallest and youngest squads and we were playing in a higher league.

What lay ahead was a huge challenge and I was greatly

encouraged by our pre-season tour of Scotland, where we played the likes of Greenock Morton and Partick Thistle. We stayed at Glasgow University – Walsall were in the same camp, funnily enough – and it was a valuable exercise in team bonding, with training morning and afternoon and a match in the evening.

While we were up there I took the whole team to watch Celtic play West Ham in a friendly and oh, what about those Celtic fans? The passion, commitment and, above all, the sportsmanship of those people is something to behold. There were over 40,000 for a match with nothing at stake and they cheered every kick and treated their new manager Martin O'Neill like the new Messiah.

I was satisfied to finish the 2000/01 season in mid-table. Wayne Turner, my assistant, made a major contribution to our consolidation with his professionalism and encouragement and development of the young players.

We had a wonderful FA Cup run, too. When we were drawn away to Chelsea in the third round I said publicly that we would be lucky to get away with 10–0. In the event we restricted them to 5–0 on what was a wonderful day for the supporters and the team. I had four players on the park that day whose earnings are £300 a week – I wonder what Jimmy-Floyd Hasselbaink, Dennis Wise and company would make of that! For my boys to compete with Chelsea was a tremendous achievement, and after the game Ken Bates, their chairman, kept us entertained for a couple of hours in the boardroom, where he said that the scoreline had flattered his club and that we had emerged from the game with a lot of credit.

Ken's an old mate, but a lot of people do not like him simply because he tells the truth, which often hurts. I've known him a long time and, like me, he has never been afraid to voice his opinion. He's my kind of guy.

A major part of our consolidation in 2000/01 involved selling Matthew Wicks to Brighton for £25,000, having signed him on a free transfer from Crewe 18 months previously. That allowed me to strike a deal in which we would pay Crystal Palace £1,000 a month over 25 months for Leon McKenzie, who finished the season as our leading goalscorer. Previously I had had Leon on loan in the Third Division when he was still a teenager. He scored eight goals in 12 games and I very much wanted to sign him then, but Steve Coppell wanted £500,000 for him. He boasts a goal-in-two-games scoring average for us and has a bright future.

We had more than our share of injury problems. Jason Lee missed the start of the campaign and we miss his presence when he is not playing. But we won our first two away games of the season at Oxford and Oldham and then managed to go on 19 journeys without winning again. It was a strange sequence because the results would not go for us despite our playing well in most of those games. I couldn't berate the lads too much because they were giving everything and performing as well as they could. The fact is that there are some big-hitters in that league. Millwall, Reading, Wigan, Bristol City, Walsall

... they are all strongly suited. Their wage bills are in the £3 million-£4 million bracket and we do well just to compete with them to be honest.

We did well at home, where our average gate was over 6,000, and we gave our fans plenty to cheer. Playing in a higher league has allowed us to play football of a better quality and the facilities when you go away are far superior. It was enjoyable and it was satisfying, but we cannot rest on our laurels. Next season will be even harder.

We only have a couple of players out of contract, so we hope to be wheeling and dealing again. Within budget, of course! The club is more important than any individual, and it is important with all the changes in football regarding player contracts that stability is maintained. Bosman affected all clubs, especially the ones lower down, because they relied on selling their players to offset their losses. The new EU ruling means that when your younger players move on, your only compensation is that calculated on what it has cost you as a club to train the individual from the age of, say, 10 to 17.

It is still to become clear what the practicalities are, but what is evident is that the two boys we sold to Tottenham, Davies and Etherington, would bring in nothing like the £1.2 million we received at the time.

This is going to cause havoc in football. All the clubs up and down the country who run a youth academy, into which heavy investment is pumped, will be faced with a decision on whether or not they can afford the money to bring along players so that they become assets when the return on them will be so severely diminished. Clubs do not want, nor can they afford, to be making kids into footballers for somebody else to reap the benefit further down the line.

Already clubs are disbanding their youth and reserve team set-ups, adopting the attitude that they will cut out all the time, effort and expense in cultivating players in favour of going along to somebody else's and nicking theirs. All they will have to pay is this vague 'training compensation'.

Nobody, and I have sought the views of all the leading figures in the game over this, is able to precisely define these costs. Is it 25 times what it has cost to bring an individual along between the ages of 10 and 17? Is it 100 times? All I know is that it will be a lot less than what we know as a normal transfer fee.

It is criminal for the game when there is absolutely nothing at all wrong with the system as it stands. All you're going to get now are hundreds of talented kids with no club to play for. Why do they not just leave us alone?

Every representative body in the country, the FA, the Football League, the League Managers' Association and many others have fought against these changes. Okay, we all know that transfer fees have become ridiculous and have gone through the roof, but it's better that than what is proposed.

The Premiership will be affected, too. At the moment

players appear on officially presented balance sheets as assets – at Manchester United Ryan Giggs is worth £30 million and David Beckham £50 million, say – and the banks are more than willing to facilitate colossal overdrafts. If, overnight, these assets are withdrawn the banks are going to demand to be shown other assets to replace them, and if these cannot be demonstrated then they are going to call in their money. The far-reaching consequences are that a lot of clubs will go to the wall.

But it was business as usual for us and we had an early disappointment when we went out of the Worthington Cup at the first hurdle, drawing 0–0 at home to Luton and then going out on the away goals rule in a 2–2 draw at London Road. Our league form stuttered and we were given an early indication of the strength of the division when we had 75 per cent of the play at home to Millwall and still lost 4–1. Their superior final ball was the difference and it was clear then that they would have a major say in the destination of the championship.

It became a recurring theme. We went to Brentford, played them off the park and lost 1–0 and Ray Lewington, whom I think is a brilliant coach, apologised afterwards. He said he felt so embarrassed at having taken three points, but that's football and it was nice of him to say that. Same at Bristol City, where we got beaten in the last minute and Danny Wilson was very complimentary towards us.

Jason Lee's return from injury was perfectly timed, because he popped up with a last-minute equaliser in the FA Cup second round against Oldham and that set us up for our memorable trip to Chelsea.

Probably the biggest disappointment of the season came against Northampton, in front of a Christmas crowd of nearly 10,000. We were 1–0 up and playing superbly, had four one-on-ones with their goalkeeper, who saved the lot, and they popped up twice at the other end and got an equaliser followed by a winner.

The campaign was going this way and that and a frustrating feature was that on only two occasions did we manage back-to-back wins. But we had a little run against quality opposition and that was good for us, while the match of the season was probably our 3–3 end-to-end draw at Notts County.

The finale was at home to Rotherham in a match that had a full bearing on the Division Two title. Their manager, Ronnie Moore, deserves to be knighted for what he has achieved at the South Yorkshire club over the last two seasons. To gain successive promotions is a fantastic feat and in Division Two everybody was waiting in vain for months for justification of their predictions that they would slip up sooner rather than later.

There were no banana skins at all.

At the other end of the spectrum, it was sad to see Luton relegated. Living near there and having played for them, I take more than a passing interest in The Hatters and it looked as though they might pull off the great escape when they brought in Joe Kinnear and proceeded to win four of their first five matches under him. But they went another eleven without winning a game and that was that.

I feel sorry for Joe because he had also been at Oxford for a time and they, too, went down. He had been a miracle worker at Wimbledon and the same was anticipated at both of these lesser clubs. But I feel confident that the summer sort-out at Luton will see them promoted. He surprised me by bringing in only one player when, with his knowledge and his contacts in the game, he might have been expected to have been more active in the transfer market.

There was one exit and one entrance at Peterborough which were of some significance. On deadline day we sold Adam Drury to Norwich in a deal which could bring us in over £500,000. Adam had served the club well and I was sorry to see him go. Although I thought he was better than that and we had received no other bids, business, as they say, is business. His departure weakened the team, but strengthened the bank balance, which is what it is all about these days. Survival.

So once Drury had left Peterborough, another player joined in the shape of my son, Adam, who had begun to make his way in life. Adam had been playing for Bedford Town and was asked over to Peterborough for a trial – nothing to do with me; it was independent of my interests and entirely on merit. One of the best things as a parent was to have a letter delivered to my house from Kit Carson, the Academy director, to give to Adam to say that he had been offered a scholarship with Peterborough.

To see the joy on the boy's face, and the happiness within, brought a lump to my throat. He's a miserable little sod at the best of times, but I have never seen him smile so much and quite rightly so. It was not so much a smile as a beam. He has dedicated himself to a single goal in his early life, to the extent that he avoids going out with his mates at the weekend and goes to bed early, and for Kirstine and myself, this was a real highlight of the year.

My wife has been like a taxi service, making constant sacrifices like waiting for him to come home from school, driving him the 40 miles from Bedford to Peterborough, sitting in a car park for two and a half hours while reading a book and then driving him home again. He hasn't been the most academic individual and Kirstine was worried that if he did not get this scholarship then there could be real problems in the summer when he left school. So the joy when he did was matched by relief.

I would take him sometimes on Sundays and either watch him or one of the other Academy games. I would never say anything to anybody about him, preferring to let the people who run the Academy just get on with it. They don't want their coaches telling them one thing and the dads, i.e., me, telling them something else, so other than quiet encouragement I would keep my thoughts to myself. Like other parents we watch and sometimes it is good and sometimes it is bad. There were plenty of times when I thought he would never make it.

A lot of people think Adam is at Peterborough because

of me, whereas that simply is not the case. He is there on his own merits and he stands on his own two feet. Finishing school in the summer meant that he would be leaving home and taking up residence in the club hostel. When we learned of his acceptance we had a happy family night, with his sisters now accepting that he would reside 40 miles away and that things would change.

What I wondered was what might have happened if that Academy letter from Kit Carson had said that Adam was not being accepted. Reality hit home when all the lads were on the phone to each other inquiring who had made it and who had not, and the successful ones rallied round the disappointed faction. You do not realise that a boy's failure to make it does not only affect the individual. He may have been at the club for five years, since the age of ten, and his whole world revolves around the football club. Rejection is heartbreaking for the boy, but it is no less harrowing for his mum and dad, whose sacrifices over all that time have been enormous. Their brothers and sisters; their grandparents, they are all in it together and the hurt is terrible.

What brings this even more sharply into focus is when you get the eight or nine boys who have grown into men, have completed their three-year apprenticeship and are still not guaranteed a career in football. I have to call in some of these aspiring Beckhams and tell them that their futures lie in another profession and that is because if they are not wanted at Peterborough they sure as hell will not be wanted elsewhere in the Football League. It's brutal, really, and it happens to a lot of people. Many of them burst out crying right there in front of you and though your instinctive emotion is to cry with them, you are there to do that job and not allow sentiment to get in the way. But it is without doubt the worst aspect of being a football manager – to look a boy in the eye and tell him you are not signing him. You have kicked him in the bollocks and he is finished.

Football is full of ups and downs and the events of the final day of the 2000/01 season in Divisions Two and Three amply demonstrated both. Our fixture at home to Rotherham potentially held the destiny of the championship, because if Millwall had slipped up against Oldham, Ronnie Moore's side could have won the title at London Road. As it happened, Millwall ran out comfortable 5–0 winners and our match finished 1–1, so it was the London team that journeyed into Division One having won the league.

Meanwhile, over at Barnet, it was a winner-takes-all crunch battle with Torquay for the retention of League status and of course I had more than a passing interest in events at Underhill. The night before the game I had been at a function at Barnet which, eerily, was designed to celebrate their ten years as a League club. Within 24 hours they were a League club no longer as Torquay rattled up a 3–0 half-time lead, withstood a comeback that saw a final score of 3–2, and finished the game with their own League status intact.

Demotion to the Conference, where I had once

enjoyed such a rollercoaster ride with this little club, was a crying shame and Torquay's manager Colin Lee adequately summed it up when he said: 'I feel for Barnet. It must be a massive blow. I wouldn't wish what we have been through today on anyone. The pressure was just immense. But it's something I just had to do.'

That's football for you. Sometimes cruel, sometimes ruthless, sometimes very sad.

But at the other end of the spectrum another of my old clubs, Birmingham, brought the promise of Premiership football when they made the play-offs.

I know that shootouts are common events for the police in America, but I can't ever remember the law getting involved in a penalty shoot-out before Birmingham's controversial play-off semi-final second leg against Preston at Deepdale on 17 May.

Brum travelled to Lancashire for the return holding a 1–0 lead from the first leg, but it was Preston who made it through to the First Division play-off final against Bolton in Cardiff on 28 May with all hell breaking loose over a dramatic penalty shoot-out.

Preston's Paul McKenna scored the winning goal after Graham Alexander, David Healy and Sean Gregan had all converted from the spot.

Rob Edwards had missed his penalty but early failures from Marcelo and Darren Purse meant it was all over for Birmingham.

Even successful kicks from Stan Lazaridis and Nicky Eaden could not save them and, as two years ago against

Watford, they lost a play-off semi-final in a penalty shoot-out.

Birmingham, also beaten in the previous season's play-offs, saw goals from Healy and Mark Rankine, with one reply from Geoff Horsfield, take the game to extra-time and then penalties.

Preston could have been back in the game when they were awarded a penalty for hand ball by Sonner, but full-back Alexander hit the spot-kick against the bar. Then Birmingham nearly secured the tie in stoppage time when Lazaridis went round Lucas, but shot across the face of goal from a narrow angle.

But the home side were back in the lead and level on aggregate in the fourth and final minute of stoppage time when Rankine shot home from close range after Bennett could only parry a Healy shot.

Preston went closest to settling it in extra-time, but Bennett saved a rising shot from Edwards and also did well to beat away an effort from Healy.

There were amazing scenes prior to the penalty shoot-out when Birmingham manager Trevor Francis ordered his players to leave the pitch following an argument over which end of the pitch the penalties should be taken. Referee Paul Danson indicated they should be taken at the Bill Shankly Kop end, which was full of home fans, instead of where the old Town End used to be situated. That end had been demolished towards the end of last season and was now a derelict building site.

Francis furiously remonstrated with the referee but

eventually the players returned to the pitch and the penalties commenced.

But the outcome of the spot-kicks made Francis even unhappier, as the defeated Worthington Cup finalists missed out on a second trip to the Millennium Stadium in the same season, while David Moyes' men danced with joy in front of their fans. Lancashire Police confirmed that the shoot-out at Deepdale was held at the home end because of safety reasons. They were apparently concerned that there could have been a surge from the crowd if the shoot-out was held at the other end.

After the furore, the Lancashire Constabulary and the host club issued a joint statement which said: 'Any decision surrounding the field of play in a football match is ultimately that of the referee.

'However, in any pre-match safety briefings, the club's ground-safety officer and police will give advice to the referee based on the safety of supporters in the stadium and the preservation of public order.

'That was the case in advance of the match at Deepdale. Public safety remains paramount on any such decision-making.'

Birmingham were not satisfied with that and decided to lodge an official complaint with the Football League, with Karren Brady maintaining: 'Trevor had a word with the referee before the start of the game and the referee had told him penalties would be taken from the neutral end. When the last kick of extra-time had been made, Trevor and the players went to that end.' Karren confirmed that club solicitor Henri Bradman had been instructed to take up the legal challenge and David Sullivan added: 'We will be taking legal advice from counsel.'

When the Blues lost the Worthington Cup final to Liverpool on penalties three months previously Karren had been upset that they also had to take those spot-kicks at the end housing opposition fans at the Millennium Stadium.

She said: 'It's all about justice. We owe it to our supporters and our players. We had to swallow this against Liverpool and we're not going to swallow it again.'

Seemingly, Preston manager David Moyes had little sympathy for Birmingham. He hit out at their objections, claiming his team had earned the right to take penalties in front of their own fans by finishing fourth in Division One, giving them a play-off semi-final at home.

Moyes said: 'If we had been Birmingham – in the same situation, at Birmingham – I would gladly have taken them at that end (in front of Birmingham's fans) because that's the way it is.

'I didn't even know what it was all about until I was told that Birmingham had gone and seen the referee before the game and asked for the penalty kicks to be taken at the empty end.

'If you are a paying supporter, you would have wanted the penalties to be taken at the other end. I think that would be an obvious situation.

'My argument would be that we went to Birmingham,

we came fourth in the division and it was our right to play here in the second game.

'Birmingham had their opportunity down there – their stadium's finished and I've got to say it's a lovely stadium – but if that had been the case there, I couldn't ask people to come and pay to get in tonight and have the penalties taken at the open end.

'I think it's very petty.'

But Moyes revealed there were no hard feelings between himself and Francis at the final whistle.

'I've shaken hands with all of the Birmingham staff and they've wished us all the best, which is nice,' he said.

Birmingham's appeal was in the hope of getting the play-off semi-final second-leg at Preston replayed.

So it was a season of high drama but little reward for two of the clubs dearest to my heart – Barnet out of the league and Birmingham's attempts to bring Premiership football to St Andrews continuing to be frustrated.

In the final analysis keeping Peterborough out of trouble was, by contrast, the season's most rewarding aspect.

CHAPTER EIGHTEEN

Small Fry

I have great worries for the future of the game that I so dearly love. Money, greed and power have become overriding concerns and have secured such a foothold that as the rich are getting richer they are not giving a toss about those less fortunate than themselves. Imagine that it has taken a century or so to build the pack of cards which is the 92 Premiership and Nationwide Football League clubs and all the blood, sweat, toil and tears that has gone into so doing. The puff of wind which is now threatening the very fabric of a great proportion of them will soon reach gale force and, as it does so, they will come tumbling down one by one.

There are 20 or so big clubs with the High Street big banks and each of them, some in the Premiership, are struggling big time. Keeping up with the Joneses is an obsession at a time when they can ill-afford such pretensions. The income is not there. The facilities to do so are not there. The Premiership is dictating to the rest.

We said before its formation that, for the good of the domestic game, there could not be a breakaway and there was no way it could ever happen. But it did. Now the Premiership is making moves towards just 16 or 18 clubs and the same noises that it cannot happen are being made. But it will. There will never be a Super League with fixtures on Mars, say some. But there will. The top five or six clubs will go their own way as they did from the Football League a few years ago.

It is greed. It is big bucks. It is business. It is no longer a sport.

What worries me as well is that in time gone recently by, the man in the street was the support, the mainstay and the backbone of all the clubs. The only thing that ever kept them going in mundane and back-breaking jobs was the prospect of spending their Saturday afternoons at their local grounds and this vital and enjoyable aspect of their lives has been taken away from them. Stolen. Joe Public has been priced out of it and has not got a cat in hell's chance as the emphasis has switched to business and corporate indulgence.

There is something very distasteful about this because many of the people you see at football grounds these days are not football people. They are high-flying businessmen using grounds as a facility for entertaining clients. So you get computer nerds who wouldn't know their free-kick from a free lunch taking the place of people who would give their right arms for the opportunity of seeing their team in action, and all in the name of the next big deal. More business is done during the 90 minutes of a match than those people will do in a week in their offices.

The national game is changing, too. When I was growing up, England were the world leaders in football. Everybody looked up to us. Now we have plummeted like a stone in the world rankings, to the degree that countries which are pinpricks and largely anonymous on the world map have not only caught us up but have overtaken us. The reason for that is simple. All too late we realised the value of getting at the kids when they are young – I mean as young as seven or eight – and putting them into academies. If you are going to create a top-class player, you need to teach him the basic skills almost as soon as he is able to kick a ball. Howard Wilkinson takes and deserves all the plaudits for initiating these methods in this country but, by the same token, they were being practised at Ajax 20 years ago and in countries who have enjoyed a recent emergence some 15 years ago.

Consequently we are country miles behind.

Now we have got this invasion of foreigners. Don't get me wrong, some of them who grace the Premiership are world class and make our domestic game better as a spectacle while improving the quality of the English players alongside them. But there are too many of them. And for every one who is any good, there are nine who bring the game into disrepute. They are making a mockery of the good, old-fashioned English game. This influx of foreigners is not restricted to players, either. The current trend is for clubs to bring in foreign coaches when there are more than enough good English, Scottish, Welsh and Irish coaches to go around the world and who are out of work now.

Not only that. The foreign coaches are getting more and more foreign assistant coaches and they are getting more and more foreign players. And now we have got the situation, as the academies spring up, that we are buying in 13-year-olds from Brazil, 14-year-olds from France and 15-year-olds from Italy. Where does that leave the English game? There will not be an England team in five years at this rate. It has gone stark-raving mad.

It has got to be stopped before the damage becomes irreparable and my suggestion would be to restrict foreign players at each club to a maximum of two. An illustratory gauge on this is that I used to know every player on the books of every Premiership team. Now I would be hard-pressed to name half of them. And wasn't that one of the joys of the English game, that if it was Arsenal versus Manchester United, or even Southend versus Barnet, that you would be able to virtually guarantee the line-ups and be familiar and comfortable with them?

The foreign force is killing our game. If you want a centre-forward you no longer go to Chester to pick up Ian Rush. If you want a goalkeeper you do not go to Scunthorpe for Ray Clemence or the same source for Kevin Keegan. It worked. The Chesters and Scunthorpes of this world would go and spend their money within the English game and that made the English game tick.

No longer. Not a single transfer deal in 1999 involved a Third Division player joining a Premiership outfit. The elite prefer to go abroad, maintaining that players are cheaper. What a load of bollocks. How can they be cheaper? They might get them for less as far as a transfer fee is concerned, but then they stick them on £20,000 a week wages. Are you sure? They are not in the real world.

They are making it more difficult for all other clubs to exist. I happen to be old-fashioned in saying that we have 92 league clubs in England and we should always have 92 league clubs. You might be a Manchester United fan, an Arsenal fan, a Leeds fan; but it should not be forgotten that there are also Halifax fans, Rochdale fans and Barnet fans. There might be only a couple of thousand of them, but they are just as passionate in their support and their feelings for their clubs. These are communities and their clubs must not be taken away from them. If you do, you take away their dream. Their impossible dream.

An exception to the general rule they may be, but Wimbledon rose from non-league to the Premiership and many millions of people around the country believe, or at least live in hope, that their club will one day do the same. Unfortunately, that will never happen again. With each passing year the gap between the divisions is getting wider and wider. There are now even divisions within divisions and it does make you wonder where the game is going.

Bosman was a disaster for the smaller clubs. There is no question about it. As things stand in the wake of that landmark ruling, a player becomes a free agent at the age of 24, but what will happen in the future is that some smart operator will make a High Court case out of a 17-year-old or 18-year-old player who is out of contract, challenge the validity of 24 being the governing age and win his case. Then we are all in trouble. All the investments in time and money will be out of the window.

Where boards of directors once had patience, understanding and a degree of ambition it is my view that they will no longer be so tolerant. Promotion from league to league means bringing grounds up to standard and that costs fortunes. You have got to part with the money before you get any Trust money back; with the amount of gate money you get, you question game by game whether it is worth the effort; you cannot afford transfer fees, signing-on fees and big wages. So what do you do?

The next stage will be a Premiership One and a Premiership Two. All the big clubs are complaining that they play too many matches and in 1999 Manchester United delivered a miracle by achieving the Championship/Champions League/FA Cup treble. But what did they do in the summer? They went to China and Australia when they were mentally and physically knackered. Why? Because money is the god and the god is money.

So eventually they will get their Premiership One with

16 or 18 teams and their Premiership Two with 16 or 18 teams. There will not be anything else. So far as they are concerned the rest can go out of business.

Yet the Nationwide Conference is run superbly. More and more of the clubs involved in it and being run properly are going full-time, while in the next step up, the Third Division, more and more clubs are talking about going part-time. At least all the Third Division clubs get £264,000 a year from central funds involving television money. The non-league clubs don't receive a penny. Getting £5,000 a week in still does not make any of these clubs successful financially, which illustrates to me that the lower league is being run better.

This is not a criticism of the Football League, more a commentary upon the way the game has gone and how many clubs have badly managed their affairs. So many are so deep in debt, even before their staffs have been paid and before a ball is kicked on a Saturday. But just look at players' wages. Over the past four years they have escalated by between 78 and 82 per cent. And gate receipts and commercial revenues are in no way matching those kind of hikes. You do not need to be Einstein, then, to deduce that most of the clubs in England are struggling. It only needs one or two of them to go and many of the rest will surely follow.

The truly frightening thing is that it could happen tomorrow. I think that for the sake of football all this money going into the Premiership – and we are talking multi-millions – should somehow be filtered down, not as handouts but as safeguards to keep the other clubs alive. There would be ructions if it were directed towards the spendthrifts, but every club needs a little bit of help from the big boys.

It is a certainty that the Premiership will in the near future pledge £1 million to every Football League club and that will be on condition that they agree to a two-up-and-two-down flow between the Premiership and Division One for the first season and two-up-and-four-down for the following one or two seasons.

As short-sighted as they are, most of our clubs will be gleeful and snatch their hands off. But what happens next year? They are in the shit again. Would it not be better for the Premiership to give each club a smaller amount per year to keep them going? One of the positive recent developments in the game is that Richard Scudamore, who was chief executive of the Football League, has now been recruited to the Premiership. Despite the impossibility of satisfying 72 league chairmen he did a very good job and understands all the trials and tribulations of life outside the Premiership. With his in-depth knowledge he is perhaps the one man who can be the saviour. He is a strong enough and genuine enough guy to want to hold it all together.

But, as a group, I am not sure about the Premiership chairmen. Again, keeping up with the Joneses is what their lives are all about. They care not a jot for the small fry. My worry for the fans of the existing clubs at the lower levels are that if their club disappears from the face of the earth then they are not suddenly going to switch allegiances. If, for instance, Brentford went under their supporters would not overnight become followers of Chelsea. For one thing, they would never get in to see a match and, consequently, these people will be lost to the game, probably forever.

Another illustration of the cash drain from the game is the comparatively recent emergence of agents. Now there are good agents and bad agents, but how the hell did we allow them into football in the first place? Why on earth didn't the Professional Footballers' Association appoint a panel of ex-players to take care of business, put them on a fixed salary and ensure that the money generated from transfer fees stays within the game? As it is, these outsiders are making £1 million with the signing of a name on a dotted line as their part of setting up the deal. That stinks.

My journey through a life in football began with Manchester United and it has been a great source of satisfaction for me to witness the marvellous things which have happened at Old Trafford over the past decade. When we are talking about the managerial greats in the game Sir Alex Ferguson stands head and shoulders above his modern-day contemporaries. He had a rough time during his first four years in the biggest job in football in this country, but it is a popular misconception that his livelihood was ever imperilled. I remember seeing Sir Bobby Charlton at a Wembley game and I observed to him that things did not appear to be going well and that all anybody ever heard about in those days was the unrest at Manchester United.

He said: 'Things are fine. There is no unrest in the boardroom at all. We have got the right man. He has built very strong foundations and he has a fantastic youth set-up which is just about to blossom and we are all very excited about it. The fellow works from seven o'clock in the morning until two o'clock the next morning. Just watch what happens.'

Hearing that, and having had a few dealings with him since, there is no doubt that Fergie has earned his success. He has been first in to the training ground and the last to leave every day of the week for a long time now and what he has achieved has been nothing short of a miracle. There has been no coincidence or accident about it, just first-class forward planning by a man who really knows what he is doing.

I first met him through the meetings of the League Managers' Association, which was Graham Taylor's baby and had a huge input from Howard Wilkinson. Fergie, whose voice in football and its affairs is so powerful, has also made a massive contribution and he shows particular concern for his colleagues at a lower level. It is alright for somebody like myself threatening that unless radio and television stations coughed up some money for interviews I would tell them to get lost, but if Fergie did that the full impact would be felt. He would volunteer to do that, and it would not be for the benefit of Alex Ferguson. It would be to help out First, Second and Third Division managers who could only ever aspire to being what he is. That is why he commands the most enormous respect from his managerial colleagues throughout the game. He will make a stand on their behalf.

He once phoned me when I was at Barnet, saying he believed that I had a good young player called Andy Clarke. At the time Clarke's agent was a guy called Ambrose Mendy, who also represented Paul Ince, and Fergie asked if I would let him have a look at Clarke. I told him I had just turned down a bid of £250,000 from Wimbledon for the player and it was arranged that he should go to Old Trafford for ten days.

Through Mendy I learned that Ince had looked after him very well during his stay and Fergie duly rang to reveal what he thought. 'The lad's done great,' he said. 'With both his long stuff and his short stuff he has been in the top three all the time and he popped in a couple of goals. I'll bring him in here and give you £25,000 for him and ...'

'Hold on, Alex. I told you what I've just rejected. What do you mean twenty-five grand?'

'No,' he said. 'I'll give you more than that, but he's got to play the games.'

'If I tell my chairman that I've turned down £250,000 for him,' I said, 'but that he is going to Manchester United for £25,000, he'll have my kneecaps blown off. No, it ain't a deal.'

With that I had to pull Clarkey back. Now he's a black bloke and he went white when I told him he could not go to Old Trafford. But within a short time I had sold him to Wimbledon for £350,000.

My next dealing with United was one day while I was at Birmingham. I took a call from Fergie's assistant Jim Ryan, who said that Eric Cantona had been done for a long period of time in the wake of his infamous kung-fu kick in the crowd and they wanted to keep him fit during his enforced absence. Jim requested that I take a team up to The Cliff for a game behind closed doors and all the lads loved it. They had a great day because the club looked after us and they had the chance to witness Cantona's class at first hand. He was outstanding.

Soon afterwards Fergie called to see if we would stage a pre-season friendly at St Andrews.

'Who with?' I asked.

'My first team,' he said.

'Are you sure?' was my astounded reaction.

'I'm just returning the favour,' he said. The game was obviously a big attraction and drew a crowd of 18,000.

Two of my boys, Mark and Adam, are Manchester United daft and when I've been up to The Cliff I have taken them along with me and they have been completely awestruck. Fergie has made sure they have gone away with signed footballs and made sure they have been treated well and I cannot speak highly enough in praise of the man.

He is as loyal as the day is long to people who are loyal to him, but woe betide those who cross him. Two days before they were to appear in a Charity Shield at

Wembley recently, one of United's former players was holding his testimonial in Bristol and Fergie made sure that players of the calibre of David Beckham turned out to support him. Nobody else at that level would do that. The reverse side of his nature was shown when a player who had criticised him in a tabloid newspaper and received £25,000 for his treachery broke his leg so badly that his career was finished. He hobbled up the stairs on crutches at Old Trafford to request a testimonial and when Fergie learned of his presence he stormed out of his office, threw the hapless individual's accessories down the stairs and sent him tumbling after them.

'Go and tell the tabloids about that and get a few more quid off them,' he boomed.

I regarded it as one of life's golden moments when, in 1999, I was invited to his testimonial. To be part of an occasion like that, and to go back to Manchester afterwards and the restaurant in which all the players were present was just something else. Money cannot buy that. And for a man so esteemed as Fergie to invite a poxy Second Division manager such as myself speaks volumes about the man.

There are thousands of stories which are the stuff of legend in our wonderful game. I hope you have enjoyed my contribution.

Index